Computational Intelligence Based Solutions for Vision Systems

Series editors

Prateek Agrawal

University of Klagenfurt, Austria and Lovely Professional University, India

Anand Sharma

Mody University of Science and Technology, India

Vishu Madaan

Lovely Professional University, India

About the series

The motive of this series is to develop a trusted library on advanced computational methods, technologies and their applications.

This series focuses on the latest developments in next generation computing, and in particular on the synergy between computer science and other disciplines. Books in the series will explore new developments in various disciplines that are relevant for computational perspective including foundations, systems, innovative applications and other research contributions related to the overall design of computational tools, models and algorithms that are relevant for the respective domain. It encompasses research and development in artificial intelligence, machine learning, block chain technology, quantum cryptography, quantum computing, nanoscience, bioscience-based sensors, IoT applications, nature inspired algorithms, computer vision, bioinformatics etc. and their applications in the areas of science, engineering, business and social sciences. It covers a broad spectrum of applications in the community, from industry, government, and academia.

The aim of the series is to provide an opportunity for prospective researchers and experts to publish works based on next generation computing and its diverse applications. It also provides a data-sharing platform that will bring together international researchers, professionals and academics. This series brings together thought leaders, researchers, industry practitioners, and potential users of different disciplines to develop new trends and opportunities, exchange ideas and practices related to advanced computational methods and promote interdisciplinary knowledge.

Computational Intelligence Based Solutions for Vision Systems

Edited by
Varun Bajaj and Irshad Ahmad Ansari
Electronics and Communication Engineering, PDPM Indian Institute of Information Technology Design and Manufacturing, Jabalpur, India

IOP Publishing, Bristol, UK

ISBN   978-0-7503-4821-8 (ebook)
ISBN   978-0-7503-4819-5 (print)
ISBN   978-0-7503-4822-5 (myPrint)
ISBN   978-0-7503-4820-1 (mobi)

DOI   10.1088/978-0-7503-4821-8

Version: 20220501

IOP ebooks

British Library Cataloguing-in-Publication Data: A catalogue record for this book is available from the British Library.

Published by IOP Publishing, wholly owned by The Institute of Physics, London

IOP Publishing, Temple Circus, Temple Way, Bristol, BS1 6HG, UK

US Office: IOP Publishing, Inc., 190 North Independence Mall West, Suite 601, Philadelphia, PA 19106, USA

Dedicated to my father the late Mahendra Bajaj and family members.

—Varun Bajaj

Dedicated to my lovely daughter 'Eimaan'.

—Irshad Ahmad Ansari

Contents

Preface   xv

Acknowledgements   xvii

Editors biographies   xviii

List of contributors   xx

1   Drone-based vision system: surveillance during calamities   1-1
*Ankit Charan Janbandhu, Sachin Sharma, Irshad Ahmad Ansari
and Varun Bajaj*

1.1   Introduction   1-1

1.2   Surveillance system   1-2

     1.2.1   The importance of surveillance systems   1-3

     1.2.2   The use of drones in surveillance system   1-6

1.3   Proposed method   1-6

     1.3.1   Detecting human faces   1-7

     1.3.2   Tracking human faces   1-10

     1.3.3   Locating and capturing human faces   1-14

     1.3.4   Counting the number of people   1-16

     1.3.5   Drone deployment and testing   1-16

1.4   Conclusion   1-16

     References   1-18

2   Use of computer vision to inspect automatically machined workpieces   2-1
Virginia Riego del Castillo and Lidia Sánchez-González

2.1   Introduction   2-1

2.2   Related works   2-2

2.3   Methods   2-3

     2.3.1   Image acquisition   2-3

     2.3.2   Surface analysis to determine workpiece quality   2-5

     2.3.3   Burr detection   2-8

     2.3.4   Classification   2-11

2.4   Experimental set-up   2-12

2.5   Experimental results   2-14

     2.5.1   Workpiece quality   2-14

     2.5.2   Burrs   2-16

2.6   Conclusions and future work   2-17

      References   2-18

3   Machine learning for vision based crowd management   3-1
      K S Kavitha and Megha P Arakeri

3.1   Introduction   3-1
3.2   Related work   3-2
      3.2.1 A review of people count detection techniques   3-2
3.3   Proposed methodology   3-4
      3.3.1 The architecture of the proposed system   3-4
      3.3.2 An objective technique for counting people   3-5
      3.3.3 The architecture of YOLOV3   3-8
3.4   Experimental results   3-11
      3.4.1 Dataset   3-11
      3.4.2 Performance analysis   3-11
3.5   Conclusion   3-14
      References   3-15

4   Skin cancer classification model based on hybrid deep feature   4-1
      generation and iterative mRMR
      Orhan Yaman, Sengul Dogan, Turker Tuncer and Abdulhamit Subasi

4.1   Introduction   4-1
      4.1.1 Background   4-1
      4.1.2 Motivation   4-2
      4.1.3 Literature review   4-2
      4.1.4 Our model   4-4
      4.1.5 Contributions   4-4
      4.1.6 Study outline   4-4
4.2   Material   4-4
4.3   Preliminary   4-5
      4.3.1 Residual networks   4-7
      4.3.2 DenseNet201 model   4-7
      4.3.3 MobileNetV2 model   4-8
      4.3.4 ShuffleNet model   4-8
4.4   The proposed framework   4-9
      4.4.1 Feature generation   4-9
      4.4.2 Iterative mRMR feature selector   4-11
      4.4.3 Classification   4-12

4.5   Results and discussion   4-13
       4.5.1 Experimental set-up   4-13
       4.5.2 Results   4-13
       4.5.3 Discussion   4-15
4.6   Conclusions and future works   4-21
       References   4-21

5   An analysis of human activity recognition systems and their   5-1
        importance in the current era
        Chaitanya Krishna Pasula and V M Manikandan

5.1   Introduction   5-1
5.2   Stages in human activity recognition   5-3
5.3   Applications of human activity recognition   5-3
       5.3.1 Security video surveillance and home monitoring   5-3
       5.3.2 Retail   5-4
       5.3.3 Healthcare   5-4
       5.3.4 Smart homes   5-5
       5.3.5 Workplace monitoring   5-5
       5.3.6 Entertainment   5-5
5.4   Approaches for human activity recognition   5-5
       5.4.1 The HAR process using 3D posture data   5-5
       5.4.2 Human action recognition using DFT   5-6
       5.4.3 The local SVM approach   5-6
       5.4.4 A robust approach for action recognition based on   5-7
              spatio-temporal features in RGB-D sequences
       5.4.5 SlowFast networks for video recognition   5-7
       5.4.6 Long-term recurrent convolutional networks for visual   5-8
              recognition and description
       5.4.7 3D convolutional neural networks for human action   5-9
              recognition
       5.4.8 Human activity recognition using an optical flow based   5-9
              feature set
       5.4.9 Learning a hierarchical spatio-temporal model   5-9
       5.4.10 Human action recognition using trajectory-based   5-10
              representation
       5.4.11 Human activity recognition using a deep neural network   5-10
              with contextual information

5.5 Challenges in human activity recognition   5-11
    5.5.1 Dataset   5-11
    5.5.2 Sensors   5-12
    5.5.3 Experimentation environment   5-12
    5.5.4 Intraclass variation and interclass similarity   5-12
    5.5.5 Multi-subject interactions and group activities 5-12
    5.5.6 Training   5-13
    5.5.7 Challenges in HAR applications   5-13
5.6 Datasets available for activity detection research   5-13
    5.6.1 Action-level dataset   5-14
    5.6.2 Interaction-level dataset   5-14
    5.6.3 Group activities level dataset   5-15
    5.6.4 Behavior-level dataset   5-16
5.7 Scope for further research in this domain   5-17
5.8 Conclusion   5-17
    References   5-18

6 A deep learning-based food detection and classification system   **6-1**
Bhan Singh, Divyanshu, Mayur Kashyap,
Himanshu Gupta and Om Prakash Verma

6.1 Introduction   6-2
6.2 Literature review   6-3
6.3 Theory   6-4
    6.3.1 YOLOv3   6-5
    6.3.2 YOLOv4   6-5
    6.3.3 SSD   6-7
6.4 Methodology/experiments   6-8
    6.4.1 Dataset   6-8
    6.4.2 Data augmentation   6-9
    6.4.3 Implementation   6-9
    6.4.4 Software and hardware   6-10
    6.4.5 Performance parameters   6-10
6.5 Results   6-11
6.6 Conclusion and future scope   6-12
    References   6-16

**7   The detection of images recaptured through screenshots   7-1
based on spatial rich model analysis**
Areesha Anjum and Saiful Islam

7.1   Introduction   7-1
7.2   Literature review   7-3
7.3   Spatial rich model   7-7
    7.3.1   Computing noise residuals   7-8
    7.3.2   Residual truncation and quantization   7-8
    7.3.3   Formation of a sub-model with co-occurrence matrices   7-9
7.4   Proposed work   7-9
    7.4.1   Selection of the neighborhood descriptor   7-10
7.5   Experimental results   7-10
    7.5.1   Screenshot dataset   7-10
    7.5.2   Detection performance of the neighborhood descriptors   7-15
    7.5.3   The detection performance of neighborhood descriptors   7-15
        with an ensemble classifier
    7.5.4   Detection performance of neighborhood descriptors   7-16
        with an SVM
    7.5.5   Performance comparison of the neighborhood descriptors   7-17
7.6   Conclusion   7-18
7.7   Future work   7-18
    References   7-19

8   Data augmentation for deep ensembles in polyp segmentation   8-1
Loris Nanni, Daniela Cuza, Alessandra Lumini and Sheryl Brahnam

8.1   Introduction   8-1
8.2   Deep learning for semantic image segmentation   8-3
8.3   Stochastic activation selection   8-4
8.4   Data augmentation   8-5
    8.4.1   Spatial stretch   8-5
    8.4.2   Shadows   8-6
    8.4.3   Contrast and motion blur   8-6
    8.4.4   Color change and rotation   8-7
    8.4.5   Segmentation   8-8
    8.4.6   Rand augment   8-8
    8.4.7   RICAP   8-9
    8.4.8   Color and shape change   8-10
    8.4.9   Occlusion 1   8-10

8.4.10 Occlusion 2   8-11

8.4.11 GridMask   8-11

8.4.12 AttentiveCutMix   8-11

8.4.13 Modified ResizeMix   8-12

8.4.14 Color mapping   8-12

8.5 Results on colorectal cancer segmentation   8-13

8.5.1 Datasets, testing protocol and metrics   8-13

8.5.2 Experiments   8-14

8.6 Conclusion   8-19

References   8-20

**9 Identification of the onset of Parkinson's disease through a   9-1
multiscale classification deep learning model utilizing a
fusion of multiple conventional features with an nDS
spatially exploited symmetrical convolutional pattern**
Ranita Khumukcham and Gaurav Saxena

9.1 Introduction   9-2

9.1.1 A comprehensive literature review   9-4

9.1.2 Contributions   9-8

9.2 Proposed methodology   9-9

9.2.1 Retrieval of voice samples   9-9

9.2.2 Pre-processing   9-10

9.2.3 Proposed multiscale multiple feature convolution with   9-11
       hybrid n-dilations (MMFCHnD) architecture

9.3 Experimental results and discussion   9-15

9.3.1 Evaluation metrics   9-15

9.3.2 Development of the training and testing images   9-17

9.3.3 Deep learning training details   9-17

9.3.4 Implementation results   9-18

9.4 Conclusion   9-21

References   9-22

**10 Computer vision approach with deep learning for a medical   10-1
intelligence system**
Monali Gulhane

10.1 Introduction   10-1

10.2 Defining computer vision   10-3

10.3 Computer vision in practice   10-4
     10.3.1 Medical imaging   10-5
     10.3.2 Cardiology   10-6
     10.3.3 Pathology   10-7
     10.3.4 Dermatology   10-8
     10.3.5 Ophthalmology   10-8
     10.3.6 Video for medical purposes   10-9
     10.3.7 The presence of humans   10-10
     10.3.8 Implementation in the clinic   10-11
10.4 A case study of vision based machine learning   10-14
     10.4.1 Networks of neurons   10-14
10.5 Data preparation overview   10-16
     10.5.1 Data access and querying   10-17
     10.5.2 De-identification   10-18
     10.5.3 Data retention   10-18
     10.5.4 Medical image resembling   10-19
     10.5.5 Choosing an appropriate label and a definition of ground truth   10-19
     10.5.6 The truth or the label's quality   10-19
10.6 The future of computer vision and natural language processing in healthcare   10-19
10.7 Research related problems in computer vision   10-20
     10.7.1 View of CNN through computer vision   10-20
     10.7.2 Visualizations based on gradients   10-20
     References   10-21

11 Machine learning in medicine: diagnosis of skin cancer using a support vector machine (SVM) classifier   **11-1**
Siddarth Shah, Dipen Gohil, Rutvik Shah and Manan Shah

11.1 Introduction   11-1
11.2 Technologies used in skin cancer detection   11-2
11.3 Support vector machines (SVMs)   11-3
11.4 The SVM in skin cancer detection   11-5
     11.4.1 Image acquisition   11-5
     11.4.2 Feature extraction   11-7
     11.4.3 SVM classification   11-8

11.5 Brief description of skin cancer detection   11-9

11.6 Challenges faced by SVMs   11-13

11.7 Future aspects in skin cancer detection   11-13

11.8 Conclusion   11-14

     References   11-14

Preface

Currently, computational intelligence (CI) is being used in a variety of applications and is thus influencing people's lives in various ways. The growth in research in advanced computing and respective fields such as intelligent vision systems (IVSs) is assisting people by allowing rapid response and ease of use. The advancement of IVSs depends jointly on the development of advanced computing and knowledge of vision systems. IVSs help to achieve highly efficient performance (comparable to human vision) to allow a profound understanding of different scenarios and applications. IVSs provide the ability to handle and examine the big data generated by vision sensors and make decisions based on specific requirements. CI enables the different issues that influence IVSs and their practical use to be addresssed. Therefore, the merger of CI with IVSs can do wonders for the wellbeing of humans.

In recent times high performance computing has seen continued growth, affecting various fields and changing the computational domain altogether for the betterment of human life. Computer vision can be deemed as one of the most important fields which affects human life in a significant way. CI based computing can be very helpful in determining solutions for advanced vision systems as they required high-end processing capabilities. The in-depth analysis of large datasets is the basis for the development of IVSs and the same can be very helpful in vision and surveillance applications. Deep computational architecture and low level feature extraction, generation and understanding can provide new directions for the current research of vision systems.

Computer vision is a significant technology covering diverse fields. It plays an important role in the fields of information technology and intelligence. The combination of vision systems with CI is giving rise to IVSs. Computer vision is affecting different areas of human life such as surveillance, medical assistance, remote sensing, target detection, tracking, etc.

Computer vision plays a significant role in industry as well. Intelligent systems and computer vision find applications in various industrial phases such as the pre-processing, production and testing phases. Computer vision techniques are an important component of security and surveillance systems. An intelligent vision system using visible and infra-red sensors can track illegal activities and alert the user in the case of any incidents.

Considering the future issues of high performance computing and the need for IVSs, this book focuses on the advancements of this domain. This book is made up of contributions by invited research scholars, academic researchers and industry professional related to high performance computing for IVSs and related applications.

The chapters of this book are as follows. Chapter 1 provides insight into a drone based vision system, and its implementation and application for surveillance. Details of the system components, implementation steps and analysis of obtained result are provided. Chapter 2 highlights an important application of computer vision to automatically detect surface imperfections using a grey-level co-occurrence matrix and a supervised classification technique. Chapter 3 demonstrates the use of machine learning for vision-based crowd management systems. This work utilizes a deep neural network based YOLOV3 model which is trained using the COCO dataset to detect the people in the frame. Chapter 4 develops a hybrid deep feature extraction model based on five pre-trained deep learning models and an ImRMR based feature selection model for skin cancer classification. Chapter 5 presents an analysis of human activity recognition systems and their importance in the current era. The author discusses the various applications of human activity recognition and the different methods available for automatic activity detection from videos. Chapter 6 explores three deep learning based object detection models, namely YOLOv3, YOLOv4 and SSD, based on mAP. A detailed description of data augmentation is also presented.

Chapter 7 introduces a forensic method to identify recaptured images by means of rich feature extraction from different noise residuals on multiple quantization values. The work focuses on a prominent feature in the spatial domain to classify the original images and screenshots taken from LED monitors. Chapter 8 offers multiple data augmentation approaches for boosting segmentation performance by utilizing DeepLabv3+ as the architecture and ResNet18/ResNet50 as the backbone. Chapter 9 proposes a novel multiscale object detection and location architecture for the classification of Parkinson's disease. The developed model utilizes 540 deep learning layers to learn from a wide range of features by using two unique attributes. Chapter 10 deals with the various AI-powered techniques that address several of the most critical societal health problems, including cardiovascular disease, cancer, dermatological conditions, neurological illnesses, breathing illnesses and gastrointestinal issues. In addition, various imaging techniques, such as computerized tomography, magnetic resonance, radiographiy ultrasonography, dermoscopy, etc, are also discussed. Chapter 11 discusses the application of machine learning techniques in medicine. This chapter focuses on the diagnosis of skin cancer using a support vector machine (SVM) classifier.

Acknowledgements

Dr Bajaj expresses his heartfelt appreciation to his mother Prabha, wife Anuja and daughter Avadhi for their wonderful support and encouragement throughout the completion of this important book. His deepest gratitude goes to his mother-in-law and father-in-law for their constant motivation. This book is an outcome of sincere efforts that could only be given to the book due to the great support from Dr Bajaj's family.

Dr Ansari expresses his gratitude and sincere thanks to his wife, family members and teachers for their constant support and motivation.

We sincerely thanks to Professor Sanjeev Jain, Director of PDPM IIITDM Jabalpur, for his support and encouragement. We would like to thank all our friends, well-wishers and all those who keep us motivated to do more and more, better and better. We sincerely thank all the contributors for their writing on the relevant theoretical backgrounds and applications in this book.

We express our humble thanks to Dr John Navas and all the editorial staff of IOP for their great support, necessary help, appreciation and quick responses. We also wish to thank IOP for giving us this opportunity to contribute on a relevant topic with a reputed publisher. Finally we want to thank everyone who, in one way or another, helped us in editing this book.

Dr Bajaj thanks in particular his family who provided encouragement throughout the editing of the book. This book is dedicated from the heart to his father who took the lead to heaven before the completion of this book.

Last but not least we would also like to thank God for showering us with his blessings and strength to do this type of novel and quality work.

Varun Bajaj
Irshad Ahmad Ansari

Editors biographies

Varun Bajaj

Varun Bajaj (PhD, SMIEEE20) has been an Associate Professor in the department of Electronics and Communication Engineering at the Indian Institute of Information Technology, Design and Manufacturing (IIITDM) Jabalpur, India since July 2021. He was an Assistant Professor at IIITDM Jabalpur from March 2014 to July 2021. He also worked as visiting faculty at IIITDM Jabalpur from September 2013 to March 2014. He worked as an Assistant Professor in the Department of Electronics and Instrumentation, Shri Vaishnav Institute of Technology and Science, Indore, India during 2009–10. He received his PhD degree in Electrical Engineering from the Indian Institute of Technology, Indore, India, in 2014. He received his MTech degree with honours in Microelectronics and VLSI Design from the Shri Govindram Seksaria Institute of Technology and Science, Indore, India, in 2009, and his BE degree in Electronics and Communication Engineering from Rajiv Gandhi Technological University, Bhopal, India in 2006.

He is an Associate Editor of the *IEEE Sensors Journal* and the Subject Editor-in-Chief of *IET Electronics Letters*. He served as a Subject Editor of *IET Electronics Letters* from November 2018 to June 2020. He is a Senior Member of IEEE (from June 2020) and was a Member of IEEE (2016–2020), and has also contributed as an active technical reviewer for leading international journals published by IEEE, IET and Elsevier, etc. He has 128 publications which include journal papers (88), conference papers (31), books (9) and book chapters (10). The citation impact of his publications is around 3375 citations, with an h index of 30 and an i10 index of 73 (Google Scholar, November 2021). He has supervised seven PhD scholars (four completed and three in progress) and seven MTech scholars. He has been listed in the world's top 2% of researchers/scientists by Stanford University, CA (October 2021). He has worked on research projects funded by DST and CSIR. He is a recipient of various reputed national and international awards. His research interests include biomedical signal processing, AI in healthcare, brain–computer interfaces, pattern recognition and ECG signal processing.

Irshad Ahmad Ansari

Irshad Ahmad Ansari has been a faculty member in the department of Electronics and Communication Engineering at the PDPM Indian Institute of Information Technology, Design and Manufacturing (IIITDM) Jabalpur, India, since 2017. He received his BTech degree in Electronics and Communication Engineering from Gautam Buddh Technical University (formally UPTU), Lucknow, India, in 2010, and his MTech degree in Control and Instrumentation from Dr B R Ambedkar National Institute of Technology Jalandhar, Punjab, India, in 2012. He completed his PhD at IIT Roorkee with an MHRD teaching assistantship, and subsequently joined the Gwangju Institute of Science and Technology, South Korea, as a postdoctoral fellow. His major research interests include image processing, signal processing, soft computing, brain–computer interfaces and machine learning. He is a Senior Member of IEEE. He is currently supervising three PhD scholars. He has authored more than 55 research papers in various reputed international journals/conferences proceedings of publishers such as IEEE, Elsevier, Springer, IOP etc. He also serves as an active and potential technical reviewer for various journals of repute.

List of contributors

Areesha Anjum
Department of Computer Engineering, Zakir Husain College of Engineering and Technology, Aligarh Muslim University, Aligarh, India

Irshad Ahmad Ansari
PDPM Indian Institute of Information Technology Design and Manufacturing, Jabalpur, India

Megha Arakeri
M S Ramaiah Institute of Technology, Bangalore, India

Varun Bajaj
PDPM Indian Institute of Information Technology Design and Manufacturing, Jabalpur, India

Sheryl Brahnam
Missouri State University, Springfield, Missouri, USA

Daniela Cuza
University of Padua, Padua, Italy

Divyanshu
Dr B R Ambedkar National Institute of Technology, Jalandhar, India

Sengul Dogan
Technology Faculty, Firat University, Elazığ, Turkey

Dipen Gohil
LJ Institute of Engineering and Technology, Ahmedabad, India

Monali Gulhane
Computer Science and Engineering, St Vincent Palloti College of Engineering and Technology, Nagpur, India

Himanshu Gupta
Dr B R Ambedkar National Institute of Technology, Jalandhar, India

Saiful Islam
Department of Computer Engineering, Aligarh Muslim University, Aligarh, UP, India

Ankit Charan Janbandhu
PDPM Indian Institute of Information Technology Design and Manufacturing, Jabalpur, India

K S Kavitha
M S Ramaiah Institute of Technology, Bangalore, India

Mayur Kashyap
Dr B R Ambedkar National Institute of Technology, Jalandhar, India

Ranita Khumukcham
Indian Institute of Information Technology Senapati, Manipur, Mantripukhri, India

Alessandra Lumini
University of Bologna, Bologna, Italy

V M Manikandan
SRM University-AP, Andhra Pradesh, India

Loris Nanni
University of Padua, Padua, Italy

Chaitanya Krishna Pasula
SRM University-AP, Andhra Pradesh, India

Virginia Riego del Castillo
Departament of Mechanical, Computer Science and Aerospace Engineering, Universidad de León, León, Spain

Lidia Sánchez-González
Departament of Mechanical, Computer Science and Aerospace Engineering, Universidad de León, León, Spain

Gaurav Saxena
Indian Institute of Information Technology Senapati, Manipur, Mantripukhri, India

Siddarth Shah
LJ Institute of Engineering and Technology, Ahmedabad, India

Manan Shah
Pandit Deendayal Energy University, Gandhinagar, India

Rutvik Shah
Silver Oak College of Engineering and Technology, Ahmedabad, India

Sachin Sharma
Research Division, Jagadish Chandra Bose Research Organisation, Gautam Budh Nagar, Uttar Pradesh, 203207, India

Bhan Singh
Dr B R Ambedkar National Institute of Technology, Jalandhar, India

Abdulhamit Subasi
Faculty of Medicine, University of Turku, Turku, Finland

Turker Tuncer
Technology Faculty, Firat University, Elazığ, Turkey

Om Prakash Verma
Dr B R Ambedkar National Institute of Technology, Jalandhar, India

Orhan Yaman
Technology Faculty, Firat University, Elazığ, Turkey

Chapter 1

Drone-based vision system: surveillance during calamities

Ankit Charan Janbandhu, Sachin Sharma, Irshad Ahmad Ansari and Varun Bajaj

This chapter describes how drones and computer vision can work together to enhance surveillance. A drone-based surveillance system is proposed that can be used in disaster situations for monitoring the location and the number of people present, and provide information about the area so that rescue teams can use this information to be more effective in their work. Moreover, this chapter demonstrates that the BlazeFace model is more efficient than the existing face detection algorithm in terms of computation. It also discusses the use of odometry to track location in an indoor environment and a description of centroid tracking in terms of tracking faces. The drone used in this chapter is DJI Tello, and the tools used are the DJI Tellopy library, OpenCV Python and the MediaPipe library.

1.1 Introduction

In the last few decades, surveillance and human detection through monitoring have become part of current technology. In terms of human rescue during calamities and disasters, surveillance has a wide scope for further advancements in terms of human face detection, recognization and observation in extreme situations such as floods, earthquakes, fires, dust storms or any other disasters. A drone-based rescue system needs to be effective and adequate for providing information about the ground level conditions. In the present scenario, the drone-based system is equipped with new technological advancements such as the incorporation of computer vision [1], convolution neural networks [2] and deep learning [3]. Previously, surveillance was performed using a limited approach using cameras during natural or artificial calamities. Now, the worst affected areas can be reached easily using drones, even in adverse conditions.

Previously surveillance was possible only through using hot-air balloons with cameras, airplanes with a camera attached to the outer surface [4] and, a later point of time when cameras became smaller in size, a camera could be attached to a bird's body to observe a location for the objective of surveillance and rescue [5]. These conventional methods are expensive, time-consuming and can provide inaccurate information, which causes a lot of ambiguity and a waste of resources. Now drones equipped with computer vision provide an efficient drone model to tackle these challenging disaster situations in an effective manner [6–9]. By using a face detection technique and moving the drone over the target location, authentic information can be provided about the number of people present and also their location, as the drone can use its computer vision to observe difficult and impenetrable areas that are impossible for humans to reach. This system of surveillance has the power to tackle calamities and disasters in a systematic manner help people be rescued as fast as possible.

During a period of disaster, this drone-based computer vision could make a significant difference in terms of the allocation of human resources. For example, during the 2013 the Uttrakhand floods in India drones provided a clear picture of the natural disaster, and thousands of people were found using drones for the first time in Indian search and rescue operations [10]. The rescue of people was the major goal of the government during the mountain tsunami in Uttrakhand. Using a drone-based vision system, surveillance and recovery were achieved by providing immediate help to the people facing disaster. As the drone detects faces, it can provide exact numbers. The Kerala floods in 2018 also demonstrated the effective use of drones [11] in hidden places where helicopters and humans could not reach. By using drone-based computer vision during a flood, tsunami, earthquake, fire or other calamity one can also obtain information about the number of people present at the location.

In this chapter the focus will be on the two primary components: the drone and computer vision. This chapter will also elaborate on the objectives of face detection and counting the number of affected people using drones.

1.2 Surveillance system

Surveillance systems have evolved in the last two decades, in which time video surveillance has, in general, transitioned towards being a larger part of society. Although there are still many debates regarding the ethics of video surveillance technology, recent advancements in technology have led to the use of this technology in many different parts of society. Companies use video surveillance to provide security and monitor employees, monitor customer activities, and handle large crowds to reduce crowding and power consumption. Video surveillance systems have been around for a long time and they have evolved from black and white cameras to color cameras, to even the ability to be fired from a drone.

The 1990s was a decade of many societal and technological changes. One of these was the emergence of widespread video surveillance systems. During World War II, Great Britain and France faced a desperate shortage of weapons after Germany had seized control of much of Eastern Europe. Britain's only means of response was to make some changes to its military, to make sure that it was ready to defend itself. One of those changes was to put cameras on the back of tanks. The tanks were fitted with cameras to make sure that the British troops would be able to see where they were going. The cameras were also used to help British troops avoid being shot by the Germans. The Germans in turn used closed-circuit television (CCTV) technology to monitor the movements of soldiers, tanks and other military equipment to ensure that German troops were following the correct procedures and to prevent any harm being done to civilians due to false information [12, 13]. A further development occurred after the war, in the 1960s, when the number of police officers participating in law enforcement was falling rapidly. One of the ways to create a safe environment for police officers was by using CCTV surveillance equipment. In the 1980s, generally large factory buildings or quiet residential areas were chosen as possible sites for multi-story CCTV surveillance systems.

Today there are many different types of CCTV cameras in homes and businesses. As cameras become more sophisticated, they prevent the threat of burglary. Facial recognition surveillance utilizes data obtained from video surveillance cameras to automate the identification of individuals. It is often used in crime-fighting applications, but it can be used by people in everyday life as well. Typically, the systems use image-recognition algorithms to identify people in video footage. CCTV cameras can collect images of intruders without having to shoot them or have other devices involved. Video surveillance is a valuable technology for anyone who needs to create a secure shop. The main benefits of video surveillance include the ability to monitor the entrance and exit points of your shop. It also gives you new options when it comes to securing sensitive areas and the online presence of a shop. Video surveillance is very easy to set up and can be used in different ways. You can install a full-body-style camera and use the image as a sales tool. There is nothing new about video surveillance systems and still we continue to see advancements in the field every year.

1.2.1 The importance of surveillance systems

The purpose of computer vision is to provide an understanding of the physical world in order to perform necessary tasks in the environment. Computer vision is involved in surveillance, video surveillance, surveillance cameras and other applications. The video surveillance industry has grown dramatically over the past few years. It is not uncommon for companies to install video surveillance systems to protect their businesses from theft of confidential data, robberies and vandalism of their property. However, the technology of video surveillance is becoming more and more sophisticated and can now identify images and audio of unusual movements of people and vehicles. These include people on foot, cars on the street, and people moving into and out of buildings. With the advancing technology of these systems it has become possible to identify individuals or vehicles on video as well as identify crime. There are various fields in which surveillance systems play an important role. Some of them are discussed below.

1.2.1.1 Retail

A shop owner can use video surveillance equipment to help him/her keep an eye on the customers coming into his/her shop, as shown in figure 1.1. The video surveillance system can be installed in different ways depending on the needs of the store owner. There are many different types of surveillance systems that are used in retail. From security cameras positioned on store walls, to scanners that can be used to check the bags of customers, many different types of surveillance systems are used to help retailers and individual employees safeguard their businesses.

1.2.1.2 Agriculture

In the ever-expanding world of agriculture, surveillance cameras have become an essential tool, as shown in figure 1.2. The free-market economy has given rise to the idea that agricultural production is possible without limits or limits on who can do it. If you are looking to start a farm, the benefits of implementing surveillance cameras are many. With the great number of cameras available on the market today, it is easy to install them with little to no up-front cost. A surveillance camera is an automated or robotic device that records images of events occurring on or near the farm. It is used to monitor farm animals, the movement of livestock, disease infestation, agricultural activities, accidents and other farm activities. The use of surveillance cameras also allows the quality of air and water to be monitored, and the environment to be preserved.

1.2.1.3 Private households

Surveillance cameras are now installed in many homes. Not everyone has access to them, but many people can access their cameras remotely. They are widely used for security purposes, as shown in figure 1.3. These cameras are designed to capture unwanted events, such as theft, vandalism, noise, accidents and so on.

Figure 1.1. A shop under video surveillance.

Figure 1.2. Drone surveillance of a farm.

Figure 1.3. A house under CCTV surveillance.

1.2.1.4 Public places
When it comes to public safety, surveillance cameras are very useful for security and law enforcement, as shown in figure 1.4. It is becoming increasingly common for us to see those cameras on our street corners, on our local shopping centers, or even on our local bus. Surveillance cameras are used to catch robbers prowling the streets, criminals committing crimes and speeding vehicles.

Figure 1.4. A street under CCTV surveillance.

1.2.2 The use of drones in surveillance system

The recent buzz around artificial intelligence (AI) and the rise of the Internet of Things (IoT) have inspired many to start experimenting with drones. Drone technology has advanced tremendously over the last few years. Today, robots are being developed to assist humans with everyday tasks. For example, an AI-powered drone could be used to harvest crops or deliver products to consumers. Surveillance is a major concern today and drones can be used to fulfill that role. There are many different types of surveillance systems you can use with drones [14], but the three most common are umbrella coverage, perimeter coverage and ground-penetrating radar (GPR).

During the past two years, the booming drone industry has grown enormously. Drones are becoming increasingly popular in dangerous situations. They are now being used to save lives and provide humanitarian assistance to people in need, as shown in figure 1.5. The military uses drones to get information about people who are kidnapped by terrorists. When it comes to aerial photography, drones are often considered an excellent alternative to fixed cameras. The advantages of using drones include their wide perspective, the possibility for high-resolution photographs and their low cost of operation. With the use of AI and computer vision technology, many drones are now used in hazardous areas where people may need help. With the use of intelligent unmanned aerial vehicles, the number of people trapped in a critical situation can be detected and counted and suitable aid can be provided in those areas.

1.3 Proposed method

This section has the primary objectives of developing an understanding of the various computer vision methods for detecting humans, and to create a system that automatically counts the people in a chaotic environment such as a natural disaster. A DJI Tello drone has been used to test the code in this work.

Figure 1.5. The use of a drone in surveillance systems.

The topics listed below will be addressed in the following sections of this chapter:

- Section 1.3.1. Detecting human faces—An overview of the various facial recognition methods available to date is given in this section, as well as the methods used to accomplish this task and their advantages.
- Section 1.3.2. Tracking human faces—This section explains how to trace a face in an image and why this is so important.
- Section 1.3.3. Locating and capturing human faces—The purpose of this section is to demonstrate how to locate a drone in an indoor environment and how to store images of different faces in a database while performing the drone's location.
- Section 1.3.4. Counting the number of people—The goal of this section is to demonstrate how to count the number of people in a frame as well as how tracking can assist us in counting people and tracking their locations.
- Section 1.3.5. Drone deployment and testing—This section shows how to deploy our code in DJI Tello, which will be compared with some test results to check the effectiveness.

1.3.1 Detecting human faces

Face discovery is a computer technology that identifies the face and dimensions of a human face in an electronic image. The face attributes are found and also any other items such as trees, buildings and bodies are disregarded from the electronic image. It can be regarded as a specific instance of object-class detection, where the work is finding the location as well as sizes of all items in an image that are related to that class. Face detection can be seen as a more general situation of face localization. In face localization the task is to identify the locations and sizes of a recognized number of faces (typically one). Primarily, there are two types of approaches to discover faces in a given electronic image—attribute based and photograph based techniques.

The feature based method tries to extract features from the image and match them with knowledge of facial features. In contrast, the picture-based strategy attempts to obtain the best match between the training and testing photos. Various methods are available for identifying faces from a still photo or video.

As illustrated by figure 1.6, various methods are available for facial recognition [15], but the image-based method is employed in this study. Drones are used for this task and they have low computational power, so we need a method that is computationally friendly.

The new BlazeFace framework provided by Google [16] allows one to detect faces with greater accuracy. BlazeFace is a lightweight model for seeing faces in images and is an adaptation of a single-shot detection (SSD) method [17].

The BlazeFace method detects faces in an image and creates a bounding box around each face to indicate its location in the frame. It also produces six facial keypoint coordinates (for the eye centers, ear tragions, mouth center and nose tip) that allow us to estimate face rotation.

The BlazeFace model uses the depthwise separable convolution method [18]. The benefit of this method over the standard convolution method [19] can be explained by the following example. If an input image is $32 \times 32 \times 3$ (the three values here refer to channels, as a color image has three channels: red, green and blue). Thus, to detect edges or some other feature, if the size of the kernel is taken as $5 \times 5 \times 3$ and it is convolved with the image and slid over the image, it gives an output that has a size of $28 \times 28 \times 1$. The total number of multiplications performed to obtain this result is $5 \times 5 \times 3 \times 28 \times 28 = 98\ 000$. For example, to detect 64 features of the image, a 64, $5 \times 5 \times 3$ kernel has been used, so now the outcome will have 64, $28 \times 28 \times 1$ image stacks back-to-back, as shown in figure 1.7. Now the total number of multiplications

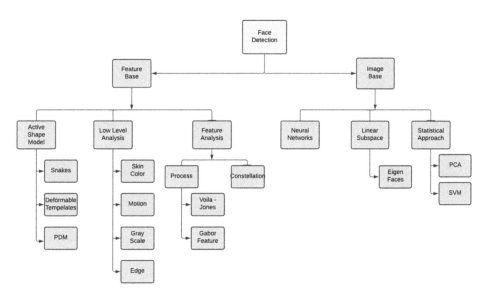

Figure 1.6. Face detection methods.

performed is $64 \times 5 \times 5 \times 3 \times 28 \times 28 = 3\,763\,200$ operations, so it can be seen that traditional convolution calculations need high computational power.

Usually, the filters for all input channels are applied in one step and then combined at the same time, while depthwise separable convolution [20] is applied in two steps:

1. *Depthwise convolution (at the filtering stage).*

   Unlike standard convolution, depthwise convolution applies convolution to a single input channel at a time. For example, if an input image of size $32 \times 32 \times 1$ is used for depthwise convolution, a $5 \times 5 \times 1$ shape kernel has been applied. That is why it is necessary to have three such kernels. After convolution its output image will be of size $28 \times 28 \times 3$. The number of multiplications will be $5 \times 5 \times 3 \times 28 \times 28 = 58\,800$ operations. This concludes the first phase. Now this will be succeeded by pointwise convolution, as shown in figure 1.8.

2. *Pointwise convolution (at the combination stage).* Pointwise convolution involves performing a linear combination of each of these layers. Here, the input is an image of size $28 \times 28 \times 1$. The filter has the shape $1 \times 1 \times 3$. This is a 1×1 operation over all three layers. If there is a need to detect 64 features, then 64 such filters are needed to see the different features, just as was done in standard convolution. It gives an output of an image size of $28 \times 28 \times 1$, and there are 64 such images stacked together. Now the number of multiplications performed is $64 \times 1 \times 1 \times 3 \times 28 \times 28 \times 1 = 150\,528$.

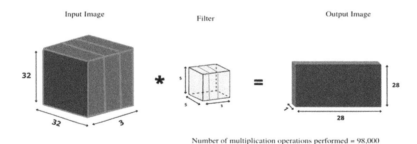

Figure 1.7. Convolution using traditional methods.

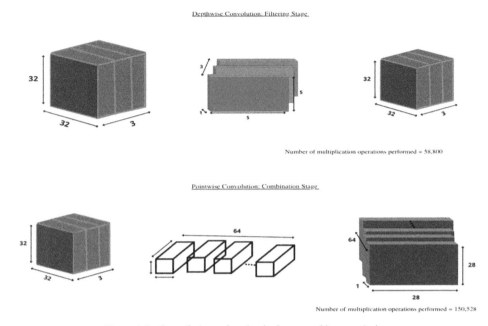

Figure 1.8. Convolution using depthwise separable convolution.

Now the total number of multiplications performed is (depthwise convolution stage + pointwise convolution stage) $58\,800 + 150\,528 = 209\,328$ multiplications, which is lower compared to the standard convolution, in which $3\,763\,200$ operations were required. Thus the BlazeFace model uses depthwise separable convolution so that it will perform fewer calculations and thus perform well in low-energy computational devices.

The BlazeFace model is adapted from SSD but there is a difference. The BlazeFace model is specially designed to detect faces and the SSD is used to detect objects having a lot of variance. The makers of the BlazeFace model claims that there is limited variance in human faces, i.e. every face has eyes, one nose and one mouth, so the number of anchors is reduced. Instead of using 4×4 and 2×2 feature map sizes, they have reduced the architecture which stops at an 8×8 feature map without further downsampling and use $2 + 2 + 2 = 6$ anchors of 8×8, which also provides extra speed to this model.

It can see in figure 1.9 how the author's face is detected by the BlazeFace model and also how the six landmarks are projected. This was done using the Google MediaPipe library which uses the BlazeFace model for face detection.

1.3.2 Tracking human faces

Although the tracking of faces is an essential part of the application, the MediaPipe library does not support active tracking, as can be seen in figure 1.10. For two people in the same image, it assigned two different IDs at two different time intervals. For this work, the faces' IDs must remain unique in the camera's frame. This is the first

Figure 1.9. Face detection using the MediaPipe library.

Figure 1.10. Proposed system without the centroid tracking algorithm.

challenge, and the second is that the camera might assign a different ID to the same face when it comes back into the frame after the drone moves. When the drone moves it is desirable that an ID be assigned to the face if it is in the frame, and if it disappears from the frame the drone it will wait for a specific number of frames. If the face reappears in this period it will again be assigned the same ID.

For solving this problem, a centroid tracking algorithm is used. It is a multi-step process, as shown in figure 1.11. The following steps are used to perform the detection and tracking of human faces using the centroid tracking algorithm.

Step 1. Calculating the centroid of the bounding box.

By using the BlazeFace model, the information of the bounding box can be traced and by applying this information the calculation of the centroid is completed, as shown in figure 1.12.

Step 2. Computing the Euclidean distances between the new bounding box and existing faces.

First, the Euclidean distance is calculated for every subsequent frame of the video stream. However, instead of assigning a unique ID to the object, first the centroid is calculated from the boundary box. This is followed by calculating the Euclidean

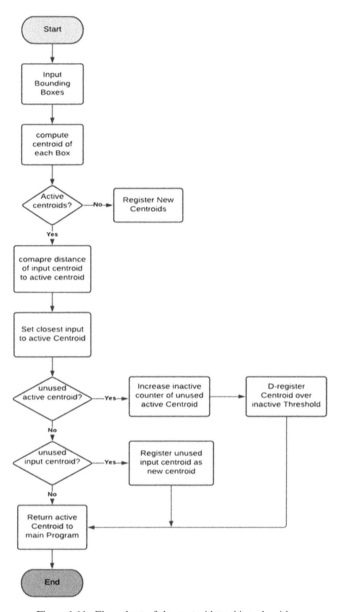

Figure 1.11. Flow chart of the centroid tracking algorithm.

distances between each pair of existing object centroids and the input object centroid. The same ID of the old object will be assigned if the distance between the old object and the newly created object is significantly less. The primary idea behind this is that if the object moves a short distance from the previous centroid (here 'object' refers to a face), it does not suddenly appear at a different location. That is why it is given the same ID for which the Euclidean distance between the

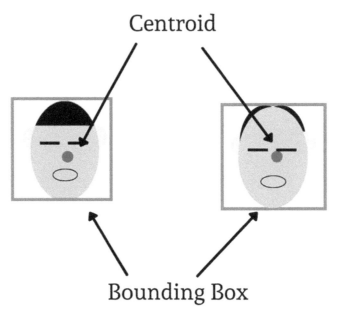

Figure 1.12. Centroid calculation using a bounding box.

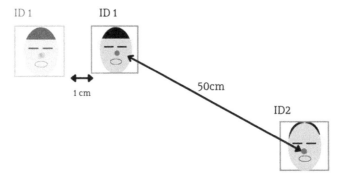

Figure 1.13. Euclidean distance calculation between the bounding boxes.

objects is very small, as shown in figure 1.13, where the face is shifted by 1 cm, but its ID is the same as the one which is closer to its new location.

Step 3. Registering of a new object.

Whenever a new face appears in the frame, to add that face to our tracking list we first assign a unique object ID, as shown in figure 1.14. We then calculate the centroid of the bounding box, store this information and repeat the process.

Step 4. Deregistering of an old object

The old object is deregistered if it cannot be matched with any existing face for N subsequent frames, as shown in figure 1.15. When a person leaves the frame, the algorithm keeps assigning the old IDs to the remaining people.

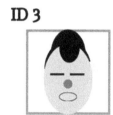

Figure 1.14. Assigning new IDs to new faces in the frame.

Location : Power & Control Lab (PDPM IIIT Jabalpur)

Figure 1.15. Deregistering of faces from the frame.

1.3.3 Locating and capturing human faces

Thus far the detection of faces and tracking them in the frame have been discussed. However, this section will demonstrate how to capture a face in the image and locate where it was taken.

A global positioning system (GPS) can be utilized to determine the drone's coordinates. However, for this work DJI's Tello is employed, which lacks GPS functionality, and if the operations are performed indoors GPS will not function. Thus, for estimating the drone's position, velocity data are used, and its angle is determined by the angular speed data; this procedure is called odometry. Using this information, the position of the drone can be calculated relative to its take-off position. There have been other advanced methods for estimating position [21–24], but in this case, odometry is employed.

For example, if the drone is at its origin, then given a velocity of 20 cm s^{-1} and a time of 1 s, after which a measurement of distance is taken, the distance is 20 cm, and a grid is created, as shown in figure 1.16.

Now if the velocity is fixed and by knowing how many seconds the forward button is pressed one can easily estimate the position of the drone relative to the take-off position.

When the drone is provided with only an angular velocity of 45° s^{-1}, it will head 45° away from the original position. If both a fixed forward velocity and a fixed angular velocity are provided, for example 20 cm s^{-1} and 45° s^{-1} for 2 s, as shown in figure 1.17 after 1 s the drone is at (14.1, 14.1) relative to its original position with a heading angle of 45°. After another second it is at (28, 28.2) relative to its original position with a heading angle of 90°.

In this way the drone position is estimated and this information is used in naming the image. Thus, one can see where a person is in relation to the take-off position. Result of which can be seen from figure 1.22.

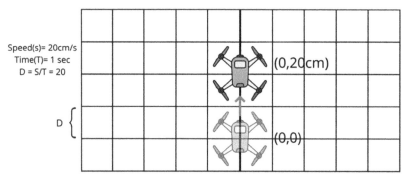

Figure 1.16. Grid cell localization.

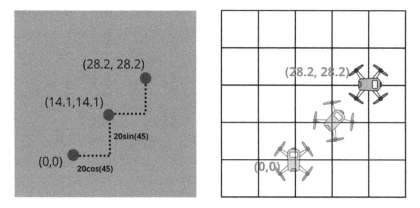

Figure 1.17. Estimating the position of drone using odometry.

Location: Power & Control Lab (P DPM IIIT Jabalpur)

Figure 1.18. Counting the people in the frame.

1.3.4 Counting the number of people

The information about how many unique IDs is generated is used in this work to count the number of people. As depicted in figure 1.18, in the left image, when there is one person in a frame ID 1 is assigned and the total person count is 1. When another person comes in ID 2 is assigned and the total person count increases to 2. So just by counting the number of unique IDs one can estimate the number of people.

1.3.5 Drone deployment and testing

Throughout this work a DJI Tello drone has been used, and for the deployment of all the methods discussed above the DJI Tello drone is programmed using the DJI Tello Python SDK. Figure 1.19 shows the flow chart of the system.

Figure 1.20(a) shows how the DJI Tello drone is locating the number of people in the frame and also assigning a unique ID to the people in the frame and, by counting the number of unique IDs assigned, it displays the number of people counted in the entire mission. It also displays the path and location where it is in reference to the take-off point, as shown in figure 1.20(b) so that rescuers know where the people are and can plan their rescue mission accordingly. It also saves the facial image of the tracked people, as shown in figure 1.20(c), so that the rescue team can make sure that all the people have been saved.

1.4 Conclusion

In this chapter an efficient surveillance system using a drone bases system is proposed and implemented. During disaster situations, the system will efficiently search areas that are beyond the reach of humans, as well as calculate the number of people trapped in these areas and their locations, so that the rescuers can perform their operations efficiently and provide first aid to these people. In addition to our system's performance during natural disasters, it can also be utilized for military surveillance to track a particular area and send useful intelligence to the military.

The system is deployed on a drone and the communication with the drone from the ground station is performed using Wi-Fi. As the distance between the drone and

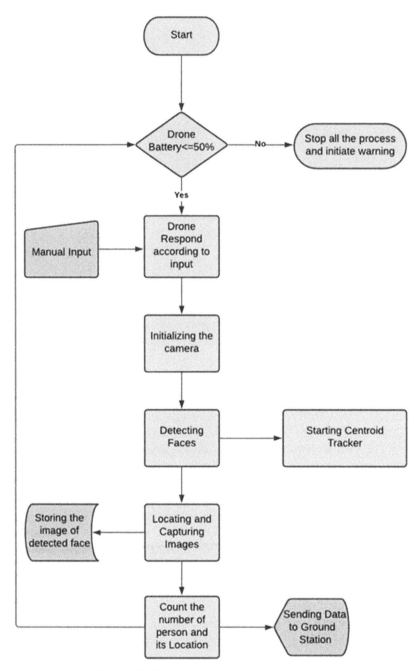

Figure 1.19. The flow chart of the proposed system.

ground station increases, the Wi-Fi signal becomes weaker. Because of that, some of the frames can be missed, which will cause an error in counting the number of people. This can be rectified by using Wi-Fi boosters or by using the LoRaWAN technology for communication between drones and ground stations.

Figure 1.20. Results of the proposed system. (a) Localization and counting of people performed by the proposed system. (b) Tracing the path of the drone. (c) Saving images of people to the database.

Acknowledgements

This research work was supported by Jagadish Chandra Bose Research Organisation (JCBRO).

References

[1] Yang J and Li J 2017 Application of deep convolution neural network *14th Int. Computer Conf. on Wavelet Active Media Technology and Information Proc. (Chengdu)* pp 229–32
[2] Goodfellow I, Bengio Y and Courville A 2016 *Deep Learning* (Cambridge, MA: MIT Press)
[3] Forsyth D and Ponce J 2011 *Computer Vision: A Modern Approach* 2nd edn (Englewood Cliffs, NJ: Prentice Hall) p 792
[4] Browning W M, Olson D S and Keenan D E 1999 High-altitude balloon experiment *Proc. SPIE* **3706** 187–95
[5] Wilkinson J 2013 Animalizing the apparatus: pigeons, drones and the aerial view *Grad. J. Vis. Mater. Cult.* **6** 1–21

[6] Mishra B, Garg D, Narang P and Mishra V 2020 Drone-surveillance for search and rescue in natural disaster *Comput. Commun.* **156** 1–10

[7] Jain A, Basantwani S, Kazi O and Bang Y 2017 Smart surveillance monitoring system *Int. Conf. on Data Management, Analytics and Innovation (ICDMAI) (Pune)* pp 269–73

[8] Menezes V, Patchava V and Gupta M S D 2016 Surveillance and monitoring system using Raspberry Pi and Simple CV *Proc. 2015 Int. Conf. Green Comput. Internet Things* pp 1276–8

[9] Alajrami E, Tabash H, Singer Y and Astal M T E 2019 On using AI-based human identification in improving surveillance system efficiency *Proc.—2019 Int. Conf. Promis. Electron. Technol.* pp 91–5

[10] Rawat M S and Dobhal R 2021 Study of flash flood in the Rishiganga and Dhauliganga Catchment in Chamoli District of Uttarakhand, India *Int. J. Georesources Environ.* **6** 84

[11] Ummer O, Scott K, Mohan D, Chakraborty A and Lefevre A E 2021 Connecting the dots: Kerala's use of digital technology during the COVID-19 response *BMJ Glob. Heal.* **6** e005355

[12] Norris C and Armstrong G 2020 *The Maximum Surveillance Society: the Rise of CCTV* (London: Taylor and Francis)

[13] Kroener I 2016 *CCTV A Technology Under the Radar?* (London: Routledge)

[14] Custers B (ed) 2016 *The Future of Drone UseInformation Technology and Law Series* vol 27 (The Hague: Asser)

[15] Kumar A, Kaur A and Kumar M 2019 Face detection techniques: a review *Artif. Intell. Rev.* **52** 927–48

[16] Bazarevsky V, Kartynnik Y, Vakunov A, Raveendran K and Grundmann M 2019 BlazeFace: sub-millisecond neural face detection on mobile GPUs ArXiv:1907.05047

[17] Liu W *et al* 2016 SSD: single shot multibox detector *European Conference on Computer VisionLecture Notes in Computer Science* vol 9905 (Berlin: Springer) pp 21–37

[18] Chollet F 2017 Xception: deep learning with depthwise separable convolutions *Proc.—30th IEEE Conf. Comput. Vis. Pattern Recognition* vol 2017 pp 1800–7

[19] Traore B B, Kamsu-Foguem B and Tangara F 2018 Deep convolution neural network for image recognition *Ecol. Inform.* **48** 257–68

[20] Yan W, Liu T, Liu S, Geng Y and Sun Z 2020 A lightweight face recognition method based on depthwise separable convolution and triplet loss *39th Chinese Control Conf. (CCC) 2020* pp 7570–5

[21] Suleiman A, Zhang Z, Carlone L, Karaman S and Sze V 2018 Navion: a fully integrated energy-efficient visual-inertial odometry accelerator for autonomous navigation of nano drone *IEEE Symp. VLSI Circuits (Honolulu, HI)* pp 133–4

[22] Nist D and Bergen J 2004 Visual odometry *Proc. of the IEEE Computer Society Conf. on Computer Vision and Pattern Recognition* (Washington, DC) vol 1 p I-1

[23] Kozák V and Pivo T 2021 Robust visual teach and repeat navigation for unmanned aerial vehicles *European Conf. on Mobile Robots (Bonn)* pp 1–7

[24] Kamsani M N L and Mohd M N 2021 Implementation of deep learning and motion control using drone *J. Electr. Electron. Eng.* **2** 57–68

Chapter 2

Use of computer vision to inspect automatically machined workpieces

Virginia Riego del Castillo and Lidia Sánchez-González

Machined workpieces in manufacturing processes must satisfy certain quality standards. Inspection by human operators involves subjectivity and is time consuming. We employ a vision system composed of a microscope camera and a boroscope to acquire images of machined workpieces. Next, we apply computer vision to detect surface imperfections automatically or to identify the type of edge finish. Using existing techniques, we classify surfaces with texture information extracted from the grey level co-occurrence matrix or the local binary pattern features. By carrying out a supervised classification of the obtained feature vectors, the system determines if a surface presents some imperfections. Regarding the edge finish, first its contour is located and represented with a feature vector obtained using an ad hoc procedure. Next, a classification stage identifies the burr type and determines if the edge finish achieves the desired quality level. This system automates daily tasks thus facilitating the manufacturing process.

2.1 Introduction

Industry is undergoing a new revolution by incorporating collaborative robots to assist in daily tasks. In the case of machined workpieces, operators perform visual inspection of the workpieces' surfaces or manual inspection to detect burrs by passing by their fingernail along the edges of the part. In order to analyse small workpieces, tools such as roughness meters are required, which make the inspection process slower and more tedious. Automating some of the decision-making tasks allows us to reduce the subjectivity and time of inspection. Moreover, there is a reduction in the costs required to achieve the high quality standards that the parts have to fulfil [1].

In this field researches have attempted different approaches, such as defect inspection in injection procedures [2]. A large number of studies has focused on the study of the surface of machined workpieces, for example, predicting surface roughness [3] or defects [4]. Manual inspection presents several drawbacks that can be solved by analysing microscopic information obtained from the acquired images using existing techniques. In fact, digital image processing is used widely in milling to analyse the condition that a given tool presents [5], for example, considering flank wear areas [6] or to automatic identification of where the tool tip is located [7].

Another problem studied in milling is the formation of burrs which, according to the ISO 13715 standard [8], is present in those machined pieces with rough remains of material making the edge not ideal geometrically. These burrs might be due to residues produced by the machining process. The importance of the presence of burrs lies in the high costs generated by cutting them. Some researchers study the relationship between the mechanisms and the production of burrs, providing different solutions to erase them with lasers or high pressure water [9]. In addition, malformations in production have several causes, such as vibration, cutting forces, surface quality or burr formation, among others [10].

In this chapter we explain different computer vision solutions to detect the two main problems in milling: surface imperfections and burr formation. The outline of this chapter is as follows. Section 2.2 summarizes the latest research in this field, while section 2.3 explains the methodological schemes of different techniques. Then section 2.4 specifies the tools and dataset required to develop all the mentioned experiments. The results obtained in the experiments are gathered in section 2.5. Finally, section 2.6 includes the conclusion and discussion of future works.

2.2 Related works

Notwithstanding that computer vision techniques have been applied to manufacturing processes since the 1990s, this is still a field of ongoing research [11–13]. Some researchers have focused on tool condition monitoring. They have proposed the use of computer vision techniques that analyse texture information provided by the grey-level co-occurrence matrix (GCLM). Among such features, entropy allows the determination of tool wear [14] and, along with the angular second moment (ASM), contrast and correlation enable monitoring of tool wear [15]. These systems build a knowledge base according to existing expertise that helps operators during the decision-making stages. More recent works use other approaches such as convolutional neural networks (CNNs), achieving an accuracy of 98.7% in recognition of the tool wear state [16] and 97.10% in the detection of tool breakage [17]. Sound signals features from Harr wavelet energy and statistical analysis have been used to determine how severe the tool wear is, achieving an accuracy of 82.41% [18].

Similar to tool monitoring, the use of texture descriptors is a fairly standard solution to study a material's surface. Whereas some methods propose wavelet statistical features to classify different textures [19] others consider entropy from the GLCM [20]. There are also studies that use local binary patterns (LBPs) in order to classify datasets, with identifications of the defects reaching an accuracy of 97.89%

[21]. Regarding deep learning, some approaches use CNN to detect defects in images with architectures such as ResNet and VGG [22] or PGA-Net [23]. In this chapter, we focus on two traditional approaches to classify surfaces according to their appearance: the use of LBPs to detect anomalies [24] and multiple GCLM properties to classify surfaces [25, 26].

Here, the study of burr presence is focused mainly on the reasons for how and why they are formed [27], defining a list of five types of burr at the edge finish. Cutting conditions are also studied in order to understand how they affect burr formation [28]. Signal processing of acoustic emission or forces employed to cut the pieces can also give enough information to be able to assess parameters such as the size of the burr [29]. In more detail, the exit angle can reduce the presence of burrs [30]. In fact, even the heterogeneity present in a microstructure of a certain material or the thickness that is present in a chip before cutting it might play a significant role in burr formation [31].

Some image processing techniques have been used to detect burr formation. In [32] the position of the burr is calculated by searching for the best-fit rectangle, whereas in [33] the burr is found considering the horizontal axis. In this chapter we use two different approaches: one based on thresholds and linear regression to determine the presence of burrs in images of milling parts and thus categorize them [34], and another based on contour properties that give a burr classification [35].

2.3 Methods

We have designed two different methods, one to analyse the surface texture of the workpieces and another to detect and classify the type of burr that a given part presents. Both methods are based on computer vision techniques such as the ones mentioned in section 2.2. First, the images of the workpieces are acquired by the vision-based system described in section 2.3.1. By applying digital image processing to the captured images two different objectives are established. On the one hand section 2.3.2 details the procedure to analyse the surface texture of the workpieces. On the other hand, section 2.3.3 explains the method to detect the end of the workpiece and extract certain features that represent the contour in order to determine the type of burr that is present. Finally, section 2.3.4 gives details about the classifiers that have been considered in experiments and evaluates their performance.

2.3.1 Image acquisition

The acquisition system comprises an industrial boroscope with an attached micro-scope camera, as shown in figure 2.1. The system counts with white LED light supplied by an optical fibre with adjustable brightness to obtain enough information about the workpiece. The system captures RGB images with 2592×1944 pixels and a resolution of 300 ppp.

The inner and outer surfaces of the machined parts, such as those shown in figure 2.2, can be visualized with the vision system. All the acquired images have

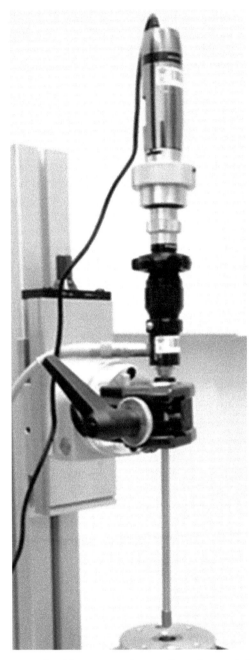

Figure 2.1. Acquisition system built with a camera that acquires microscopic images from the boroscope visualization [37].

been labelled manually by experts using visual inspection. The obtained dataset with surface images that are classified according to surface wear is available in [36]. The dataset with a collection of burr images labelled considering three categories is available in [26].

Figure 2.2. Examples of the machined workpieces used for the experiments.

2.3.2 Surface analysis to determine workpiece quality

Undoubtedly, texture is one important characteristic of an image and it is highly correlated with tone. However, tone refers to the situation when a given area of the image presents certain variation, while texture presents a wide variation. That is the reason why Haralick *et al* [38] proposed the grey-tone spatial-dependence matrices, commonly called the grey-level co-occurrence matrix (GCLM). The GCLM is computed considering the grey values of the image pixels for a chosen distance and angle.

Step 1. Image pre-processing
This approach is based on the use of grey-level images. For that reason, the first step converts the original image to grey values using the construction of luminance, as explained in [39], that converts the three channels (RGB) into only one channel of grey levels called G by applying the weighted addition

$$G = 0.299 \times red \text{ channel} + 0.587 \times green \text{ channel} \\ + 0.114 \times blue \text{ channel.} \tag{2.1}$$

Figure 2.3 shows the obtained image after applying equation (2.1). Then the image is enhanced to improve its contrast quality by applying contrast-limited adaptive histogram equalization (CLAHE). Specifically, in this work it is applied with a contrast limit of three and a grid for histogram equalization of 8×8, as these are the values for the parameters of CLAHE that achieve a better image visualization.

Step 2. Image analysis
Afterwards, the histogram of the grey-level image I is calculated with the number of times that a certain value j appears from a given value i. That histogram generates a normalized matrix called M. From this matrix, the following texture features can be obtained [38]:
- *Contrast* measures the intensity difference between a certain pixel and the pixels that are around it:

$$\sum_{i,j=0}^{levels-1} M_{i,j}(i-j)^2. \tag{2.2}$$

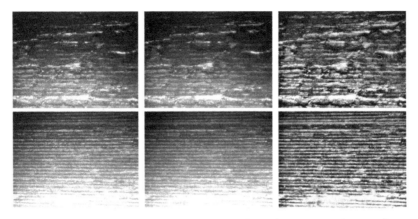

Figure 2.3. Samples of images that present certain defects on the surface (upper row) or not (lower row) and how they appear originally (left), when converted to grayscale (middle), and after histogram enhancement (right).

- *Dissimilarity* gives information about abrupt change considering linear weights:

$$\sum_{i,j=0}^{\text{levels}-1} M_{i,j} \mid i - j \mid. \tag{2.3}$$

- *ASM* (angular second moment) uses each value $M_{i,j}$ as a weight; a high values indicates that the image is homogeneous:

$$\sum_{i,j=0}^{\text{levels}-1} M_{i,j}^2. \tag{2.4}$$

- *Energy* is the square root of the ASM:

$$\sqrt{\text{ASM}}. \tag{2.5}$$

- *Homogeneity* gives information about how close the matrix elements are to the diagonal:

$$\sum_{i,j=0}^{\text{levels}-1} \frac{M_{i,j}}{1 + (i - j)^2}. \tag{2.6}$$

- *Correlation* gives information if there is a linear dependence of the pixel values within a neighbour:

(a) (b) (c) (d)

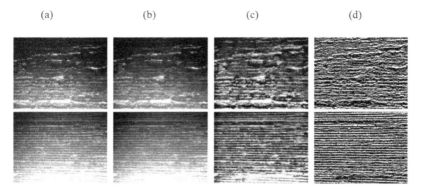

Figure 2.4. Samples of images of part surfaces that present certain defects (upper row) or not (lower row). The original image (a) is converted to grayscale (b) and CLAHE is applied (c). Finally, horizontal stripes are obtained with a Sobel edge filter (d).

$$\sum_{i,j=0}^{\text{levels}-1} M_{i,j} \left[\frac{(i - \mu_i)(j - \mu_j)}{\sqrt{(\sigma_i^2)(\sigma_j^2)}} \right], \tag{2.7}$$

where the μ_i, μ_j, σ_i, and σ_j variables are calculated as

$$\mu_i = \sum_{ii} \sum_j M_{i,j} \tag{2.8}$$

$$\mu_j = \sum_{jj} \sum_i M_{i,j} \tag{2.9}$$

$$\sigma_i = \sum_i (i - \mu_i)^2 \sum_j M_{i,j} \tag{2.10}$$

$$\sigma_j = \sum_j (j - \mu_j)^2 \sum_i M_{i,j}. \tag{2.11}$$

Another way to describe the surface texture is the use of a local binary pattern (LBP), which defines the texture of a pixel considering its neighbourhood. After the pre-processing stage the horizontal stripes are highlighted by employing a Sobel edge filter, as is shown in figure 2.4. That is the reason why it is calculated with the first horizontal (y) derivate and a small kernel of 5×5 pixels. After that, the LBP [40] is computed as follows: for a circle whose radius is R centred in each pixel x_0, the sign of the difference between the grey level of such pixel ($I(x_0)$) and the grey levels of the pixels that belong to that circle (neighbour P) are considered as the following equation shows:

$$\text{LBP}_{P,\ R}(x_0) = \sum_{k=1}^{P} s\left\{ I(x_k) - I(x_o) \right\} \times 2^{k-1}, \tag{2.12}$$

where the signal is defined as

$$s = \begin{cases} 1, & \text{if} \quad \{I(x_k) - I(x_o)\} \geqslant 0 \\ 0, & \text{if} \quad \{I(x_k) - I(x_o)\} < 0 \end{cases}. \tag{2.13}$$

2.3.3 Burr detection

Another problem to consider in manufacturing processes is the presence of burrs in the machined parts. In this case, the first stage involves the end detection of the machined workpiece. In other words, the location where the workpiece ends, and the background starts must be determined. In this section the method proposed by the authors in [34] to determine the edge finish of a certain part is explained in detail.

Step 1. Image pre-processing.
As in surface analysis, this procedure also starts with the original image that is denoised using non-local means [41], replacing a pixel with the mean of similar patches. In this case we use a template window to compute the weight of seven pixels, a search window to compute the weighted average of 21 pixels and a regulation filter strength of 10. Next, the obtained image is converted to grayscale as was explained previously. Figure 2.5 gives information about the image evolution along this pre-processing stage.

Step 2. Image analysis.
In order to preserve as much information as possible, as was mentioned above, the image is enhanced by applying CLAHE (see figure 2.6(a)). Next, the image is converted to zeros and ones with Otsu thresholding so as to distinguish the workpiece (white pixels) from the background (black pixels), figure 2.6(b). As we want to obtain the line that limits the end of the piece, we apply morphological operations to the binary image, specifically a closing operation

(a)   (b)   (c)

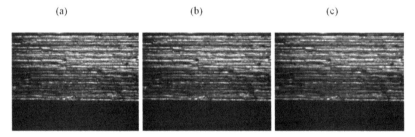

Figure 2.5. Machined workpiece images are pre-processed to detect the edge. First, the original image (a) is denoised with non-local means (b) and then it is converted to grayscale (c).

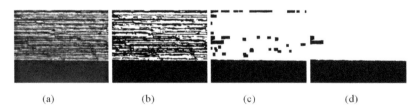

(a)   (b)   (c)   (d)

Figure 2.6. The end finish of the workpiece image is detected as follows: first the image is enhanced (a), then Otsu thresholding converts it into a binary image (b), next a closing operation is applied (c) and finally small objects are removed (d).

with a kernel of 35 × 35. This operation consists of a dilation operation followed by an erosion that allows us to merge the near white sections of the image (figure 2.6(c)). Finally, small objects in the image whose number of pixels is lower than 10 000 pixels are deleted, keeping just the bigger areas, as figure 2.6(d) shows.

The final step involves determining the right location of the end of the workpiece. To deal with this, as we proposed in [35], divide the image uniformly by height, obtaining a set of horizontal regions of the image in the region where the part ends. For each horizontal region the percentage of white pixels that correspond to the part is calculated. This information can be shown in the chart of figure 2.7, represented by a dashed line. As can be observed, it defines a function similar to a step function, so we focus on the change section. The criterion to determine where the edge finishes is established as follows. Let be y the percentage of white pixels for each horizontal region x; we consider only those points whose difference to the next point is greater than 5. Then we focus on the y values in order to group points whose difference is less than 5. Finally, we study the highest difference between the x values of each group to select the group whose distance is the highest. Finally, the points of the selected group are the potential points of the section of the image corresponding to the end of the workpiece. As we can see in figure 2.7, the chart (left side) shows all the points (discontinuous line) that are then filtered (circle points) and grouped in regions (blue areas). The group with the greatest distance between the points (orange continuous line) is the region of interest and it is marked by a red box in the original image (figure 2.7, right).

We can observe in figure 2.8 that this algorithm works properly for images where the background is at the top of the image as well as for those where the background is at the bottom. Figure 2.8 shows the chart of the points used to detect the end of the piece. As can be observed, the blue area that contains the orange line determines where the end is located. In the right-hand panel of figure 2.8 we can see the original image with the potential section highlighted in red which corresponds to the blue area with the orange line determined by the chart.

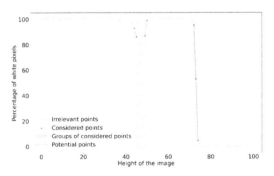 

Figure 2.7. Detection of the end of a machined workpiece and the obtained region of interest.

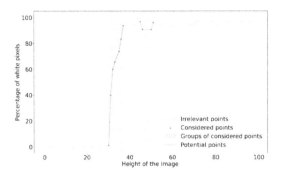

Figure 2.8. Detection of the end of a machined workpiece that presents a burr-breakage whose background is located at the top of the image.

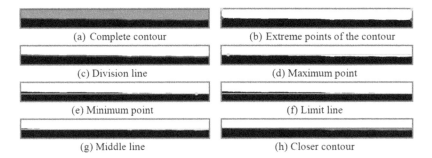

Figure 2.9. Process for extracting information from a contour.

The obtained potential points generate an equation that can be adjusted to a linear model. We can apply linear regression to the points in order to define a linear equation that keeps the distances to the points at a minimum. In every step of the procedure, the weights are updated to reduce the distance from the equation to the points. Normally the distance is calculated using the sum of squares.

In [35] another approach is proposed to extract a feature vector of the binary edge image that represents the contour of the part. As previously, the original image is pre-processed and then binarized to separate the background and object. This approach extracts information from the contour specified by the end of the part. Thus the first step deals with the longest contour identification by considering the region where the part ends, since it presents the greatest area (number of pixels). That is to say that we understand that a contour is formed with continuous points with the same value (figure 2.9). Next, we create a feature called *sign* that indicates if the workpiece is located at the top of the image or at the bottom by considering the percentage of white pixels of the top and bottom sections.

The limit of the workpiece with the background is the contour to be determined (figure 2.9(a)), as well as a division line that allows us to extract certain features. In order to obtain that division line we identify four points: the ones located on the left and right sides of the contour are shown in blue and the corners of the region of interest are shown in green in figure 2.9(b). They help us to extract the division line from the end of the workpiece (the blue line in figure 2.9(c)) because two points give us the beginning and end of the line, and the other two are used to close the contour in the limits of the region of interest of the image. Then we extract the points that are located at the maximum M and minimum m positions for future operations (the green points in figures 2.9(d) and (e), respectively) and draw one horizontal line that crosses M and another that crosses Mm (the green line in figures 2.9(d) and (e)). These horizontal lines allow us to calculate the lower part of the contour (figure 2.9(f)) and the middle point between m and M where we draw another horizontal line (figure 2.9(g)). Finally, a new region is defined by closing the area described by the division line and passing through the m and M points (figure 2.9(h)).

After these calculations we can extract multiple features that can help us to classify the contours. The features are shown in figure 2.10 and are the following:

- *Distance*, which is the divergence of the contour, defined as the distance between the previously defined points m and M.
- *Percentage of white pixels (PWP) considering the limit line*. To compute this feature, the region of interest that holds the end of the part is divided using the limit line (figure 2.9(f)). Then the PWP is calculated in each section (figure 2.10(a)). If the workpiece is in the top of the image (considering the previously computed sign), the value corresponds with the top section. If not, the value is the one in the bottom section.
- *PWP considering the middle line*. Similarly, in this case the region of interest is divided using the middle line (figure 2.9(g)) and the PWP is calculated as in the previous step (figure 2.10(b)).
- *Slope*. The slope is obtained using a linear regression model (figure 2.10(c)) whose input is formed by the points of the contour (figure 2.9(c)).
- *Extent* is the ratio of the closed contour area (figure 2.9(h)) and the bounding rectangle area that defines the region of interest (the blue rectangle in figure 2.10(d)).

2.3.4 Classification

As we have mentioned in previous sections, images are divided into multiple categories and the ground truth has been labelled by an expert using visual inspection. With this information we can establish that the final problem is a supervised classification, in which final categories are known and make it possible to

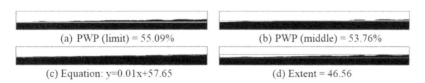

(a) PWP (limit) = 55.09%   (b) PWP (middle) = 53.76%

(c) Equation: y=0.01x+57.65   (d) Extent = 46.56

Figure 2.10. Some of the features extracted from the contour of the binary edge image. PWP in the limit and middle line (first row). Equation using linear regression and the extent (second row).

fit the considered models. In this section, we mention some classifiers that are commonly used for this type of problem and that have been considered in the experiments so as to evaluate the methods.

a) *k*-nearest neighbours

is one of the simplest methods; it generates k centroids of the dimension of the input vector. For example, if we are creating an LBP with six-bin histograms to classify images with and without defects, we should establish two centroids with dimensions of six. During the training the position of the centroids is optimized to be the closest one to the neighbouring points of the same class [42].

b) An SVC

is a support vector machine (SVM) with a parameter to control the regularization (C). SVMs are based on the optimization of a hyperplane to distinguish between two categories in the data. The C parameter [43] adds a penalty for each misclassified point. Thus if we choose a small C, the penalty will be lower and the margin greater. When C is larger, the number of misclassified examples is smaller because of the high penalty.

c) Decision tree classifiers [44] establish a set of rules structured hierarchically with the knowledge extracted from the training set. The tree representation provides an easier interpretation of the model. This has been improved with some ensemble methods:

- Random forest [45] ensembles decision trees that are joined to achieve a higher accuracy while keeping a stable prediction. The final output is the mean of the prediction of some decision trees.
- Extremely randomized trees, also known as extra-trees, are similar to random forest. The difference is found when the node has to establish the threshold—while random forest searches for the optimal value, extra-trees assign a random value. This change makes it possible to obtain a forest with higher randomness, reducing the risk of overfitting during the training.

(d) Boosting methods train certain weak learners sequentially so as to improve the results step by step. Adaptive boosting [46], also known as AdaBoost, uses the failures from the previous weak learner to train another one. Gradient boosting [47] is an improvement of AdaBoost in which a loss function indicates how good each weak learner is during the training. Finally, extreme gradient boosting, known as XGBoost, uses the previous idea and incorporates several regularization techniques.

2.4 Experimental set-up

All the experiments have been developed using Python since it is one of the most used tools in data science and is multiplatform, which facilitates experiment reproducibility. In addition to this, multiple libraries have been employed to speed up the development. In order to deal with images, filters and different operations available in OpenCV have been applied. Scikit Learn has also been used to develop machine learning models and evaluate their results.

For experiments, the dataset was formed by images that were acquired by employing the vision-based system explained in section 2.3.1. In order to analyse the surface of a workpiece, 587 images were captured. The class of images with imperfections is formed by 437 samples. The remaining 152 samples satisfied the quality standards according to the classification made by human operators. This dataset is available in [36].

For the burr detection, although researchers consider different types of burrs in the literature [27], we assume just three of those categories which allow us to determine how significant is the burr. Therefore, if a part presents a clean finish that is the ideal situation and is called a knife-type burr (K). If the end shows small splinters it is called a saw-type burr (S) because of the irregularities. Lastly, large deformations in the edge finish are categorized as burr-breakage (B), that is a part that would be considered unusable by the industry. A sample image of each category can be seen in figures 2.11 and 2.12. The burr dataset contains 1073 images with 429 samples of the K category, another 400 images belong to the S class and the remaining 244 are of type B. This dataset is public and is available in [48].

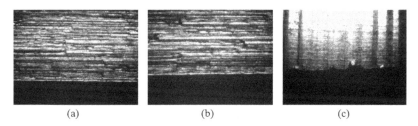

(a)   (b)   (c)

Figure 2.11. Samples of different burr categories: knife-type or ideal (a), saw-type burr (b) and burr-breakage (c).

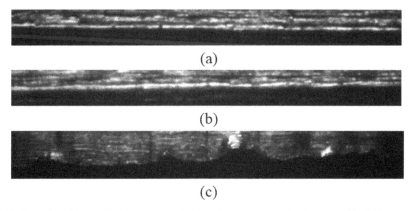

(a)

(b)

(c)

Figure 2.12. Samples of the region of interest of different burr categories: knife-type or ideal (a), saw-type burr (b) and burr-breakage (c).

2.5 Experimental results

Using the datasets and tools explained in section 2.4, some experiments have been developed to classify the quality of surface of the workpieces (section 2.5.1), and also to detect and categorize the edges that a given machined part presents (section 2.5.2). For reproducibility purposes, all the experiments carried out for this chapter and the images that form the dataset are publicly available in a repository [49].

2.5.1 Workpiece quality

Surface finish pays an important role to determine if a machined part satisfies the expected quality. Therefore, we want to determine if the surface image of a certain workpiece presents some type of defect to determine its quality. This might be considered a regression problem if we had metrics to quantify it, such as the ones obtained with a roughness meter. Otherwise, as the images were labelled visually, two categories are established for experiments: 'good' for those surfaces that present no imperfections and 'with defects' for surfaces with a higher heterogeneity and defects such as scratches or pitches.

The GLCM can be calculated considering different distances and angles, so we establish a neighbour distance of three pixels and nine different angles between 0° and 180°. These features are calculated for the original image in grayscale and also for the enhanced image obtained after using CLAHE. Figure 2.13 shows that, in general, there is a higher distance between the features when the image has been enhanced (continuous line). Consequently, higher distances between features make it easier to classify them correctly.

Furthermore, the LBP descriptor can be calculated for different values of the radius and points and, after that, they are expressed as a histogram of a determined number of bins. Figure 2.14 shows the final descriptors for an image with no defects

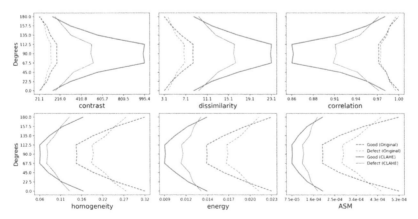

Figure 2.13. GLCM properties, from 0° to 180°, calculated from surface images labelled as good (red) and images with defects (green) at the surface considering the original images (discontinuous line) and the enhanced images (continuous).

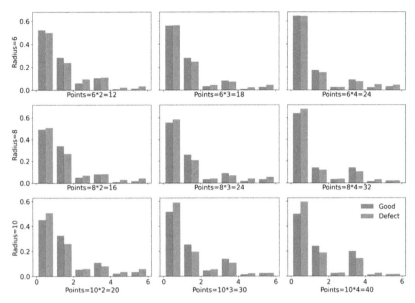

Figure 2.14. LBP descriptors for images labelled as with no defects (good) and with defects, generating histograms with six bins and multiple radius and points.

Table 2.1. The results of published papers using texture descriptors to compare the quality of the surface.

Paper	Descriptor	Results	Classifier
[24]	LBP	Hit rates of 86%	Random forest
[25]	GLCM	Hit rate of 91.8%	Decision tree
[26]		Precision of 96.2%	Extra-trees

and an image with defects considering six bins and a combination of different values for the radius and the number of points.

For each image of the dataset mentioned in section 2.4, the set of features described in section 2.3.2 have been extracted. All this information has been used to feed multiple classifiers (explained in section 2.3.4). Table 2.1 summarizes the results obtained in the experiments. A comparison of LBP with six and four bins applying some classifiers (decision tree, k-nearest neighbours, random forest and support vector) is presented in [24]. The results determine that random forest is the best classifier with a hit rate of 84.3% with four bins and an 86% with six bins.

Using features extracted from the GLCM, homogeneity and ASM are used for a ten-fold cross validation with different classification approaches (decision tree, k-nearest neighbours, naïve Bayes and multi-layer perceptron) [25]. The best hit rate is yielded by the decision tree classifier (89.6%). The final results with the hold-out dataset (30%) achieved 91.8%, improving the LBP results and reducing the set of features. A deeper study with more classifiers was developed in [26], using SVC, decision tree classifiers (decision tree, extra-trees and random forest) and boosting

classifiers (bagging, gradient boosting, AdaBoost and XGBoost). The best performance was achieved with the extra-tree classifier with 19 weak classifiers. A precision
of 94.7% was reached during training with ten-fold cross validation and 96.2% with
the hold-out dataset (30%).

2.5.2 Burrs

In [34] the method proposed to classify burrs in images of workpieces includes the
detection of their edge and computing the percentage of white pixels of the contour
so as to define a linear equation of those points. Linear regression is used to calculate
the most accurate equation for the potential points. Figure 2.15 shows the charts
with the points and calculated equations for the sample images in figure 2.11. As can
be observed there is a huge difference in the slope of the burr-breakage (B) if it is
compared with the others, although the difference between the knife-type (K) and
saw-type (S) is not so significant. In [34] a manual threshold was established to
categorize the burrs presented in 126 images of workpieces (using 88 for training and
38 for testing). The results show a precision of 76.32% in the test set.

A deeper study of results can be done for each category, yielding a better precision
in the detection of big deformations labelled as burr-breakage (B) with an 88.89% of
hit rate. However, 75% of the images that present higher quality standards (knife-
type and saw-type) are classified correctly.

Considering a larger image dataset, formed of 1073 images with 429 samples of the
K category, 400 images of the S category and 244 of the B category, the method
proposed in [35] represents the contour where the part finishes by a set of features
formed by characteristics explained in section 2.3.3. The data were passed to multiple
classifiers (AdaBoost, gradient boosting, random forest and k-nearest neighbours) with

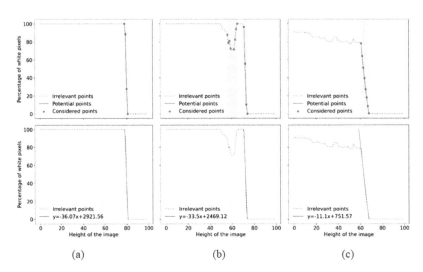

(a)   (b)   (c)

Figure 2.15. Graphs of the generated equation for samples of knife-type (a), saw-type (b) and burr-breakage
(c). The first row shows the complete process to select the potential points and the second row shows the points
determined by the linear regression.

a grid search of parameters. The final results establish random forest as the best classifier of the ten-fold cross validation with an accuracy of 74.94%. The best performance was achieved when 14 was the maximum depth of the tree and 95 was the maximum number of trees in the forest. The model evaluation obtains a 90% precision for the test set (formed by 20% of the dataset). The obtained results improve those obtained by the method that uses only linear regression.

2.6 Conclusions and future work

Computer vision techniques can be applied to a huge variety of problems. In this chapter we have focused on the study of the quality of machined workpieces. The main objective in industrial production is to generate parts with the highest quality and the lowest costs. Resources and money are often spent on assessing quality standards and correcting possible defects that may occur during production.

A complete computer vision methodology has been developed, including the pre-processing step for each image, which has a high relevance because it involves an improvement of the information that we can obtain from the image (which usually presents noise and illumination problems). Also, the extraction of different features from the image is proposed to adapt the image processing to the dataset samples. Last but not least, the use of classifiers such as SVC, decision trees or boosting methods, among others, allows us to carry out a supervised classification.

On the one hand, we focused on the study of the surface of the workpiece images in order to detect wear and imperfections that might devalue the production. We propose two methods based on well-known computer vision techniques to extract texture descriptors that allow us to classify images according to the type of texture they show. One is the use of LBP, obtaining a hit rate of 86%, and the other is the use of descriptors computed from the GLCM, achieving 94.2% precision in detecting if the image presents wear or not. These results can provide intelligence to decision-making systems, ensuring that industry standards are satisfied.

On the other hand, detection and classification of the edge finish of the part is another problem to study. After the pre-processing, we propose to binarize the image so as to differentiate which pixels correspond to the workpiece and which pixels belong to the background. Once the binary image is obtained, so as to determine the region of the image where the edge finish of the part is located, we divide the image by its height in homogeneous horizontal sections. For each section we calculate the percentage of white pixels that defines a function similar to the step one function, if the edge is located at a certain step section. To classify this burr, linear regression of the function can be used, obtaining a precision of 76.83%. We also propose a feature vector computed from the obtained contours achieving 90% precision. Detection is a very important task for the automation of capturing images and allows the evaluation of the surface, but the classification of the burrs is relevant for the fulfilment of industry quality standards.

These two approaches provided results that fulfil the quality standards and also reduce personnel costs with the automation of some tasks. However, the results could be improved with techniques that detect the edges more precisely or the use of convolutional neural networks (CNN). In both cases, there is a need to upgrade the datasets in terms of the number of images, but also in different situations such as changing lighting, pieces or materials, among others.

Acknowledgements

We are grateful for grant PID2019–108277GB-C21 funded by MCIN/AEI/ 10.130339/501100011033. VR would also like to thank Universidad de León for its funding support for her doctoral studies. Finally, we gratefully acknowledge Centro de Supercomputación de Castilla y León (SCAYLE) for its infrastructure support.

References

[1] Dornfeld D and Min S 2010 A review of burr formation in machining *Burrs—Analysis, Control and Removal* (Berlin: Springer) pp 3–11

[2] Chaves M L, Vizán A, Márquez J J and Ríos J 2010 Inspection model and correlation functions to assist in the correction of qualitative defects of injected parts *Polym. Eng. Sci.* **50** 1268–79

[3] Bustillo A and Correa M 2012 Using artificial intelligence to predict surface roughness in deep drilling of steel components *J. Intell. Manuf.* **23** 1893–902

[4] Hu H, Liu Y, Liu M and Nie L 2016 Surface defect classification in large-scale strip steel image collection via hybrid chromosome genetic algorithm *Neurocomputing* **181** 86–95

[5] Dutta S, Pal S K, Mukhopadhyay S and Sen R 2013 Application of digital image processing in tool condition monitoring: a review *CIRP J. Manuf. Sci. Technol.* **6** 212–32

[6] Dai Y and Zhu K 2017 A machine vision system for micro-milling tool condition monitoring *Precis. Eng.* **52** 183–91

[7] López-Estrada L, Fajardo-Pruna M, Sánchez-González L, Pérez H, Fernández-Robles L and Vizán A 2018 Design and implementation of a stereo vision system on an innovative 6DOF single-edge machining device for tool tip localization and path correction *Sensors* **18** 3132

[8] ISO 2017 Edges of undefined shape—indication and dimensioning *Technical product documentation* ISO 13715:2017

[9] Aurich J C, Dornfeld D, Arrazola P J, Franke V, Leitz L and Min S 2009 Burrs—analysis, control and removal *CIRP Ann.—Manuf. Technol.* **58** 519–42

[10] Balázs B Z and Takács M 2020 Experimental investigation and optimisation of the micro milling process of hardened hot-work tool steel *Int. J. Adv. Manuf. Technol.* **106** 5289–305

[11] Malamas E N, Petrakis E G M, Zervakis M, Petit L and Legat J D 2003 A survey on industrial vision systems, applications and tools *Image Vis. Comput* **21** 171–88

[12] Oyeleye O and Lehtihet E A 1998 A classification algorithm and optimal feature selection methodology for automated solder joint defect inspection *J. Manuf. Syst.* **17** 251–62

[13] Magee M and Seida S 1995 An industrial model based computer vision system *J. Manuf. Syst.* **14** 169–86

[14] Li L and An Q 2016 An in-depth study of tool wear monitoring technique based on image segmentation and texture analysis *Measurement* **79** 44–52

[15] Peng R, Liu J, Fu X, Liu C and Zhao L 2021 Application of machine vision method in tool wear monitoring *Int. J. Adv. Manuf. Technol.* **116** 1357–72

[16] Cao X C, Chen B Q, Yao B and He W P 2019 Combining translation-invariant wavelet frames and convolutional neural network for intelligent tool wear state identification *Comput. Ind.* **106** 71–84

[17] Wu X, Liu Y, Zhou X and Mou A 2019 Automatic identification of tool wear based on convolutional neural network in face milling process *Sensors* **19** 3817

[18] Ravikumar S and Ramachandran K I 2018 Tool wear monitoring of multipoint cutting tool using sound signal features signals with machine learning techniques *Mater. Today Proc.* **5** 25720–9

[19] Arivazhagan S and Ganesan L 2003 Texture classification using wavelet transform *Pattern Recognit. Lett.* **24** 1513–21

[20] Li L and An Q 2016 An in-depth study of tool wear monitoring technique based on image segmentation and texture analysis *Meas. J. Int. Meas. Confed.* **79** 44–52

[21] Song K and Yan Y 2013 A noise robust method based on completed local binary patterns for hot-rolled steel strip surface defects *Appl. Surf. Sci.* **285** 858–64

[22] He Y, Song K, Meng Q and Yan Y 2019 An end-to-end steel surface defect detection approach via fusing multiple hierarchical features *IEEE Trans. Instrum. Meas.* **69** 1493–504

[23] Dong H, Song K, He Y, Xu J, Yan Y and Meng Q 2020 PGA-net: pyramid feature fusion and global context attention network for automated surface defect detection *IEEE Trans. Ind. Informatics* **16** 7448–58

[24] Sánchez-González L, Riego V, Castejón-Limas M and Fernández-Robles L 2020 Local binary pattern features to detect anomalies in machined workpiece: hybrid artificial intelligent systems *Int. Conf. on Hybrid Artificial Intelligence Systems* (Lecture Notes in Computer Science vol 12344) ed E A de la Cal *et al* (Cham: Springer) pp 665–73

[25] Castejón-Limas M, Sánchez-González L, Díez-González J, Fernández-Robles L, Riego V and Pérez H 2019 Texture descriptors for automatic estimation of workpiece quality in milling: hybrid artificial intelligent systems *Int. Conf. on Hybrid Artificial Intelligence Systems* (Lecture Notes in Computer Science vol 11734) ed H Pérez *et al* (Cham: Springer) pp 734–44

[26] Riego V, Castejón-Limas M, Sánchez-González L, Fernández-Robles L, Pérez H, Diez-Gonzalez J and Guerrero-Higueras A M 2021 Strong classification system for wear identification on milling processes using computer vision and ensemble learning *Neurocomputing* **456** 678–84

[27] Lin T R 2000 Experimental study of burr formation and tool chipping in the face milling of stainless steel *J. Mater. Process. Technol.* **108** 12–20

[28] Chern G L 2006 Experimental observation and analysis of burr formation mechanisms in face milling of aluminum alloys *Int. J. Mach. Tools Manuf.* **46** 1517–25

[29] Niknam S A, Tiabi A, Zaghbani I, Kamguem R and Songmene V 2011 Milling burr size estimation using acoustic emission and cutting forces *Int. Mech. Eng. Congr. Expo.* vol 3 (New York: ASME) pp 901–9

[30] Póka G, Mátyási G and Németh I 2016 Burr minimisation in face milling with optimised tool path *Procedia CIRP* **57** 653–7

[31] Régnier T, Fromentin G, Marcon B, Outeiro J, D'Acunto A, Crolet A and Grunder T 2018 Fundamental study of exit burr formation mechanisms during orthogonal cutting of AlSi aluminium alloy *J. Mater. Process. Technol.* **257** 112–22

[32] Chen X, Shi G, Xi C, Zhong L, Wei X and Zhang K 2019 Design of burr detection based on image processing *J. Phys. Conf. Ser.* **1237** 032075

[33] Sharan R V and Onwubolu G C 2011 Measurement of end-milling burr using image processing techniques *J. Eng. Manuf.* **225** 448–52

[34] del Castillo V R, Sánchez-González L, Fernández-Robles L and Castejón-Limas M 2020 Burr detection using image processing in milling workpieces: soft computing models in industrial and environmental applications *Int. Workshop on Soft Computing Models in Industrial and Environmental Applications* (Advances in Intelligent Systems and Computing vol 1268) ed A Herrero *et al* (Cham: Springer) pp 751–9

[35] Riego del Castillo V, Sánchez-González L and Álvarez-Aparicio C 2021 Classification of burrs using contour features of image in milling workpieces: hybrid artificial intelligent systems *Int. Conf. on Hybrid Artificial Intelligence Systems* (Lecture Notes in Computer Science vol 12886) ed H Sanjurjo *et al* (Cham: Springer) pp 209–18 (Bilbao, 2021)

[36] del Castillo V R and Sánchez-González L 2021 Use of computer vision to inspect automatically machined workpieces—datasets https://open.scayle.es/dataset/workpieces-image-dataset

[37] Olivera D C 2019 Using a borescope prototype: specifications, virtual modelling and practical application *Master's Thesis* University of León, Spain

[38] Haralick R M, Dinstein I and Shanmugam K 1973 Textural features for image classification *IEEE Trans. Syst. Man Cybern.* **SMC-3** 610–21

[39] ITU Radiocommunication Assembly 2011 Studio encoding parameters of digital television for standard 4:3 and wide-screen 16:9 aspect ratios *Recommendation ITU-R* BT.601-5

[40] Smolka B and Nurzynska K 2015 Power LBP: a novel texture operator for smiling and neutral facial display classification *Procedia Comput. Sci.* **51** 1555–64

[41] Buades A, Coll B and Morel J M 2011 Non-local means denoising *Image Process. Line* **1** 208–12

[42] Cunningham P and Delany S J 2020 *k*-nearest neighbour classifiers—a tutorial *ACM Comput. Surv.* **54** 128

[43] Chang C C and Lin C J 2021 LIBSVM: a library for support vector machines www.csie.ntu.edu.tw/

[44] Breiman L, Friedman J H, Olshen R A and Stone C J 1984 *Classification and Regression Trees* (Monterey, CA: Wadsworth and Brooks/Cole)

[45] Breiman L 2001 Random forests *Mach. Learn.* **45** 5–32

[46] Zou H, Zhu J, Rosset S and Hastie T 2009 Multi-class AdaBoost *Stat. Interface* **2** 349–60

[47] Friedman J H 2001 Greedy function approximation: a gradient boosting machine *Ann. Stat.* **29** 1189–232

[48] del Castillo V R and Sánchez-González L 2021 Burr detection and classification using RUSTICO and image processing—datasets *SCAYLE*

[49] del Castillo V R and Sánchez-González L 2021 Computer vision workpieces: use of computer vision to inspect automatically machined workpieces *GitHub* https://github.com/uleroboticsgroup/computer_vision_workpieces

Chapter 3

Machine learning for vision based crowd management

K S Kavitha and Megha P Arakeri

Artificial intelligence tasks that would normally require human eyesight are best served by computer vision. As a result, people counting, usually referred as crowd counting, is an important computer vision application. People counting is a technique for counting people in public or estimating the amount of people in a certain area. Large crowds in public places risk people's health in the current COVID-19 pandemic situation. Manually restricting the number of people in public places is tedious. Hence, this chapter proposes a crowd management technique using a machine learning approach. The proposed system counts the people in a video frame captured from CCTV installed in public places. A deep neural based network is used for crowd computing in real time. The work uses the YOLOV3 model which is trained using the COCO dataset to detect the people in the frame. Even in difficult situations, such as crowded heads and incomplete visibility of heads, the model performs well. In a densely populated area this method provides high accuracy in determining the human count within a predetermined time frame and the accuracy achieved by the model is 95%.

3.1 Introduction

The COVID-19 pandemic began in late 2019 in China and spread around the world. It has had a tremendous influence on society worldwide. Its economic, social and environmental consequences have touched a large number of people. Many governments have implemented substantial transportation and public space restrictions. The number of pedestrians in public spaces has dropped drastically as a result of this circumstance. Private video monitoring systems, in addition to public video surveillance systems, may be used to detect and count people. Several types have been operational for a number of years, allowing for comparisons with the pre-pandemic era.

The suggested system's major goal is to is to support society by economizing in terms of time and help in the reduction of the spread of the coronavirus that has escalated worldwide. The suggested method will track the number of individuals by combining modern AI technologies such as computer vision and deep learning algorithms with geometrical methodologies to create a powerful model that includes three aspects: detection, tracking and validation [1]. The main task of the people count detector is to first identify a person in a real-time frame and then count the detected people in the frame and display the results on a monitor. The proposed method acquires the data using real-time cameras and publicly available datasets are used for training purposes. This not only helps meet actual needs, but it also ensures an excellent accuracy rate. Hence in this work a real-time monitoring system is proposed using computer vision and deep neural based network techniques to help in overcoming the COVID-19 pandemic .

3.2 Related work

The goal of this section is to examine the crowd computing strategies used in this study and present peer reviewed papers that cover our current knowledge, as well as research pertaining to crowd computing. COVID-19 is a worldwide pandemic causing great suffering and we are trying to manage this dangerous respiratory disease. Many researchers have published excellent papers on ways to overcome this disease and help our society. There is a lot of ongoing research on developing automated systems based on advanced technologies for monitoring COVID-19 safety violations in public areas. A thorough overview of the techniques for counting the number of people in public places is provided in the following section.

3.2.1 A review of people count detection techniques

It is very important to prevent crowding in public areas in the COVID-19 situation. Publications on methods for counting the number of people in crowded settings are described below.

Bhangale *et al* [2] developed a deep convolution neural network (DCNN) based system which was used for real-time computing of a crowd. The proposed method used an NVIDIA GPU processor to utilize a parallel computing framework. The CSR Net neural network architecture was used to obtain output accuracy using the max-pooling operation. This work had the benefits of high-performance computing, but the method requires additional research to remove extra complications of the images from the video stream.

Sang *et al* [3] proposed a scale-adaptive convolution neural network (SaCNN) model that used a CNN to acquire a density map of the high-quality crowd images and combined these to obtain the head count. Along with SaCNN, a random cropping method was used on the training samples to improve the network generalization. The ShangaiTech Public dataset was used, which showed more accuracy, but further work must be done to enhance the reusability of the model.

Pandey *et al* [4] implemented an orthographic projection of a crowd that was captured using a camera attached to a drone to reduce the effect of obstruction and scaling.

The information that was captured was given as input to the CNN for training the model to produce a head count of the people in the frame. After feeding through the CNN, the max-pooling operation was performed to achieve the right prediction for the approach and some geometrical calculation was performed to obtain the highest accuracy. However, model prediction was quite difficult if there was an increase in the occlusion of the images.

Zhang *et al* [5] proposed an approach that used a crowd computing code framework (C^3F) to detect the crowd using the open-source tool PyTorch. This framework achieved better results and allowed the cost of the human training process to be reduced. However, the performance of the system using different models was a challenging task and it was too risky.

Bhoominathan *et al* [6] developed a method that used a convolution deep network and shallow network and it worked with the largest dataset of the studies mentioned here (UCF-CC-50) and showed the best results. Their approach used the VGG-16 architecture trained for the purpose of object classification and segmentation. The mean absolute error was used as the quantifier to check the performance of the method. However, there was an intrinsic difficulty in dealing with high density crowds.

Zeng *et al* [7] proposed a method that used a multi-scale CNN (MSCNN) for single-image crowd counting. Their approach worked on the ShanghaiTech and UCF-CC-50 datasets with a small number of parameters. The MSCNN was designed to learn scale-relevant density maps from the original images. The method achieved greater accuracy and robustness with the fewest number of parameters. However, the model was more accurate and robust for only the far smaller number of parameters which was used to calculate the density of the crowd.

Huang *et al* [8] proposed a unique approach to efficiently calculate a crowd in images. Two semantic models were developed to extract the semantic information from the images. A CNN model was constructed to learn the tasks. However, this proposed model could not function as a real-time application as it mainly focused on still images.

Wang *et al* [9] constructed a huge scale NWPU crowd counting dataset which had the characteristics of high resolution, negative samples and enormous appearance differentiation. Using this dataset, they applied 14 different types of machine learning algorithms to measure the accuracy and performance of the system. However, using this dataset they obtained some estimation errors in extremely congested crowds and it was difficult to track very small sized images and if there was very large crowd.

Zhang *et al* [10] proposed a scale-adaptive convolution neural network (SaCNN) to calculate the density of a crowd and the number of people in the images. The model combined multiple feature maps to develop a strong scale-adaptive crowd counter for the image captured and calculates a relative count of the crowd. However, the model could not apply the correct data as a weight layer into the SaCNN. It produced undesired output for the different weights applied.

3.3 Proposed methodology

The proposed system, shown in figure 3.1, aids in the safety of people in public settings by automatically detecting, tracking and validating the people detected in a real-time frame, thereby helping authorities to restrict the entry of the people into public places. This section discusses the solution architecture and how the suggested system will automatically function to avoid problems occurring.

3.3.1 The architecture of the proposed system

To automatically detect people in public places from a real-time video frame, the proposed method will use deep learning algorithms and computer vision techniques. The proposed method takes the input from the real-time video frame, feeds it into the people count detector and finally displays the results of how many people were detected in the frame and stores the output in local storage. The people count detector reads the input frame, detects the person inference and creates the bounding box along with the score labels. The detector then looks for the centroid, accepts the bounding box coordinates and computes the centroids of the bounding box, and then calculates the distance between the new centroid and the existing centroid. Then it assigns associate object IDs to the centroids marked on the frame. If new objects are detected in the frame the detector registers this and assigns a new object ID.

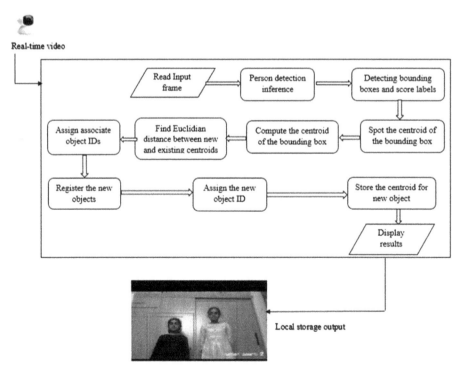

Figure 3.1. The architecture of the proposed system.

Finally, it stores the centroid of the new object and displays the results on the output frame as the human count.

3.3.2 An objective technique for counting people

Artificial intelligence tasks that would normally require human eyesight are best served by computer vision. As a result, people counting, usually referred to as crowd counting, is a common computer vision application. People counting is a method of counting pedestrians moving past or estimating the number of individuals in a certain area or the density of a crowd. Furthermore, people-counting data provide significant information for event identification and strategy planning in a monitored region.

The objective of the model is to develop a system which counts the people in a captured video frame. The pre-trained YOLOV3 model is trained using the COCO dataset to detect the people in the frame. There are only a few top-down views among the COCO dataset's person images, which contains mostly front and side views. As a result the pre-trained YOLOV3 model will give a better performance for a front view. The proposed people count detector is as shown in figure 3.2. First, the input is given as a video frame. Starting from the initial step object detection will be performed, generating the bounding box and allocating the centroid for the object detected, serially manipulating the centroids, assigning a unique ID for every person detected in the frame, keeping track of the people counted when they are in and out of the frame, and subsequently showing the count of people as the result.

A detailed explanation of all the steps is provided below. The people-counting system is made up of a number of interconnected nodes, each of which will execute a different task in order to complete the ultimate effective model.

1. *Input video.* To begin, we must first specify the video source, or the location from which the frames will be drawn. Whether our application receives images from an Internet protocol camera, a PC camera, or a compatible device will be determined by these parameters. The first step is to grab the frames from the correct source before delivering them to the next node.

2. *Region of interest (ROI).* In this phase, we need to instruct the model where to apply the algorithm and where the counting should happen in the image.

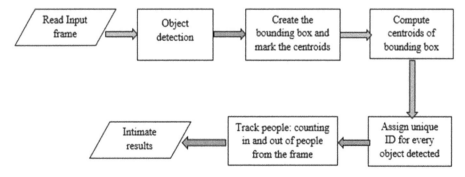

Figure 3.2. The people count detector.

This will save processing time and set up the counting area of the system. A rectangle, polygon, or segment can also be used to define an ROI.

3. *Detection of object.* This stage involves detecting the objects, in this case 'people', from the pre-processed frames. The object detection node allows us to choose from a selection of pre-trained AI models for various hardware architectures using readily available types such as a vision processing unit (VPU) or tensor processing unit (TPU).

4. *Counting the object.* In this step, the system performs the counting of the detected persons. The object count node allows us to select the detection and aggregation intervals, as well as the upload interval for submitting the findings to the cloud.

5. *Output.* The view of the video node produces a display endpoint for the processed video stream, which includes real-time detection and counting. While not necessary for our production system, it is a valuable tool for analyzing and fine-tuning parameters while testing.

The nodes must be connected appropriately for the system to function properly. For further processing, the input frames from the video source should be transferred to the ROI node. Simultaneously, the frames should be sent to the output evaluation node, which will display the results so that testing can be done. Hovering over the connection dots displays each node's output, making it easy to comprehend.

A coordinate tracking algorithm is used in the suggested model. The centroid tracking algorithm is a multi-step procedure that is described in detail in this section and is illustrated in figure 3.3.

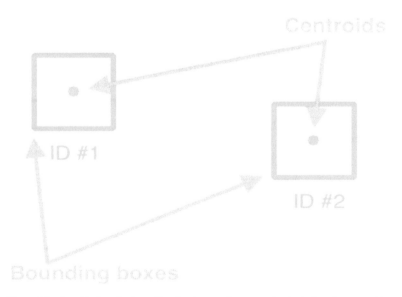

Figure 3.3. Considering the bounding box's coordinates and calculating the centroids.

Step 1. Considering the bounding box's coordinates and calculating the centroids.

Each recognized item in each frame is given a set of bounding boxes with (a, b)-coordinates via the centroid tracking technique. These bounding boxes can be generated by any type of object detector as long as they are computed for each frame in the video. Considering the bounding box's coordinates and the calculating centroids is demonstrated in figure 3.3. A unique ID is assigned because this is the first set of bounding boxes provided to our algorithm.

Step 2. Calculating the Euclidean distance between the newly created bounding boxes and the existing objects.

For each subsequent frame in the video stream, repeat step 1 of computing object centroids. However, instead of assigning a different ID to each identified object, we must first determine if the new object centroids can be related to the previous object centroids. Calculating the distance measure between each pair of existing object centroids and then calculating the distance between each pair of existing object centroids is how this is done. Figure 3.4 shows that three things have been spotted in the image this time. Two extant objects make up the two pairings that are close together.

Step 3. Changing the existing objects' (a, b) coordinates.

The essential assumption of the centroid tracking technique is that an item can move between frames, but the distance between the centroids for frames $F(x)$ and $F(x + 1)$ will be smaller than all the other distances between objects. As a result, there will be a construction of an object tracker by associating centroids with minimal distances between consecutive frames. The centroid tracker system chooses to connect centroids that have the shortest Euclidean distance between them, as is shown in figure 3.5.

Step 4. Registering the new objects detected.

If there are more input detections than there are tracked objects, we must register the new object. The process of adding a new object to our list of tracked objects is referred to as 'registration' and involves the following steps: (i) a new object ID is assigned, (ii) then step 2 is repeated and (iii) this is repeated for each frame in our

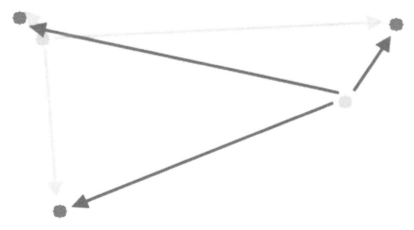

Figure 3.4. Computing the Euclidean distance.

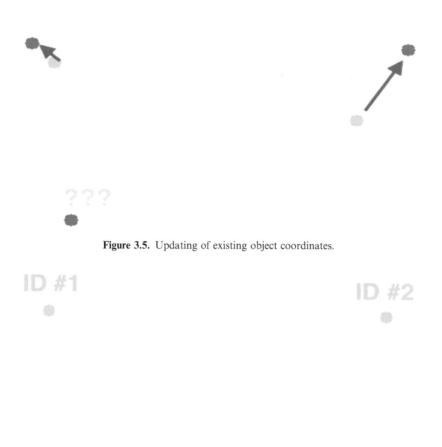

Figure 3.5. Updating of existing object coordinates.

Figure 3.6. Registering the new objects detected.

video stream. Before registering a new item, the process of correlating current object IDs with minimum Euclidean distances is carried out, as depicted in figure 3.6.

Step 5. De-registering the earlier objects.

Any suitable object tracking system must be capable of managing scenarios in which an object has departed, vanished, or is obscured from view. Old objects are deregistered if they cannot be matched to any existing objects for a total of N frames, depending on where our object tracker is planned to be deployed.

3.3.3 The architecture of YOLOV3

In this work YOLOV3 is used for person detection since it improves predictive accuracy, in particular for small-scale objects. The network topology has been altered for multi-scale object recognition, which is the main benefit. Furthermore, for object categorization it employs a range of distinct metrics [11]. Figure 3.7 depicts the model's overall architecture, which shows that the assessment of models is accomplished via convolutional layers, also known as intrinsic blocks. The blocks are made up of many fully connected layers and skip connections. The model's distinguishing feature, as illustrated in figure 3.7, is that it recognizes objects at three different scales. To down-sample the feature map and transmit invariant-sized features, convolutional layers are used. For object recognition three feature maps are used.

To calculate the distance between two people, use the triangle's matching algorithm to detect the person's distance d from the camera, and then use the camera's perceived focal length to compute the distance between them, assuming the person's real height $H = 165$ cm. The following formula can be used to compute the focal length of the camera using these data:

$$FL = (p \times d)/H. \tag{3.1}$$

The person's distance from the camera is then calculated using the real person's height p, the person's pixel height PH and the camera's focal length FL. The following formula can be used to calculate the distance from the camera:

$$D = (H \times FL)/PH. \tag{3.2}$$

We determine the distance between two persons in the video after measuring the depth of the person in the camera. A video has the potential to reveal a vast number of people. Bounding box T represents the actual manually labelled data in the dataset to be trained, whereas bounding box P represents the predicted data. Area represents the insertion of the area. A suitable region is expected and determined for each observed individual in the input frame. Following the prediction, the confidence value is utilized to choose the box of confinement. x, y, h and w are calculated for each structuring element predicted, with x, y denoting the bounding box's coordinates and w, h denoting its width and height. The bounding box values are predicted by the model as follows:

$$\text{IoU (predicted, actual)} = \text{area} \frac{\text{bounding box } T \cap \text{bounding box } P}{\text{bounding box } T \cup \text{bounding box } P} \tag{3.3}$$

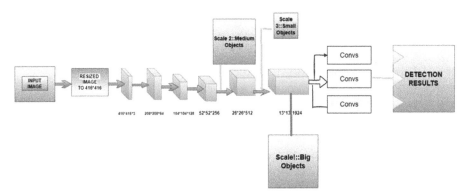

Figure 3.7. The architecture of YOLOV3.

$$B_x = \sigma(T_x) + C_x$$

$$B_y = \sigma(T_y) + C_y$$

$$B_W = P_w e_w^t \tag{3.4}$$

$$B_H = P_w e_h^t.$$

In equation (3.4) B_x, B_y, B_W and B_H are the estimated bounding box coordinates where the centre of the coordinates are represented by x and y, and width and height by W and H. T_x and T_y are the outputs of the network and C_x and C_y are used to identify the grid cell's left-top coordinates, while P_W and P_H are the width and height of the object presented.

Once persons are discovered in the video frames, the centre of each detected person's bounding boxes (shown as green boxes) is utilized to compute the distance. Using the identified bounding box coordinates, the centroid of the bounding box is determined (x, y). The centroid is calculated using a set of bounding box coordinates. Each detected bounding box is given a unique ID when the centroid is computed. The distance between each measured centroid is then calculated using the Euclidean distance, as given in

$$D = \sqrt{(y_2 - y_1)^2 + (z_2 - z_1)^2}, \tag{3.5}$$

where y_1, y_2, z_1 and z_2 are the coordinate points and D is the distance between the points.

For the arrangement of bounding boxes, the pairwise L2 standard is determined, as given by the condition

$$\|D\|_2 = \sqrt{\sum_{j=1}^{n}(q_j - p_j)^2}. \tag{3.6}$$

The algorithms below explain the entire code execution of the people count detector.

Algorithm 1. Training and pre-processing on the YOLO custom dataset
INPUT: Real-time video sequence and pre-trained COCO dataset [12].
OUTPUT: Model trained.
Step 1: Convert the video into a sequence of frames.
Step 2: Load the frames along with their pixel values.
Step 3: Processing of the frames will be done.
Step 4: Load the object names along with their respective labels.
Step 5: Data augmentation will be performed which then splits the data into training and testing batches.
Step 6: The pre-trained COCO dataset will be loaded to the YOLOV3 object detector for the detection of the objects.

Algorithm 2. Implementation of the people count detector (object detection and tracking)

INPUT: Real-time video sequence.

OUTPUT: Detection of persons in a real-time feed captured by the outsource camera, calculating the distance between the persons and outputting the total count of the people detected in the real-time camera frame.

Step 1: Capture the real-time video feed from the camera.

Step 2: Load the pre-trained COCO dataset.

Step 3: Detect the objects that have entered the view of the real-time feed.

Step 4: Using object tracking, accept the set of bounding box coordinates (x, y) and calculate the corresponding centroids.

Step 5: Assign a unique ID to a particular detected object.

Step 6: Compute the pairwise Euclidean distance between the new and existing centroids.

Step 7: Attempt to associate the object IDs.

Step 8: Register the new objects detected.

Step 9: Simply unregister an object if it is lost or has departed the range of vision.

Step 10: Display information of the total number of objects detected as the human count on the output screen.

Step 11: Exit screen when q is pressed.

3.4 Experimental results

3.4.1 Dataset

Object detection custom dataset. The system uses the YOLOV3 custom dataset [12] for the people count detection. These are the neural network's pre-trained weights, which are kept in the yolov3.weights folder.

3.4.2 Performance analysis

Performance analysis is a quantitative approach for designing the system to meet the objectives of the proposed solution. The evaluation measures explain how well the system has been developed and met the goals, and objectives can be developed to obtain better output results

Visual results. The number of individuals detected in the frame is shown in figure 3.8 and the findings are displayed as human count.

Metrics. The performance of the proposed model is analysed by calculating the analysis metrics and system is as follows:

$$\text{accuracy} = \frac{\text{true positive} + \text{true negative}}{(\text{true positive} + \text{false positive} + \text{false negative} + \text{true negative})} \quad (3.7)$$

$$\text{precision} = \frac{\text{true positive}}{(\text{true positive} + \text{false negative})} \quad (3.8)$$

Figure 3.8. Real-time people count detection.

Table 3.1. Definition of people-counting detection.

	Counting of people	No people counted
Detected within the frame	TP	FP
Not detected within the frame	TN	FN

$$\text{recall} = \frac{\text{true negative}}{(\text{true positive} + \text{false negative})} \tag{3.9}$$

$$F_1 \text{ score} = 2 \times \frac{\text{recall} \times \text{precision}}{\text{recall} + \text{precision}}. \tag{3.10}$$

Table 3.1 shows the definition of the people count detection. TP indicates true positive values (related to the number of people actually detected in the frame), FP indicates false positive values (that the persons are detected in the frame but there is no counting of the people), TN indicates true negative values (related to the counting of people not detected in the frame) and FN indicates false negative values (showing none of the people detected in the frame and hence no counting of the people).

If the object detection happens, the loss of confidence, which measures the box objectiveness, is given by

$$\text{Loss}_{\text{conf}} = \sum_{j=0}^{s^2} \sum_{i=0}^{b} \left\| \right._{ij}^{No\ obj} (c_i - c_i^*)^2, \tag{3.11}$$

where $\text{Loss}_{\text{conf}}$ is the confidence loss and c_i^* is the score confidence of the box.

In the vast majority of circumstances, Adam is the best adaptive optimizer, as the adaptive learning rate is ideal for sparse data. The people count detector has been trained using the Adam optimizer for compiling with the Keras model and the number of epochs used for training the model is 50, with a learning rate of 0.01 and 34 fps (frames per second) obtained for every 30 frames of detecting the people.

Evaluation measures. The models are trained with 600 frames using the COCO custom dataset [12]. For the model training, the phase value is 45 and the sampling rate is 65. The training loss and the curves of accuracy are as shown in figure 3.9. The model will be tested for different video sequences. Figure 3.9 (a) shows the training loss of YOLOV3 using the overhead dataset and figure 3.9(b) shows the training accuracy of YOLOV3 on the same overhead dataset.

From the curves we can see that the loss percentage is decreasing and there is a gradual increase in the accuracy plot. In the loss curve, the maximum loss in one epoch is up to 0.62% and it is gradually minimized and reaches 0.30%. In the accuracy plot, in the initial epoch the percentage was 92% and for the final batch size the accuracy achieved was up to 95%. Thus, overall, the model has achieved an acceptable accuracy compared to other models.

Figure 3.10 provides the comparison of the proposed model to other models.

Table 3.2 gives the true detection rate (TDR) and false detection rate (FDR) of the model in deep learning, in which different pre-trained object detection models are tested with the dataset that the proposed model is using and with others.

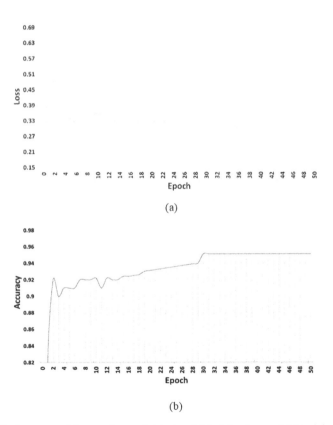

(a)

(b)

Figure 3.9. Performance of the people count detector: (a) training loss and (b) training accuracy.

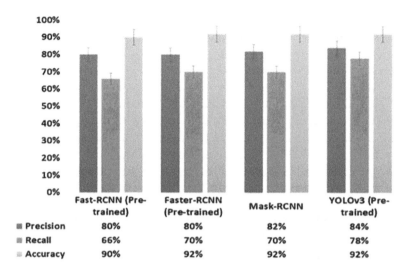

Figure 3.10. Comparison of the proposed model to other models.

Table 3.2. Comparison of the people count detector with different models.

Models	TDR	FDR
Fast-RCNN [13]	91%	0.8%
Faster-RCNN [14]	93%	0.7%
Mask-RCNN [15]	93%	0.4%
Proposed method	95%	0.2%

3.5 Conclusion

The proposed work presents a real-time deep learning-based system for automating the counting of the people via object detection and tracking methodologies, in which each participant is detected in real time using bounding boxes. The resulting bounding boxes assist in locating groups of people that satisfy the pairwise vectorized approach's proximity property. The experiments included comparisons to popular state-of-the-art object identification models such as fast-RCNN, faster-RCNN, mask-RCNN and YOLOV3, with YOLOV3 demonstrating the most improved results. The key challenge in this dataset is the tilted camera perspective, which defies popular dataset-trained person detectors yet correlates to the usual sensor location in this type of scenario.

Future research will focus on enhancing the utilization of the model's signals offered by video sequences in a detection-by-tracking method, rather than the current uni-directional sequential process, which may leave a tracker subject to detection errors. More statistical tests will help to improve the findings by refining definitions and adding data.

References

[1] Udrea C G, Alionte G, Ionaşcu G and Apostolescu T C 2021 New research on people counting and human detection *13th Int. Conf. on Electronics, Computers and Artificial Intelligence* pp 1–6

[2] Bhangale U, Patil S, Vishwanath V, Thakker P, Bansode A and Navandha D 2020 Near real-time crowd computing using deep learning approach *Third Int. Conf. on Computing and Network Communications* **171** 770–9

[3] Sang J, Wu W, Luo H, Xiang H, Zhang Q, Hu H and Xia X F 2019 Improved crowd counting method based on scale-adaptive convolutional neural network *IEEE Access* **7** 24411–9

[4] Pandey A, Pandey M, Singh N and Trivedi A 2020 KUMBH MELA: a case study for dense crowd counting and modelling *Multimed. Tools Appl.* **79** 17837–58

[5] Zhang J, Chen S, Tian S, Gong W, Cai G and Wang Y 2021 A crowd counting framework combining with crowd location *J. Adv. Transp.* **43** 1–14

[6] Boominathan L, Kruthiventi S S S and Babu R V 2016 CrowdNet: a deep convolutional network for dense crowd counting *Int. Computing Education Research Workshop* pp 640–4

[7] Zeng L, Xu X, Bolun C, Suo Q and Tong Z 2017 Multi-scale convolutional neural networks for crowd counting *IEEE Int. Conf. on Image Processing* pp 465–9

[8] Huang S, Li X, Zhang Z, Wu F, Gao S, Ji R and Han J 2018 Body structure aware deep crowd counting *IEEE Trans. Image Process.* **27** 1049–59

[9] Wang Q, Gao J and Lin W 2020 NWPU-crowd a large-scale benchmark for crowd computing and localization *IEEE Trans. Pattern Anal. Mach. Intell.* **43** 2141–9

[10] Zhang L, Shi M and Chen Q 2017 Crowd counting via scale-adaptive convolutional neural network *IEEE Winter Conf. on Applications of Computer Vision* pp 1113–21

[11] Yu J, Amores J, Sebe N and Tian Q 2006 A new study on distance metrics as similarity measurement *Proc. of ICME. IEEE Int. Conf. on Multimedia and Expo* **10** 533–66

[12] Roboflow Object Detection Datasets https://public.roboflow.com/object-detection

[13] Girshick R B 2015 Fast R-CNN *IEEE Int. Conf. on Computer Vision* vol 9 (Piscataway, NJ: IEEE) pp 1440–8

[14] Ren S, He K, Girshick R and Sun J 2017 Faster R-CNN: towards real-time object detection with region proposal networks *IEEE Trans. Pattern Anal. Mach. Intell.* **39** 1137–49

[15] Kumar G and Shetty S 2021 Application development for mask detection and social distancing violation detection using convolutional neural networks *Proc. of the 23rd Int. Conf. on Enterprise Information Systems* **1** 760–7

Chapter 4

Skin cancer classification model based on hybrid deep feature generation and iterative mRMR

Orhan Yaman, Sengul Dogan, Turker Tuncer and Abdulhamit Subasi

Skin cancer is a major public health issue, as it is the most prevalent form of cancer, representing more than half of all cancers diagnosed worldwide. In this study a novel deep learning-based framework is developed for the classification of skin lesions. The primary objectives of this research are to reach a high classification rate on a public skin cancer image dataset and use the effectiveness of the different deep feature generators together. The presented model uses five pre-trained deep learning models as feature generators. By generating 1000 features from each model, 5000 features are extracted in total. In the features selection phase an iterative and improved version of the minimum redundancy maximum relevance (mRMR) feature selection technique, called ImRMR, is used. The proposed hybrid deep feature extraction and ImRMR based feature selection model reached 96.58% accuracy on the dataset used. The calculated results were also compared to other state-of-the-art skin cancer detection models, and the proposed model achieved better results than previous works.

4.1 Introduction

4.1.1 Background

Global warming, one of the largest problems facing humans in recent years, harms the environment and affects people's health negatively [1]. With the changes to the structural features of the ozone layer, people are exposed to more harmful sun rays. Therefore, cases of skin cancer have been increasing rapidly in recent years [2–4]. When the studies in the literature are examined, it is seen that many image processing methods have been developed for skin cancer detection [5, 6]. this disease is classified with artificial intelligence methods by using pretreatment steps such as segmentation of images of skin cancer [7]. Datasets in the literature present skin cancer types such as actinic keratoses, basal cell carcinoma, benign keratosis, dermatofibroma, melanocytic nevus, melanoma and vascular lesion [8–11]. Many datasets are used in the literature to detect and classify skin cancer, such as the ISIC (2017, 2018), Dermofit, DERMIS, PH2, SPC, NIH and HAM10000 datasets which are used widely in the literature [12].

4.1.2 Motivation

Machine learning techniques now have a wide field of implementation. In particular, deep learning models have higher classification abilities. Therefore, many problems have been addressed using deep learning models, and large image datasets have been collected to test the capability of the deep learning methods. This research focuses on automated skin cancer classification using the HAM10000 skin cancer image dataset. This dataset is a large and heterogeneous dataset, and since it is difficult to achieve a high classification performance for such a dataset, the feature engineering and deep learning frameworks have been used to overcome this problem. An appropriate and sufficient feature generator, feature selector and classifier must be used to yield high accuracies. To generate features comprehensively, five pre-trained CNN models are utilized as a feature generation function. An iterative feature selector is deployed to generate features to select the best number of features automatically without employing a trial and error strategy and these features are classified using a deep neural network (DNN) [13].

4.1.3 Literature review

Many classification frameworks have been developed in the literature using HAM10000 and other datasets [14–16]. The studies in the literature include methods which can be applied on mobile phones and have been developed separately from the techniques developed on servers [17, 18]. Cherif *et al* [17] developed a skin cancer detection method for mobile devices using the MobileNetV2 CNN model. It achieved 91.33% success by using 48 373 dermoscopic images in total. Dascalu and David [18] proposed a method that detects skin cancer by using bidirectional communication between mobile devices and the Cloud. In their proposed method, a dermoscopic image taken from a mobile phone is sent to the Cloud system and classified in deep learning models. The results of the deep learning model are transmitted to the mobile phone and the user is informed of the image recognition results. Dai *et al* [19] provided a machine learning and CNN-based skin cancer detection method that can be used on mobile phones. In the proposed method, seven different classes were determined using the HAM10000 dataset. Wati *et al* [20] used image processing and a multilayer perceptron neural network (MLPNN) method for skin cancer detection. Approximately 85.71% success was achieved with the proposed method. The datasets, methods and success criteria used by the current studies in the literature are summarized in table 4.1.

As can be seen in table 4.1, deep networks, in particular CNNs, are the flagship of the state-of-art automated skin cancer detection/classification methods. Therefore we present a fused deep CNN feature generator based model. As stated, CNNs have high time complexity in the training phase. To overcome the time complexity of CNNs, transfer-learning models have been used. Herein, deep features are generated

Table 4.1. Summary of the studies in the literature.

Studies	Year	Method	Dataset	Criteria
Mai et al [12]	2018	InceptionV3, ResNet50, VGG16, VGG19	PH2 [21]	Accuracy, precision, recall, specificity, F_1 score
Lee et al [22]	2018	WonDerM	HAM [14]	Accuracy
Gessert et al [23]	2018	Densenet121, ResNet50, SeNet154	HAM [14], ISIC [24]	Accuracy
Li and Li [25]	2018	DenseNet201, ResNet152, InceptionV4	HAM [14]	Accuracy
Majtner et al [26]	2018	VGG16, GoogLeNet	ISIC [24]	Accuracy
Goyal et al [27]	2018	FRCNNInceptionV2, SSD-InceptionV2, DeepLabV3, VGG16, ResNet50	PH2 [21], HAM [14], ISIC [24]	Accuracy, precision, recall, F_1 score
Shahin et al [28]	2018	ResNet50, InceptionV3	HAM [14]	Accuracy, precision, recall
Tschandl et al [29]	2019	UNet16, LinkNet34, LinkNet152	HAM [14]	Accuracy
Hagerty et al [30]	2019	ResNet50	NIH [30], HAM [14]	Accuracy
Dai et al [19]	2019	CNNs	HAM [14]	Accuracy
Tschandl et al [31]	2019	CNN	EDRA [32], ISIC2017 [24], PRIV [31]	Accuracy, recall, specificity
Barata et al [33]	2019	LSTM	ISIC2017 [24]	Accuracy, recall, specificity
Gessert et al [34]	2019	InceptV3, Dense121, SE-RX	SPC [35], HAM [14], ISIC [24]	Sensitivity, specificity, F_1 score
Tschandl et al [36]	2020	ResNet34	HAM [14]	Accuracy
Chaturvedi et al [37]	2020	MobileNet	HAM [14]	Accuracy, precision, recall, F_1 score

using transfer learning. Table 4.1 shows that the different CNNs result in different scores on the skin cancer image datasets. This situation shown that the different CNNs have different benefits and disadvantages in image classification. Therefore we used a fused deep feature generator (by using five pre-trained CNNs) to use the advantages of different CNNs together, and propose a highly accurate and cognitive skin cancer image classification model.

4.1.4 Our model

In this study, the proposed model is developed using the HAM10000 dataset. The HAM1000 dataset contains 10 015 samples with seven classes. In this model, we used ten CNNs for testing and the CNNs used are ResNet18 [38], ResNet50 [38], ResNet101 [38], DenseNet201 [39], MobileNetv2 [40], VGG16 [41], VGG19 [41], ShuffleNet [42], AlexNet [43] and GoogLeNet [44]. The five CNNs with the best results are selected as deep feature generators. According to tests, the best-attained five CNNs are Resnet50, Resnet101 Densenet201, Mobilenetv2 and ShuffleNet. By applying these models to the skin cancer images, $5 \times 1000 = 5000$ features are generated. The used ImRMR selector chooses the most informative 1093 features from the 5000 generated features and the selected 1093 are fed to the DNN classifier. The classification accuracy is found to be 96.58% by deploying the presented model on the HAM10000 dataset.

4.1.5 Contributions

The contributions of this research are as follows:
- Fused deep feature extraction is presented in this model by employing five pre-trained deep CNN models. This feature generation network is named a deep feature generator. The presented model is applied to the HAM10000 dataset with *seven* classes. This model reaches 96.58% classification accuracy.
- A new iterative feature selector is presented and this feature selector is named ImRMR. The main purpose of the ImRMR is to select the optimal number of features automatically. By applying ImRMR the most informative features are chosen and the effectiveness of the selected deep networks is used together.

4.1.6 Study outline

This paper is structured as follows. In section 4.2 the properties of the HAM10000 dataset are given. The used CNN models are explained in section 4.3. In section 4.4, the proposed framework, feature generation, iterative mRMR feature selector and classification are explained. The experimental set-up, results and discussion are presented in section 4.5. The results and information about future research are explained in section 4.6.

4.2 Material

HAM10000 dataset was used to test the proposed method in this study and it can be downloaded at https://dataverse.harvard.edu/dataset.xhtml?persistentId=doi: 10.7910/DVN/DBW86T. There are 10 015 skin cancer images in this dataset. It is a large and commonly used dataset in machine learning application. Therefore the

HAM10000 dataset is selected as the test-bed for this work. These images are in RGB color format and the size of each image is $600 \times 450 \times 3$. The HAM10000 dataset consists of seven classes. The properties/attributes of the HAM10000 dataset are also listed in table 4.2 [14].

As can be seen in table 4.2 the HAM10000 dataset consists of seven classes. The number of images is given for each class. There are 327 for actinic keratoses (Akiec), 514 for basal cell carcinoma (Bcc), 1099 for benign keratosis (Bkl), 115 for dermatofibroma (Df), 1113 for melanocytic nevus (Mel), 6705 for melanoma (Nv) and 142 images for vascular lesion (Vasc). Four different methods were used in labeling these images. These were confirmed by histopathology (histo) follow-up examination (follow_up), expert consensus (consensus), or *in vivo* confocal microscopy (confocal). Most of the images were confirmed by histopathology. The HAM10000 dataset images consist of males and females, while the gender of 57 images is unknown. Sample images are presented in figure 4.1.

4.3 Preliminary

Convolutional neural networks (CNNs) are one of the most commonly utilized automatic image classification models in the literature and many CNNs have been presented to solve computer vision problems. They generally consist of convolution, pooling, batch normalization, drop-out, fully connected layer(s) and classification using softmax phases [43]. Generally, CNNs are multi-layered deep networks, hence they can generate features at low, moderate and high levels. CNNs have used backpropagation to assign optimum weights [45]. Figure 4.2 presents the general architecture of a CNN [46].

The layers of the CNN are explained comprehensively in the following.

The input layer is the first layer of the CNN. In this layer the images used are fed to the CNN. The size of the image or other data introduced affects the test time and the size of memory needed. Therefore it is essential to choose the CNN model according to the input data or the size of the input data according to the CNN model.

The convolution layer is used to extract features from the data coming from the previous layer. Convolution is performed on the matrix using filters of different sizes such as 2×2, 3×3, or 5×5.

The rectified linear units (ReLu) layer is used after the convolution layer. After certain mathematical operations in the convolution layer, the network turns into a linear structure. The ReLu layer is used to prevent this linearity.

The pooling layer is generally used after the ReLu layer and before the convolution layer. The purpose of the pooling process is to reduce the size of the data to be given to the convolution layer.

The fully connected layer comes after the convolution, ReLu, and pooling layers used in CNN architecture. All layers are found before it is combined.

The drop-out layer is used in the CNN architecture to prevent memorization/ overfitting rather than the network's self-training.

Classification layer output values are equal to the number of objects to be classified. In our classification, *seven* different objects produce a specific range of output in the range of 0–1.

Table 4.2. The properties of the HAM10000 dataset [14].

Abr.	Number of images	Name of the class	Dx_type				Gender		
			Histo	Confocal	Consensus	Follow-up	Male	Female	Unknown
Akiec	327	Actinic keratoses	327	—	—	—	221	106	—
Bcc	514	Basal cell carcinoma	514	—	—	—	317	197	—
Bkl	1099	Benign keratosis	766	69	264	—	626	463	10
Df	115	Dermatofibroma	55	—	60	—	63	52	—
Mel	1113	Melanocytic nevus	1113	—	—	—	689	424	—
Nv	6705	Melanoma	2498	—	503	3704	3421	3237	47
Vasc	142	Vascular lesion	67	—	75	—	69	73	—

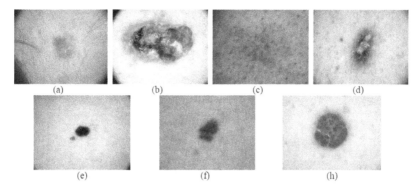

Figure 4.1. Sample images of seven classes in the HAM dataset [14]: (a) actinic keratoses, (b) basal cell carcinoma, (c) benign keratosis, (d) dermatofibroma, (e) melanocytic nevus, (f) melanoma and (h) vascular lesion.

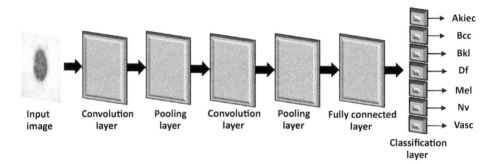

Figure 4.2. CNN general architecture [46].

In this study the Resnet50, Resnet101, Densenet201, Mobilenetv2 and ShuffleNet models, which are widely used in CNN architectures, were used. Hence transfer learning is used to generate features. The networks used were trained on the ImageNet dataset and 1000 features were generated using the fully connected layer.

4.3.1 Residual networks

ResNet is a comprehensively designed deep learning model. It was originally designed as a 34-layer network architecture in 2016. This architecture consists of residual blocks. In convolution, the ReLu of the x input in the residual block gives an $F(x)$ result after the convolution processes. The $F(x)$ value continues by adding it to the x input. The residual block structure is given in figure 4.3 [47].

4.3.2 DenseNet201 model

The DenseNet model is a deep learning model developed by Huang *et al* [48]. In this network model the network structures are hierarchical. The primary purpose of the DenseNet model is that each layer in the network is connected to the front layers. Therefore it ensures the number of feature maps accumulates continuously. Thus a

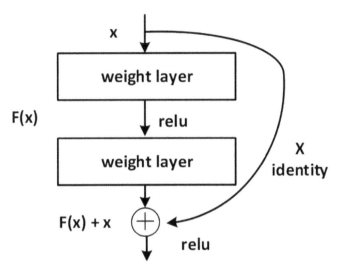

Figure 4.3. The residual block structure.

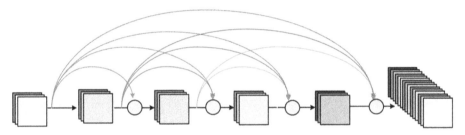

Figure 4.4. The general architecture of the DenseNet model.

large number of feature maps with few convolutional cores are obtained. One of the advantages of the DenseNet model is that very deep models can be designed with dense connections using only a few parameters. It is also less likely to be over-fitted than other models. The general architecture of the DenseNet model is given in figure 4.4 [39].

4.3.3 MobileNetV2 model

MobileNetV2 is a deep network model developed for image processing or classification applications in mobile devices and embedded systems, since it is a lightweight model. This architecture has enabled higher performance operation using decomposed convolutions. In the MobileNetV2 model inverted residuals and linear bottleneck operators are used. It is an improved version of the MobileNet model.

4.3.4 ShuffleNet model

ShuffleNet is one of the commonly preferred lightweight networks for computer vision applications. The ShuffleNet model has been developed by making use of

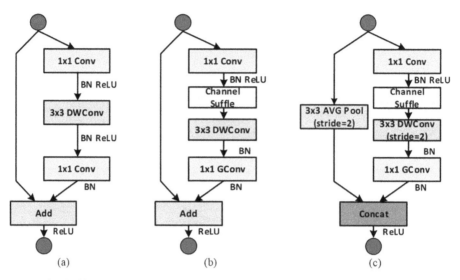

Figure 4.5. The ShuffleNet model: (a) bottleneck unit with depthwise convolution (DWCont), (b) ShuffleNet unit with pointwise group convolution (GConv) and channel shuffle and (c) ShuffleNet unit with stride = 2.

channel mixing processes. These model features give successful results for small networks. The primary phases of this network are the bottleneck unit, shuffle unit and shuffle unit with stride two. The ShuffleNet model is shown in figure 4.5 [42].

4.4 The proposed framework

This research presents a fused deep feature extraction network with an iterative feature selector. This model has three main phases: a fused deep feature generation model using five CNNs, informative feature selection using ImRMR and classification with DNN. An graphical summary of the presented model is shown in figure 4.6.

The pseudocode of the presented deep features and iterative mRMR based framework is shown in figure 4.7. The $D201(.)$, $R50(.)$, $R101(.)$, $M(.)$ and $S(.)$ functions are defined to express DenseNet201, ResNet50, ResNet101, MobileNetv2 and ShuffleNet, respectively, for expression of the proposed skin cancer classification model. The details of the phases of this model are presented in the following subsections.

4.4.1 Feature generation

The widely preferred variants of the pre-trained CNN models were tested in the presented feature generation model and the five pre-trained CNN models which achieved the best results were selected as feature generators. The selected pre-trained models are DenseNet201, ResNet50, ResNet101, MobileNetv2 and ShuffleNet. The common characteristics of these models are that they generate 1000 features and they achieved a more than 80% accuracy rate for the used HAM10000 skin cancer dataset. Therefore they are considered as feature generation functions in the proposed model. In this respect, we present a hybrid deep feature generation model and the steps of this deep hybrid feature generator are as follows.

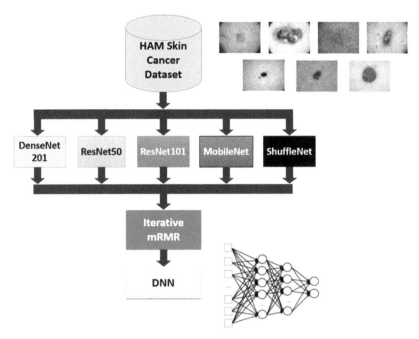

Figure 4.6. A graphical illustration of the presented fused deep feature and ImRMR based skin cancer classification framework. In the feature generation phase five pre-trained networks are applied to cancer images and each network generates 1000 features. Then the generated features are combined with the final feature vector with a size of 5000. Iterative mRMR selects the most valuable features, and these features are forwarded to the DNN classifier.

Procedure: *FusedDeep − ImRMR(Im)*

Input: Skin cancer image (Im) with a size of W x H, actual output ($target$) with a length of d (number of images)

Output: Predicted value (pv)

00: Load skin cancer dataset with a length of d

01: **for** k=1 to d **do** // Read and process each skin cancer image.

02:     $feature^1 = D201(Im)$; // Extract features deploying DenseNet201.

03:     $feature^2 = R50(Im)$; // Extract features deploying ResNet50.

04:     $feature^3 = R101(Im)$; // Extract features deploying ResNet101.

05:     $feature^4 = M(Im)$; // Extract features deploying MobileNetV2.

06:     $feature^5 = S(Im)$; // Extract features deploying ShuffleNet.

07:     **for** i=1 to 5 **do**

08:         $X(k, (i − 1) * 1000 + 1 : i * 1000) = feature^i$; // Feature concatenation

09:     **end for i**

10: **end for k**

11: $last = ImRMR(X, target)$; // ImRMR feature selection

12: $pv = DNN(last, target, 10)$; // Classification using DNN with 10-fold cross-validation

Figure 4.7. The pseudocode of the proposed combined deep feature and ImRMR based cancer image classification model. Lines 01–10 express the feature generation model, ImRMR is defined in line 11 using the $ImRMR(.,.)$ function. DNN based classification is shown in line 12.

Step 0: Load skin cancer image (Im).

Step 1: Generate features using the selected CNNs.

$$\text{feature } 1 = D201(Im) \tag{4.1}$$

$$\text{feature } 2 = R50(Im) \tag{4.2}$$

$$\text{feature } 3 = R101(Im) \tag{4.3}$$

$$\text{feature } 4 = M(Im) \tag{4.4}$$

$$\text{feature } 5 = S(Im). \tag{4.5}$$

Step 2: Combine the features generated to obtain the final feature vector (X) with a length of 5000:

$$X((i - 1) \times 1000 + j) = \text{feature } i(j), \quad i = \{1, 2, \ldots, 5\},$$
$$j = \{1, 2, \ldots, 1000\}. \tag{4.6}$$

4.4.2 Iterative mRMR feature selector

An iterative version of the mRMR selector is developed to choose the informative features, and this feature selector is called ImRMR. The primary aim of this feature selector is to select the optimal number of features from the generated features with a length of 5000. The flow diagram of the presented ImRMR selector is shown in figure 4.8.

The steps of this selector are as follows:

Step 1: Load the combined features.

Step 2: Apply mRMR to X. To simplify this step mRMR is defined using the $mRMR(.,.)$ function. This function takes *two* parameters, and they are features and target values. This function returns the sorted indices of the features ordered by descending (idx):

$$idx = mRMR(X, \text{target}). \tag{4.7}$$

Step 3: Choose a lower bound (LB) and upper bound (UB) to decrease the time complexity of the ImRMR. In this work, the LB and UB are selected as 100 and 1100, respectively.

Step 4: Select features iteratively (f^i):

$$f^i(t) = X(idx(t)), \quad t = \{1, 2, \ldots, k\}, \quad k = \{\text{LB}, \text{LB} + 1, \ldots, \text{UB}\},$$
$$i = \{1, 2, \ldots, \text{UB} - \text{LB} + 1\}. \tag{4.8}$$

Step 5: Calculate the loss values of each selected feature using a linear discriminant (LD) classifier with ten-fold cross-validation:

$$\text{loss}(i) = \text{LD}(f^i, \text{target}, 10). \tag{4.9}$$

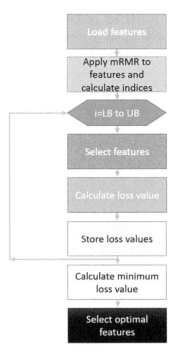

Figure 4.8. The flow diagram of the ImRMR feature selector. Here, LB and UB represent the lower bound and upper bound of the number of features. These variables are used to decrease the time complexity of the ImRMR.

Step 6: Find the minimum loss value:

$$[\text{minimum, id}] = \min(\text{loss}) \tag{4.10}$$

$$\min(x, y) = \begin{cases} x, & x \leqslant y \\ y, & y < x \end{cases}, \tag{4.11}$$

where id describe the indices of the minimum value.

Step 7: Chose the optimal feature vector (X^O) using the *idx, id, LB* and *X* values:

$$X^O(h) = X(idx(h)), \quad h = \{1, 2, \dots, \text{id} + \text{LB} - 1\}. \tag{4.12}$$

The steps given above (steps 1–7) define the presented feature selection procedure of the ImRMR feature selector. This selector is utilized to generated 5000 features and the upper bound is selected as 1100. It selects 1093 features. These features are forwarded to the DNN classifier, details are given in the following section.

4.4.3 Classification

The DNN classifier, which is an improved version of the artificial neural network (ANN) [49], is employed for the classification [13]. ANNs with a number of hidden layers greater than *one* are called DNN. The used DNN is a backpropagation network, and a scaled gradient conjugate (SCG) is used to assign optimal weights.

The selected 1093 features are utilized as the input of the DNN. The learning rate and momentum rate are set to 0.7 and 0.3, respectively. The batch size used is 100. The classification performance is evaluated using the ten-fold CV. The DNN used has three hidden layers, and the sizes of these layers are 270, 150 and 50, respectively.

4.5 Results and discussion

The experimental set-up, results and discussion are given in this section.

4.5.1 Experimental set-up

The presented hybrid deep feature generation and ImRMR based model was implemented on a workstation, and MATLAB (2020a) was chosen as a programming environment for feature generation, selection and classification. To generate features from the deep networks used, these networks were utilized as a feature generator using an m file. ImRMR was implemented as a separate function. The range of the features was selected as from 100 to 1100.

4.5.2 Results

The key objective of the developed model with hybrid deep features and ImRMR based feature selection was achieved, with high classification performance compared to the state-of-the-art models on skin cancer image datasets. The ten widely employed pre-trained CNN models were utilized to develop a hybrid feature generation network as feature generators. The tested networks were ResNet18, ResNet50, ResNet101, MobileNetv2, VGG16, VGG19, ShuffleNet, AlexNet and GoogleNet. We used transfer learning to generate features from the CNNs. The hyperparameters used are as follows: the mini batch size was [8, 16], the maximum epoch number was [5, 20], the decay factor for weights was 0.01, the initial learning ratio was 1e-4 and the optimizer was selected as SGDM. According to the test, the SVM [50] classifier was the best conventional classifier. Therefore, appropriate deep CNNs were selected according to the SVM results. Ten-fold cross-validation (CV) was also the selected validation technique. In this study an 80% classification accuracy was determined as a threshold value for the selection of the most appropriate CNNs. These CNNs were employed on the HAM10000 dataset and the calculated results without employing ImRMR are listed in table 4.3.

The highlighted pre-trained models in bold font achieved greater than 80% accuracy rates. Therefore we selected these pre-trained models as feature generation functions and 5000 features were generated using them. ImRMR selected 1093 features from the generated 5000 features. The distributions of the chosen features according to the used networks are shown in figure 4.9.

The selected 1093 features were fed to the DNN classifier and ten-fold CV was used in the DNN. In the ten-fold CV, 90% of the skin cancer images were utilized for training and 10% of them were used for testing. This process is repeated *ten* times to evaluate robust results. A schematic overview of the ten-fold CV is shown in figure 4.10.

Table 4.3. The calculated results of the pre-trained CNNs using SVM with ten-fold CV.

CNN	Accuracy (%)
ResNet18 [38]	78.30
ResNet50 [38]	**82.81**
ResNet101 [38]	**81.82**
DenseNet201 [39]	**81.73**
MobileNetv2 [40]	**81.09**
VGG16 [41]	79.69
VGG19 [41]	78.46
ShuffleNet [42]	**80.33**
AlexNet [43]	78.44
GoogleNet [44]	76.60

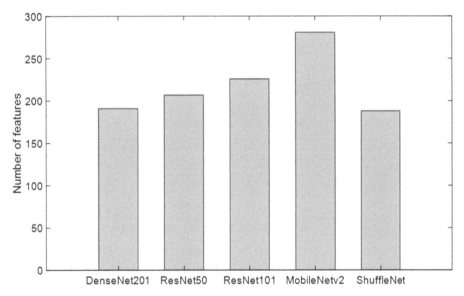

Figure 4.9. The distributions of the features that were generated using the selected deep networks. The ImRMR selected 191, 207, 226, 281 and 188 features from DenseNet201, ResNet50, ResNet101, MobileNetv2 and ShuffleNet, respectively.

Table 4.4 lists the fold-wise accuracies of the developed model. Furthermore, in order to evaluate the developed model comprehensively, the confusion matrix and the average classification performance of the proposed model with hybrid deep features and ImRMR feature selection is shown in table 4.5.

Table 4.5 presents accuracy, precision and recall rates of the proposed model. By using this table, F_1-scores, unweighted average recall (UAR), unweighted average precision (UAP) and average F_1-score (AF) can be calculated [51, 52]. The calculated recall, precision and F_1-score values per each class are also shown in

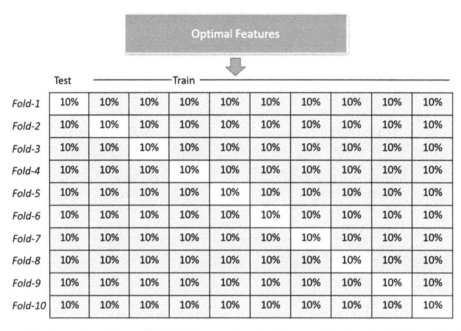

Figure 4.10. Illustration of the ten-fold CV. The selected optimal features with a length of 1093 are utilized as the input of the DNN, and the results are calculated using the ten-fold CV, as seen above.

Table 4.4. The calculated accuracy rates of the DNN using ten-fold CV.

Folds	Classification accuracy (%)
Fold-1	90.81
Fold-2	95.31
Fold-3	97.50
Fold-4	97.50
Fold-5	97.21
Fold-6	96.81
Fold-7	97.70
Fold-8	98.40
Fold-9	96.60
Fold-10	97.90
Average	96.58

figure 4.11. The used HAM10000 dataset is a heterogeneous dataset. Therefore UAR, UAP, AF, Cohen's kappa (CK) and Mathew's correlation coefficient (MCC) scores must be calculated for clear evaluation. These results are listed in table 4.6.

4.5.3 Discussion

The primary objective of the presented research is to achieve high performance on a large and heterogeneous skin cancer dataset, that is HAR10000. To realize this

Table 4.5. The calculated confusion matrix of the presented hybrid deep features and ImRMR model using the DNN classifier with a ten-fold CV.

True class	Predicted class							Recall (%)
	1	2	3	4	5	6	7	
1	289	14	15	2	7	0	0	88.38
2	14	493	7	0	0	0	0	95.91
3	10	8	999	7	50	24	1	90.90
4	3	2	6	91	2	11	0	79.13
5	5	1	49	0	1014	44	0	91.11
6	0	0	10	5	37	6652	1	99.21
7	0	3	1	0	0	4	134	94.36
Precision (%)	90.03	94.63	91.90	86. 67	91.35	98.77	98.53	**96.58**

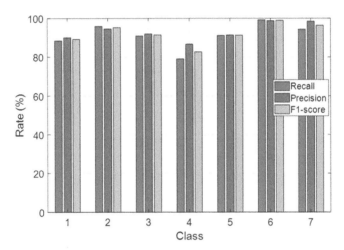

Figure 4.11. The obtained recall, precision and F_1-score rates for each class.

objective a hybrid deep feature generation model is presented. Five pre-trained CNN models have been utilized as a feature generation model. These pre-trained CNN models are selected based on their classification performance as a single feature generator. In the first phase, the widely used ten pre-trained CNN models are utilized as a feature generator, since these pre-trained models generate 1000 features. Then, the generated features were forwarded to an SVM with a third-degree polynomial kernel, since this classifier is the best-result classifier for all deep features in the MATLAB classification learner toolbox. A threshold value (80% classification accuracy) was determined to select the effective classifiers, and the used deep networks were selected per this threshold value. The five deep networks that reached more than 80% classification accuracy were utilized as feature generation functions, and 5000 features were generated. The most valuable features were selected by

Table 4.6. The calculated UAR (%), UAP (%) and AF results of the proposed hybrid deep feature and ImRMR based model.

Performance metric	Rate
UAR	91.29
UAP	93.13
AF	92.17
CK	93.43
MCC	91.47

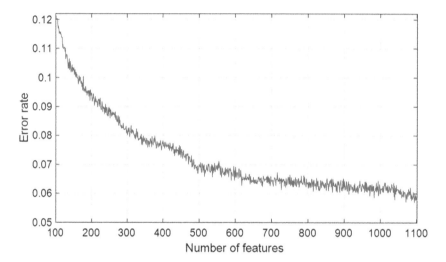

Figure 4.12. Feature selection process of the ImRMR selector using an LDA classifier as the error rate calculator.

deploying the presented ImRMR feature selector. In the ImRMR feature selector an LDA classifier has been utilized as an error value calculator since the time complexity of the LDA is low. The feature generation process of the ImRMR using LDA is presented in figure 4.12 schematically.

The ImRMR selected 1093 features and these features were classified with the DNN classifier. The DNN reached 96.58% classification accuracy, but these results are not enough to evaluate the proposed hybrid deep features and ImRMR based skin cancer image classification model since the used HAM10000 dataset is heterogeneous, i.e. unbalanced. Therefore the precision, recall, F_1-score, UAR, UAP and AF rates were also calculated. By calculating these performance metrics a comprehensive evaluation is presented for our model. The obtained confusion matrix is also given (see table 4.3). According to table 4.3, the best result and worst result classes are the sixth and fourth classes, since the most significant class is the sixth class and the lowest class is the fourth class. The results of the other state-of-the-art skin cancer classification models are listed in table 4.7 to validate the high

Table 4.7. Comparison with the state-of-the-art (%).

Study	Method	Dataset	Accuracy	Precision	Recall	Specificity	F$_1$-score
Tschandl *et al* [36]	ResNet34	HAM	80.3	—	—	—	—
Tschandl *et al* [29]	UNet16	HAM	87.6	—	—	—	—
	LinkNet34		89	—	—	—	—
	LinkNet152		88.6	—	—	—	—
Hagerty *et al* [30]	ResNet50PCS	NIH	83	—	—	—	—
	HC Ensemble		90	—	—	—	—
	HC+DL Ensemble		94	—	—	—	—
	ResNet50PCS	HAM	88	—	—	—	—
	HC Ensemble		86	—	—	—	—
	HC+DL Ensemble		90	—	—	—	—
Gessert *et al* [34]	InceptV3	SPC, HAM, ISIC	—	—	72.4	96	84
	Dense121		—	—	75.2	96	78
	SE-RX		—	—	73.6	95.8	83.4
Dai *et al* [19]	CNNs	HAM	75.2	—	—	—	—
Goyal *et al* [27]	FRCNNInceptionV2	PH2	—	100	100	—	—
	SSD-InceptionV2		—	98.5	98.5	—	—
	DeepLabV3		—	95.5	05.5	—	—
	FRCNNInceptionV2	HAM	—	83.3	82.4	—	—
	SSD-InceptionV2		—	80.8	72.8	—	—
	DeepLabV3		—	69.5	68.8	—	—
	VGG16	ISIC2017	78.7	85.7	88.2	39.3	87
	InceptionV3		80.3	86.3	89.9	41	88
	ResNet50		82.7	87.5	91.5	46.1	89.5
	DeepLabV3		94.7	—	89.8	96.4	—

Reference	Model	Dataset					
Li and Li [25]	DenseNet201	HAM	84.8	—	—	—	—
	ResNet152		86	—	—	—	—
	InceptionV4		85.7	—	—	—	—
Shahin et al [28]	ResNet50	HAM	87.1	78.6	77	—	—
	InceptionV3		89.7	84.9	80	—	—
Chaturvedi et al [37]	MobileNet	HAM	95.3	89	83	—	83
Lee et al [22]	WonDerM	HAM	89.9	—	—	—	—
Gessert et al [23]	Densenet121	HAM, ISIC	82.7	—	—	—	—
	ResNet50		86.3	—	—	—	—
	SeNet154		85.4	—	—	—	—
Majtner et al [26]	VGG16	ISIC	80.1	—	—	—	—
	GoogLeNet		79.7	—	—	—	—
Maia et al [12]	InceptionV3 + LR	PH2	92.5	87.8	72.5	97.5	79.4
	ResNet50 + SVM		91	84.3	67.5	96.8	75
	VGG16 + LR		91.5	79.4	77.5	95	78.4
	VGG19 + LR		92.5	85.7	75	96.8	80
Tschandl et al [31]	CNN	EDRA	76.2	—	86.6	70.7	—
		ISIC2017	75.9	—	70.9	77.6	—
		PRIV	62.9	—	87.2	66.2	—
Barata et al [33]	LSTM	ISIC2017	93.9	—	63.7	95.6	—
Proposed method	**Hybrid deep features + ImRMR + DNN**	**HAM**	**96.58**	**93.13**	**91.29**	**—**	**92.17**

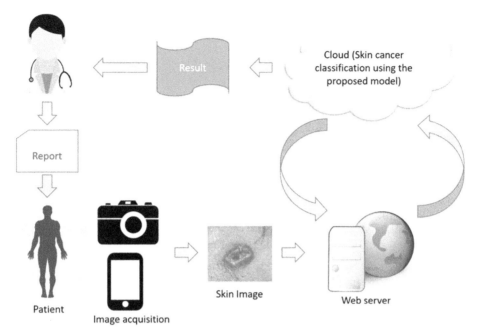

Figure 4.13. Intelligent assistant system planned for skin cancer classification from images using the proposed hybrid deep features and ImRMR based model. By using this system skin cancer diagnosis faults can be minimized.

classification capability of the proposed hybrid deep feature and ImRMR based classification model.

As can be seen from table 4.7, the best-result model for skin cancer classification on the HAM dataset is our model. This model attained a high classification accuracy rate on the HAM dataset. Li and Li [25], Shahin *et al* [28] and Chaturvedi *et al* [37] applied different CNNs to HAM datasets and the best accuracy rate among them was 95.3%, deploying MobileNet, while our proposed method attained 96.58% classification accuracies a using five deep feature generator, ImRMR selector and DNN classifier together. Table 4.7 clearly shows that our deep feature generation architecture increases the skin cancer classification capability of the deep feature generators. According to these results, the following points should be highlighted as advantages of the proposed model:

- A deep feature generation model is presented using pre-trained networks. Hence, a lightweight model is proposed.
- ImRMR solves the optimal automated number of features selection problem.
- The presented hybrid deep features and ImRMR based model significantly increased the classification capability of the deep meshes used (see table 4.3).
- High classification results were achieved using the proposed hybrid deep features and ImRMR based skin cancer images classification model (see tables 4.4–4.6).

- Robust results were achieved by employing a ten-fold CV.
- The proposed hybrid deep CNN and ImRMR based model outperformed other models (see table 4.7).

4.6 Conclusions and future works

This work has presented a hybrid deep feature generation and iterative feature selector to classify skin cancer images accurately. By employing this framework, a fully automated skin cancer classification model has been presented. The presented hybrid deep features and ImRMR based classification model reached 96.58% classification accuracy on the HAM10000 dataset. This model increased the classification capability of the pre-trained networks on the used skin cancer image dataset (see table 4.3). The UAR, UAP and AF scores of this model were also calculated as 91.29%, 93.13% and 92.17%, respectively. The presented model was also compared to other skin cancer detection/classification models, and table 4.7 denoted the high classification capability of our method.

Based on the calculated results and the structure of the presented skin cancer classification model, future research directions are as follows:

- By using other pre-trained CNN models and handcrafted feature extraction functions, a novel hybrid feature generation framework can be presented.
- The ImRMR model is an iterative and improved version of the mRMR feature selection algorithm. New generation feature selectors can be presented by applying an iterative search model on other widely used feature selectors.
- Using the proposed framework, we plan to develop a real-time intelligent decision support system (DSS) to assist medical practitioners in skin cancer classification. The intended DSS and monitoring system is schematically summarized in figure 4.13.

References

[1] Nerguizian V, Alazzam A, Stiharu I and Burnier M 2017 Characterization of several cancer cell lines at microwave frequencies *Measurement* **109** 354–8

[2] Lei B, Xia Z, Jiang F, Jiang X, Ge Z, Xu Y, Qin J, Chen S, Wang T and Wang S 2020 Skin lesion segmentation via generative adversarial networks with dual discriminators *Med. Image Anal.* **64** 101716

[3] Mirzaalian H, Lee T K and Hamarneh G 2016 Skin lesion tracking using structured graphical models *Med. Image Anal.* **27** 84–92

[4] Thomas S M, Lefevre J G, Baxter G and Hamilton N A 2021 Interpretable deep learning systems for multi-class segmentation and classification of non-melanoma skin cancer *Med. Image Anal.* **68** 101915

[5] Dawes A J, Igoe D P, Rummenie K J and Parisi A V 2020 Glass transmitted solar irradiances on horizontal and sun-normal planes evaluated with a smartphone camera *Measurement* **153** 107410

[6] Balaji V R, Suganthi S T, Rajadevi R, Krishna Kumar V, Saravana Balaji B and Pandiyan S 2020 Skin disease detection and segmentation using dynamic graph cut algorithm and classification through naive Bayes classifier *Measurement* **163** 107922

[7] Pérez E, Reyes O and Ventura S 2021 Convolutional neural networks for the automatic diagnosis of melanoma: an extensive experimental study *Med. Image Anal.* **67** 101858

[8] Reddy N D Classification of dermoscopy images using deep learning arXiv:1808.01607

[9] Kaymak S, Esmaili P and Serener A 2018 Deep learning for two-step classification of malignant pigmented skin lesions *14th Symp. Neural Networks and Applications NEUREL* 2018 pp 1–6

[10] Chen E Z, Dong X, Li X, Jiang H, Rong R, Wu J, Tech V and Haven N 2019 Lesion attributes segmentation for melanoma detection with multi-task U-Net East China University of Science and Technology, Shanghai, China UT Southwestern Medical Center, Dallas, TX, USA Cleerly Inc, New York City, New York, USA *IEEE 16th Int. Symp. Biomedical Imaging* pp 485–8

[11] Passos M L C and Saraiva M L M F S 2019 Detection in UV–visible spectrophotometry: detectors, detection systems, and detection strategies *Measurement* **135** 896–904

[12] Maia L B, Lima A, Pinheiro Pereira R M, Junior G B, Dallyson Sousa De Almeida J and De Paiva A C 2018 Evaluation of melanoma diagnosis using deep features *Int. Conf. Systems, Signals, and Image Processing (June 2018)*

[13] Ciregan D, Meier U and Schmidhuber J 2012 Multi-column deep neural networks for image classification *Proc. IEEE Computer Society Conf. Computer Vision and Pattern Recognition* pp 3642–9

[14] Tschandl P, Rosendahl C and Kittler H 2018 Data descriptor: the HAM10000 dataset, a large collection of multi-source dermatoscopic images of common pigmented skin lesions *Sci. Data* **5** 1–9

[15] Abraham N and Khan N M 2019 A novel focal Tversky loss function with improved attention u-net for lesion segmentation *Proc. Int. Symp. Biomedical Imaging (April 2019)* pp 683–7

[16] Weber P, Tschandl P, Sinz C and Kittler H 2018 Dermatoscopy of neoplastic skin lesions: recent advances, updates, and revisions *Curr. Treat. Options Oncol.* **19** 1–17

[17] Ech-Cherif A, Misbhauddin M and Ech-Cherif M 2019 Deep neural network based mobile dermoscopy application for triaging skin cancer detection *2nd Int. Conf. Computer Applications and Information Security* pp 1–6

[18] Dascalu A and David E O 2019 Skin cancer detection by deep learning and sound analysis algorithms: a prospective clinical study of an elementary dermoscope *eBioMedicine* **43** 107–13

[19] Dai X, Spasic I, Meyer B, Chapman S and Andres F 2019 Machine learning on mobile: an on-device inference app for skin cancer detection *4th Int. Conf. Fog Mobile Edge Computing* pp 301–5

[20] Wati M, Haviluddin, Puspitasari N, Budiman E and Rahim R 2019 First-order feature extraction methods for image texture and melanoma skin cancer detection *J. Phys. Conf. Ser.* **1230** 012013

[21] Mendonca T, Ferreira P M, Marques J S, Marcal A R S and Rozeira J 2013 PH2–a dermoscopic image database for research and benchmarking *Proc. Annu. Int. Conf. IEEE Engineering in Medicine and Biology Society* pp 5437–40

[22] Lee Y C, Jung S-H and Won H-H 2018 WonDerM: skin lesion classification with fine-tuned neural networks arXiv:1808.03426

[23] Gessert N, Sentker T, Madesta F, Schmitz R, Kniep H, Baltruschat I, Werner R and Schlaefer A 2018 Skin lesion diagnosis using ensembles, unscaled multi-crop evaluation and loss weighting arXiv:1808.01694

[24] ISIC 2020 The International Skin Imaging Collaboration: Melanoma Project *ISIC* https:// isic-archive.com

[25] Li K M and Li E C 2018 Skin lesion analysis towards melanoma detection via end-to-end deep learning of convolutional neural networks arXiv:1807.08332

[26] Majtner T, Bajić B, Yildirim S, Hardeberg J Y, Lindblad J and Sladoje N 2018 Ensemble of convolutional neural networks for dermoscopic images classification arXiv:1808.05071

[27] Goyal M, Hassanpour S and Yap M H 2018 Region of interest detection in dermoscopic images for natural data-augmentation arXiv:1807.10711

[28] Shahin A H, Kamal A and Elattar M A 2019 Deep ensemble learning for skin lesion classification from dermoscopic images *2018 9th Cairo Int. Biomedical Engineering Conf.* pp 150–3

[29] Tschandl P, Sinz C and Kittler H 2019 Domain-specific classification-pretrained fully convolutional network encoders for skin lesion segmentation *Comput. Biol. Med.* **104** 111–6

[30] Hagerty J R, Stanley R J, Almubarak H A, Lama N, Kasmi R, Guo P, Drugge R J, Rabinovitz H S, Oliviero M and Stoecker W V 2019 Deep learning and handcrafted method fusion: higher diagnostic accuracy for melanoma dermoscopy images *IEEE J. Biomed. Heal. Informatics* **23** 1385–91

[31] Tschandl P, Argenziano G, Razmara M and Yap J 2019 Diagnostic accuracy of content-based dermatoscopic image retrieval with deep classification features *Br. J. Dermatol.* **181** 155–65

[32] Argenziano G *et al* 2000 *Interactive Atlas of Dermoscopy* (Milan: Edra Medical)

[33] Barata C, Marques J S and Celebi M E 2019 Deep attention model for the hierarchical diagnosis of skin lesions *IEEE Computing Soc. Conf. Computer Vision and Pattern Recognition (June 2019)* pp 2757–65

[34] Gessert N, Sentker T, Madesta F, Schmitz R, Kniep H, Baltruschat I, Werner R and Schlaefer A 2020 Skin lesion classification using CNNs with patch-based attention and diagnosis-guided loss weighting *IEEE Trans. Biomed. Eng.* **67** 495–503

[35] Kawahara J, Daneshvar S, Argenziano G and Hamarneh G 2019 Seven-point checklist and skin lesion classification using multitask multimodal neural nets *IEEE J. Biomed. Heal. Informatics* **23** 538–46

[36] Tschandl P *et al* 2020 Human–computer collaboration for skin cancer recognition *Nat. Med.* **26** 1229–34

[37] Chaturvedi S S, Gupta K and Prasad P S 2021 Skin lesion analyser: an efficient seven-way multi-class skin cancer classification using MobileNet *Adv. Intell. Syst. Comput.* **1141** 165–76

[38] Kaiming H, Xiangyu Z, Shaoqing R and Jian S 2006 Deep residual learning for image recognition *Indian J. Chem.* B **45** 1951–4

[39] Huang G, Liu Z and van der Maatens L 2017 Densely connected convolutional networks *IEEE Conf. Computer Vision and Pattern Recognition* pp 2261–9

[40] Howard A G, Zhu M, Chen B, Kalenichenko D, Wang W, Weyand T, Andreetto M and Adam H 2017 MobileNets: efficient convolutional neural networks for mobile vision applications arXiv:1704.04861

[41] Simonyan K and Zisserman A 2015 Very deep convolutional networks for large-scale image recognition *3rd Int. Conf. on Learning Representations* pp 1–14

[42] Zhang X, Zhou X, Lin M and Sun J 2018 Shufflenet: An extremely efficient convolutional neural network for mobile devices *Proc. of the IEEE Conf. on Computer Vision and Pattern Recognition* pp 6848–56

[43] Gopalakrishnan K, Khaitan S K, Choudhary A and Agrawal A 2017 Deep convolutional neural networks with transfer learning for computer vision-based data-driven pavement distress detection *Constr. Build. Mater.* **157** 322–30

[44] Szegedy C, Liu W, Jia Y, Sermanet P, Reed S, Anguelov D, Erhan D, Vanhoucke V and Rabinovich A 2015 Going deeper with convolutions *IEEE Comput. Vis. Patt. Recogn. Conf.* **91** 2322–30

[45] Goodfellow I J, Bulatov Y, Ibarz J, Arnoud S and Shet V 2014 Multi-digit number recognition from street view imagery using deep convolutional neural networks *2nd Int. Conf. on Learning Representations* pp 1–13

[46] Lawrence S, Giles C L, Tsoi A C and Back A D 1997 Face recognition: a convolutional neural-network approach *IEEE Trans. Neural Netw.* **8** 98–113

[47] He K, Zhang X, Ren S and Sun J 2015 Delving deep into rectifiers: surpassing human-level performance on ImageNet classification *Proc. IEEE Int. Conf. Computer Vision* pp 1026–34

[48] Huang G, Sun Y, Liu Z, Sedra D and Weinberger K Q 2016 *Deep Networks with Stochastic Depth* (Lecture Notes on Computer Science vol 9908) (Berlin: Springer) pp 646–61

[49] Fine T L 2005 Fundamentals of artificial neural networks *IEEE Trans. Inf. Theory* **42** 1322

[50] Keerthi S S, Shevade S K, Bhattacharyya C and Murthy K R K 2000 A fast iterative nearest point algorithm for support vector machine classifier design *IEEE Trans. Neural Netw.* **11** 124–36

[51] Dogan S, Akbal E and Tuncer T 2020 A novel ternary and signum kernelled linear hexadecimal pattern and hybrid feature selection based environmental sound classification method *Measurement* **166** 108151

[52] Shakeel P M, Burhanuddin M A and Desa M I 2019 Lung cancer detection from CT image using improved profuse clustering and deep learning instantaneously trained neural networks *Measurement* **145** 702–12

Chapter 5

An analysis of human activity recognition systems and their importance in the current era

Chaitanya Krishna Pasula and V M Manikandan

Human activity recognition (HAR) can be defined as the task of automatically identifying and analyzing human activities. It is amongst the most fascinating and actively researched topics in computer vision. HAR has been of increasing importance in everyday applications such as security video surveillance, smart homes, healthcare, human–computer interaction, virtual reality, robotics and digital entertainment. In this chapter we discuss the various applications of HAR, the different methods available for automatic activity detection from videos and the advantages of the HAR systems. This chapter also discusses the challenges in the design and implementation of human activity detection schemes. Furthermore we describe the publicly available datasets for training and evaluating the systems for HAR. The parameters of efficiency that are used to evaluate the performance of HAR systems are also outlined briefly. We conclude by comparing the methodologies and speculating on the possibilities for future research in this field.

5.1 Introduction

Human activity recognition (HAR) is the problem of detecting human actions/gestures via sensory input and then recognizing/classifying them. Since we need data from a sequence of data points to obtain an accurate classification of an action, HAR is considered a time series classification problem. According to activity theory [8], activities (for example, 'make some pasta') can be structured in a hierarchical fashion into actions such as 'prepare the sauce', 'boil a pan of water', etc, that are performed in a temporal sequential order. These actions are further composed of atomic steps called operations such as 'stand up', 'open the dough container' and so on [37]. Typically, an activity must be completed within a specified time frame and can be performed by one person or a group of individuals.

An activity can be performed using only one part of the body or through a combination of several parts of the body. Thus in HAR we analyze the movements of a subject's body parts individually [5, 9], e.g. the arms [12], head, legs, etc. This analysis allows us to describe the highlighted action and provide some important information about it. However, many studies also focus on tracking the entire body to recognize human actions [4, 10].

Activity recognition is a very important problem as it helps in understanding the concepts and issues of human actions in a real-world setting. Since the 1980s, research on HAR systems has garnered the attention of many computer science communities due to its numerous applications, such as smart surveillance [1], video search/retrieval, robots [6], monitoring systems [2], healthcare [3, 11] and management. These systems reduce the need for manually driven systems which are highly time-consuming and more expensive.

Traditionally, recognizing human activities had to be done manually, where an operator had to sit in front of a screen to monitor and guide human activities. This process was expensive, time-consuming and prone to human errors, bias and negligence. Modern human activity recognition systems are trained on data from sensors such as accelerometers, gyroscopes, cameras, body inertial sensors, depth sensors, etc, to automatically analyze and recognize human actions. HAR system implementations involve the following types of sensor technologies:

- *Contact-based methods.* These systems require physical interaction between the user and the device, e.g. accelerometers, gyroscopes, multi-touch screens, magnetometers and wearable sensors. They translate the movements performed during the activity into digital signals for recognizing the activity. However, the use of contact-based sensors requires a certain amount of skill and sophisticated equipment, which limits its accessibility to only experienced users. Also, these sensors need to be of proper size, easy to wear and not obstruct the user from performing the task itself. There is also the issue of users' privacy in continuously performing tasks while being monitored. The performance of these systems is also significantly affected by variations in position. In practical situations such as theft, we will not have access to other sensor data and thus video footage from CCTV cameras might be the only available data. These factors limit the usability of contact sensors in practical situations. As a result of recent technological advancements, smartwatches [13] and smartphones [14] equipped with a variety of sensors were also introduced in activity monitoring tasks. They overcome the issue of privacy but their limited computing and memory capabilities might restrict the diversity of their applications.
- *Vision-based remote methods.* This method simplifies the human–computer interaction task as it is natural and intuitive to use. These systems use captured video sequences or images for activity recognition. Users would not be required to wear several devices on various body parts and hence this approach might be more readily accepted by society. However, vision-based systems also face many challenges, such as the inability to capture if the subject is out of shot, accuracy, privacy concerns due to constant monitoring,

the cost of installation, infrastructure support, etc. In 2014 Theng *et al* [6] showed the use of RGB cameras for HAR and, although the approach had the benefit of being simple, it was still inefficient and, as a result, wearable and depth sensors remain more popular than the vision-based methods.

In this chapter we will be discussing only vision-based methods to keep the discussion simple.

5.2 Stages in human activity recognition

The procedure of HAR is generally broken down into the following stages:

1. *Pre-processing*: The stream of raw data from the sensors is processed to handle unwanted noise and missing information, and then is aggregated and normalized to handle redundant information.
2. *Segmentation*: The most important segments of data in the video are identified at this step.
3. *Feature extraction*: The temporal and spatial features are extracted from the data that has been segmented in the previous step.
4. *Dimensionality reduction*: The number of features is lowered in order to reduce the amount of computing resources required for the classification and to produce higher quality results.
5. *Classification*: The core machine learning techniques are applied here to identify and classify the given activity. Previously, features were extracted manually and activities were classified using techniques such as support vector machines and hidden Markov models. Lately, deep learning algorithms such as long short-term memory (LSTM) have been on the rise to automatically extract relevant features.

5.3 Applications of human activity recognition

Developing systems in HAR has been of major interest lately due to its extensive variety of applications from elderly care and surveillance, to daily life monitoring. Most of the tasks performed by humans in their daily lives can be automated through HAR systems.

5.3.1 Security video surveillance and home monitoring

Traditionally, human operators monitor surveillance systems, but this requires continuous awareness and careful monitoring of human activities via cameras for long periods of time. To effectively identify unauthorized activities, multiple cameras need to be installed at every corner of a street. This makes recognizing anomalous activities an extremely difficult and stressful task which leads to poor results. This can turn out to be a deadly and expensive mistake in crowded and sensitive places such as airports, banks, railway citations, stadiums and shopping malls.

HAR technologies [1] can automate this process by analyzing human–human interactions and detect any prohibited activities at an earlier stage. These systems can track crowd movements, human–human interactions, human–object interactions, etc, to discriminate between legal and illegal activities.

The video surveillance interpretation platform (VSIP) introduced by Brémond *et al* in 2006 [15] is a surveillance platform that recognizes fighting, vandalism and other such events that might take place in a metro system. In 2010 Chang *et al* [16] showed that this system can also be used in prisons to identify and anticipate suspicious and hostile behavior in inmates. In 2007 Fusier *et al* [17] proposed an airport surveillance system that can recognize 50 kinds of complex events, such as unloading luggage, refueling aircraft and preparations for aircraft arrival, etc.

5.3.2 Retail

Every retail environment has the goal of maximizing customer sales. In the most recent retail environment, involving consumers more directly plays a key role in increasing sales and satisfaction. The physical interaction between the customer and technology can make the experience complete and involving. It is very important to make use of the technology to monitor and evaluate interactions between customers and products (shelf-interaction analysis), customers and the store's environment, and also group interactions among the customers themselves.

In 2013 Frontoni *et al* [18] addressed this issue by developing an approach that tracks customers in retail stores and recognizes the different activities performed by them that may be useful for studying the market. This system is used for tracking customers and detecting various actions (shelf interactions, interacting with other people, picking up an item, etc) in complex retail scenarios using techniques such as low-level segmentation

5.3.3 Healthcare

A combination of HAR systems such as cognitive assistance, human tracking, fall detection, etc, can be installed in residential environments, hospitals and rehabilitation centers. These systems can make use of data from wearable and visual sensors to detect early signs of heart strokes, brain-related issues, injured people, etc, and notify medical personnel for immediate assistance. It can also be used to encourage rehabilitation patients to exercise, and support post-stroke recovery patients [20], children suffering with motor disorders [19], cognitive dysfunction patients, etc.

The smart assisted living (SAIL) system is a HAR system introduced by Zhu *et al* in 2011 [21] to monitor the wellbeing of the elderly and disabled individuals. It makes use of human–robot interaction (HRI) through a variety of devices such as smartphones, a network of body sensors, companion robots and a remote health provider to contact a health provider for assistance through the user's smartphone. HAR systems can also enhance the wellbeing of aged and handicapped individuals by acting as a life routine reminder to remind such individuals of their daily tasks that they tend to forget (e.g. taking medication). They can also be used by parents to remotely monitor infants at home and be notified of their sleeping status and predict their demands for food, etc. The GER'HOME project assists elderly individuals to improve their daily quality of life. Thus the costs of long hospitalizations after an accident, surgery, or illness are reduced as their wellbeing can be monitored from the comfort of their homes by examining data from a network of sensors, both wearable and in the environment.

5.3.4 Smart homes

A smart home system [2] is an environment that is used for monitoring and analyzing the activities of the residents and their interaction with their environment through a network of sensors to provide safety, and cognitive and physical functional support. These smart home systems provide users with an increase in the quality and independence of their lives.

The HERMES system provides cognitive assistance for people suffering from mild memory problems. HERMES uses a varied combination of computer vision applications such as speech and speaker recognition, visual processing, audio processing, and face detection and recognition.

The SWEET-HOME project [22] is a smart home solution presented by the French National Research Agency that interacts with elderly or disabled people through its speech and sound recognition systems that were trained on audio data acquired from interactions with healthy individuals.

5.3.5 Workplace monitoring

HAR applications can be developed to ensure proper hygienic measures (such as washing hands, using the proper items to cover hair) are being followed by employees at a workplace. It can also assist newer employees by ensuring they are following the proper procedures to perform various tasks in their daily work (e.g. the proper steps to cook a dish, serve a customer, etc).

5.3.6 Entertainment

Through HAR systems [7], older people [23] and people with a neurological injury can also enjoy gaming and exergaming. Simple human body gestures can be recognized for easy interaction with games. Kinect [24] and Nintendo Wii are examples of such systems.

5.4 Approaches for human activity recognition

The HAR applications can recognize activities performed in the videos and categorize them according to the activity recognized. We have reviewed a few HAR methodologies in this section.

5.4.1 The HAR process using 3D posture data

In 2015 Gaglio *et al* [29] introduced a framework for recognizing human activities using 3D posture data collected from a Microsoft Kinect RGB-D camera. The system automatically understands the activity being performed as a collection of postures that were previously known, with the individual postures representing a repeating pattern of joint configurations. The following steps are followed:

1. Feature detection: 11 joints are detected with Kinect sensors for distinguishing different body postures.
2. The K-means algorithm is used for clustering the set of joints to detect the postures that are part of a given activity.
3. Support vector machines (SVMs) are used to classify these postures after which hidden Markov models (HMMs) are used to recognize the activity.

The technique was evaluated on the following two datasets:
1. The Kinect Activity Recognition Dataset (KARD), a new publicly available dataset collected by the authors.
2. The Cornell Activity Dataset (CAD-60), which gave an overall value of 77.3% for precision and 76.7% for recall performance metrics.

This solution outperforms the relevant state-of-the-art and captures a general model of the activity independent of the subject and the speed of performance of the action. This approach can also be scaled up to accommodate several new actions. It has the ability to recognize activities belonging to the same class with varying lengths of performance duration. Frame loss and body occlusions due to the inability of Kinect to provide a stable video stream were the main causes of misclassification.

5.4.2 Human action recognition using DFT

In a 2011 paper by Kumari *et al* [30], first four different background subtraction algorithms were tested on the individual frames of the video for the extraction of the foreground, which is the object of interest. This test revealed that the improved adaptive Gaussian mixture model provides the best quality and fastest result and hence it is selected for the further process. Next, the video frames are normalized and divided into small blocks. Then the discrete Fourier transform (DFT) is calculated and averaged for each block to extract important features of the foreground object. A feature vector is used to represent the action being performed. Since the K-nearest neighbors algorithm performs well for large databases, it is preferred for feature classification. The approach is trained and evaluated using a synthetic low contrast video with 150 frames taken from the advanced computer vision dataset. When a single frame along with four continuous appended frames is used for running the experiment, it is observed that the model performance is inversely related to the value of K. Hence a value of $K = 1$ is determined to be the optimum value for activity recognition in all cases. More cameras may be used to produce a more robust recognition result in the case of occlusions.

5.4.3 The local SVM approach

In 2004 Schuldt *et al* [25] demonstrated how local spatio-temporal features that can be adjusted to the size, speed and frequency of moving patterns can be used to capture local events for recognizing complex motion patterns. Thus representations of videos that are stable with respect to corresponding transformations are constructed in terms of local spatio-temporal features. The video representations are then integrated with SVMs to recognize human actions.

The following three representations are used:

1. LFs: local features described by spatio-temporal jets of fourth order.
2. HistLFs: histograms of local features with 128 bins.
3. HistSTGs: histograms of normalized space time gradients that were computed at four temporal scales.

In addition, the following two classifiers are combined:

1. An SVM with a local feature kernel combined with LFs or an SVM with a χ^2 kernel.
2. A nearest neighbor classifier combined with HistSTGs and HistLFs.

A new database that contains 2391 sequences of 25 subjects performing a total of six actions in four different types of backgrounds was introduced for evaluation. The results showed that LFs have a significantly higher recognition performance than HistSTGs for all training subsets, excluding those with scale variations.

5.4.4 A robust approach for action recognition based on spatio-temporal features in RGB-D sequences

A new framework [31] is introduced to recognize human activities through a combination of RGB image data and depth maps based on spatio-temporal features and segmentation techniques. The following steps are followed:

1. Spatio-temporal interest points are detected on both the depth and RGB channels using spatio-temporal interest points (STIPs).
2. The following descriptors are applied to the channels to capture important information such as the motion, appearance and shape of the action
   i. The HOG3D descriptor is applied to the RGB channel
   ii. The 3DS-HONV descriptor is applied to the depth channel.
   iii. HOF2.5D is extracted from fusing the RGB and depth channels.
3. The video is segmented and GMM is applied to create the following three feature vectors for each segment: HOG3D, 3DS-HONV and HOF2.5D.
4. These feature vectors are combined with max-pooling to attain a final vector which describes the temporal structure for action representation.
5. Actions are classified using SVMs.

This proposal was evaluated on the following three benchmark datasets: 3D Action Pairs, UTKinect-Action and MSRDaily Activity 3D. The obtained action recognition accuracies were 93.5%, 99.16% and 89.38%, respectively, which is superior to the state-of-the-art proposals.

5.4.5 SlowFast networks for video recognition

In 2019 Feichtenhofer *et al* [32] proposed a SlowFast network approach for recognizing activities. It contains a fast and a slow pathway that are fused by lateral connections. The raw video is treated at different temporal rates by the two pathways, so that each of them can model the video individually.

The model contains:

1. A slow pathway that operates at low frame and refresh rates while focusing on capturing spatial semantic data given by images.
2. A fast pathway that works at high frame and refresh rates while focusing on capturing swiftly changing movements at a fine temporal resolution.

Although the fast pathway has a higher temporal rate, it is made very lightweight (~20% of total computation) by designing it to have a lesser number of channels and weaker spatial information processing ability. As a result, temporal pooling does not need to be performed and it can operate on all intermediate layers at a high frame rate and maintain temporal fidelity. This is done since the slow pathway can provide such information in a less redundant manner. Despite this, the fast network provides useful temporal information.

State-of-the-art results were reported for the Charades, AVA, Kinetics 400 and Kinetics 600 datasets in both action classification and detection from videos.

5.4.6 Long-term recurrent convolutional networks for visual recognition and description

In 2017 Donahue *et al* [26] proposed a long-term recurrent convolutional network (LRCN) model through a combination of a deep hierarchical visual feature extractor with a model that can learn to recognize temporal dynamics for sequential data. LSTM style recurrent neural networks provide good improvements over other methods when the models are trained and refined with a good amount of training data, which makes them suitable for large-scale tasks aimed at understanding visual data.

It has been shown in this study that the following methods can be improved upon with a deep sequence model by learning sequential dynamics:

- Existing techniques that learn a deep hierarchy of parameters only in the visual domain.
- Techniques which take a fixed visual representation of the input and only learn the output sequence dynamics.

The architecture was evaluated on the UCF-101 dataset by splitting it into three parts; each part's training set contained around 8000 videos. The LRCN has shown a noticeable performance increase in comparison to the baseline single-frame system. It has even shown better performance over other deep models [27, 28]. Thus using LRCN models for HAR is shown to be more advantageous than state-of-the-art approaches. These LRCN techniques can also be simple to integrate into existing visual recognition pipelines. They also do not require any hand-designed features or much pre-processing for the input to handle perceptual problems where the input is visual and varies with time or when the output is sequential.

5.4.7 3D convolutional neural networks for human action recognition

In 2013 Ji *et al* [33] proposed a method to develop a 3D CNN architecture that extracts spatio-temporal features by performing 3D convolutions. This architecture can be employed for HAR in airport surveillance videos. The channels generated from adjacent video frames are considered individually for convolution and subsampling operations. The final feature is represented as a combination of information from these channels. The performance of the architecture can be boosted by combining the predictions of multiple varieties of architectures and with regularization of the outputs with high-level features. This model was also used to construct a multi-module event detection system which demonstrated the highest performance in all three action categories at the TREC Video Retrieval Evaluation (TRECVID) 2009 evaluation for surveillance event detection.

The model was evaluated on the KTH dataset and the TRECVID 2008 dataset consisting of London Gatwick Airport surveillance footage. The results show that the model has much better performance than the frame-based 2D CNN and baseline methods on the TRECVID dataset and offers superior performance on the KTH dataset for real-world scenarios, making it ideal for such real-life surveillance applications.

5.4.8 Human activity recognition using an optical flow based feature set

In 2009 Kumar *et al* [35] proposed an optical flow feature set based approach that is both simple and efficient for recognizing human action interaction in video surveillance applications. Optical flow vectors on the borders of an individual performing the activity are used to build a feature extraction procedure utilizing a local descriptor.

The model records the changes in the action performer's silhouette over time in an efficient manner by reducing the computational complexity involved in computing an independent feature vector. An SVM is employed to classify the actions. The algorithm was trained and evaluated on the KTH, Weizmann and UT interaction datasets. The recognition rates observed were the following:

- Weizmann dataset: 95.69%.
- KTH dataset: 94.62%.
- UT interaction set_1 (ten videos): 92.7%.
- UT interaction set_2 (ten videos): 90.21%.

These results of the model are comparable to recently proposed sophisticated algorithms and thus it could be considered a good alternative for HAR in video surveillance applications.

5.4.9 Learning a hierarchical spatio-temporal model

In 2017 Xu *et al* [36] proposed a novel hierarchical spatio-temporal model (HSTM) to incorporate feature learning in a two-layer hierarchical classification (HCRF) model simultaneously. This unified algorithm is used to train the model effectively in a bottom up manner and measure both spatial and temporal similarities between the activities simultaneously to obtain greater classification performance. The aim was to exploit both the descriptive capability advantage offered by the hierarchical model and also the strong discriminative power offered by the two-layer model. The two-layer HCRF model consists of the following:

- A spatial layer at the bottom that learns high-level representations and captures spatial relations for a given video frame.
- A temporal layer at the top that characterizes temporal relations in the video using the learned features.

The model outperformed the state-of-the-art approaches when evaluated on KTH and UCF (for one-person actions), CASIA (for human–human interactions) and Gupta video datasets (for human–object interaction).

5.4.10 Human action recognition using trajectory-based representation

In their 2015 paper, Azim *et al* [51] proposed a trajectory-based approach for local representation that overcomes the limitations of previous models in capturing sufficient spatial or temporal relationships. The trajectories are extracted to reduce the redundancy and noise level when the STIPs detected by the cuboid detector are tracked using scale-invariant feature transformation (SIFT)-matching. Finally, the classification technique used is an SVM. After the extracted trajectories are enhanced, the trajectories of the actions are formed using the trajectory points and the surrounding volumes of these points are described using a bag-of-words (BOW) model. The trajectories are extracted even under any disturbances due to the movement of the camera, changes in viewpoint, occlusions or scale variations. An SVM is used to obtain the classifications and the final evaluation was performed on the Weizmann, KTH and UCF sports datasets. A 2% improvement over the baseline approach was observed when evaluated using the UCF sports dataset. A 0.4% improvement was observed compared to the dense trajectories approach on the KTH dataset and similar results were observed for the Weizmann dataset.

5.4.11 Human activity recognition using a deep neural network with contextual information

In 2017 Wei *et al* [34] proposed designing a deep neural network to recognize human activity from videos through a combination of motion and context features. The high-level mobility and low-level motion features describe the motion information of the subject. The context information consists of the following:

1. Scene based context:
    a. Scene prior: describes the scene in the frame globally.
    b. Scene context: describes the scene surrounding the subject locally.
2. Group based context:
    a. Group interaction: describes the interaction of the target person with the group members.
    b. Group structure context: describes the distribution of the group members' positions in space relative to the target person.

STIP is used as an extension to the Harris operator to extract feature points in spatio-temporal dimensions. Feature words for a histogram of optical flow (HOF) and histogram of gradient (HOG) are derived with K-means clustering. The two vectors are combined to make the motion descriptor of the person and fed into the network with four fully connected layers. The evaluation results of the model shows that it provides better performance than the state-of-the-art approaches on the collective activity dataset (CAD).

5.5 Challenges in human activity recognition

In this portion of the chapter we talk about the various challenges that may reduce the recognition ability of HAR systems. These challenges could be the specific methodologies used for the sensor devices to acquire the information, experimentation environments, the datasets used to train and evaluate models, etc. We also discuss a few ideas presented by researchers to effectively face such challenges and make the system more robust. The major challenges are discussed in the following sections.

5.5.1 Dataset

The major challenges with datasets are as follows:

- *Quantity*: Collecting, storing and annotating a large number of videos in realistic scenarios is a challenging job. This causes the number of datasets available to train and evaluate models to be limited. The majority of the existing datasets contain a very low average of 15 classes. Many researchers create their own datasets for evaluating their models which limits the publicly available benchmark dataset and makes comparing different approaches even harder. However, in 2019 Ghadiyaram *et al* [50] suggested that pre-training the model on a large amount (> 65 000 000 videos) of noisy social media data has demonstrated a significant improvement in performance when compared to existing state-of-the-art approaches on three challenging HAR datasets.

- *Diversity*: To produce maximum results the datasets used for training should be of sufficient quality. Ideally, a dataset should include a variety of human poses for the same action, in complex situations, and also variations in the quality of the videos and the methods used to capture them [38]. However, most of the benchmarks focus on simple actions.

- *Quality*: Many of the current datasets were recorded in a controlled environment with non-complex backgrounds with hired actors performing a specific set of actions. These datasets fail to meet the criteria for ideal datasets and do not cover the realistic situations required to develop real-world applications. Another problem in making an ideal dataset is with the process of manual annotation of the tasks which makes the task biased. Many datasets such as Weizmann and KTH have reached the end of their life cycles as several methods [39, 40] trained on them have achieved 100% recognition rates [38]. Such datasets with insufficient data and diversity cannot be used for training advanced and effective architectures.

5.5.2 Sensors

A 2014 review article by Theng *et al* [6] shows that because it is limited in capturing human gestures and a scene in 3D space, the RGB camera has not received as much attention as depth sensors in HAR research. Privacy is also another important issue in using RGB cameras. Being watched and recorded by a camera all the time might cause discomfort and a feeling of intrusion to the subject. As a result, depth sensors and wearable sensor technologies have been becoming more popular in HAR research of late. Depth sensors also have the advantage of low cost and a higher sample rate, and are also capable of combining visual and depth information. However, depth sensors also have their disadvantages, such as occlusion and limitations of the sensor viewpoint. Wearable sensors could tackle these challenges faced by RGB cameras and depth sensors.

5.5.3 Experimentation environment

Real-world scenarios involve dynamic backgrounds, self or partial occlusions, variance in lighting and viewpoint changes. Background noise and variation in scale as the person in the frame moves closer and farther from the camera also affect the quality of the videos. Systems designed to operate using single view acquisition devices would be limited in the amount of information they could extract from the activities being analyzed. A few earlier methods have suffered from extracting information when such complex backgrounds are present. Pruning can be used to overcome this problem. The method proposed by Wei *et al* in 2017 [34] makes use of the context to overcome the above-mentioned challenges.

5.5.4 Intraclass variation and interclass similarity

Human activity is complex and varies from subject to subject even for the same activity. Different people tend to perform the same activity in different ways due to various factors such as limb length, human structure, performing speed and strength. Even external factors such as occlusions, viewpoints of the camera, the appearance of the subject and the layout of the scene also exist. These factors lead to larger intraclass variations. In contrast, similar forms and shapes may be used in different activities which cause intraclass similarity. To tackle this, it is necessary to extract distinctive features with high accuracy.

5.5.5 Multi-subject interactions and group activities

Low-level human activities such as running, walking, etc, involve only a single subject. But in realistic scenarios, people perform activities that involve interaction with several people and objects. Different people will also be performing different activities simultaneously. Detecting abnormal/fraud activities in retail environments, casinos, workplaces, manufacturing, daily life monitoring, etc, are examples that involve such complex interactive activities. The objects tend to be small in size and similar in appearance, which makes activity recognition in such applications a difficult task. Using radio frequency identification technology (RFID) as suggested by Beddiar *et al* in 2020 [41] could be a potential solution.

5.5.6 Training

Training on large-scale datasets typically suffers from a slow learning rate, which leads to a low recognition rate. Higher computer processing power is required to process large amounts of data at a time. Also, training on datasets with very little or missing data also poses challenges. More robust methods need to be developed to deal with such uncertain cases where there is missing data.

5.5.7 Challenges in HAR applications

Videos used for applications such as video surveillance require that the target person is clear enough to detect abnormal activities. However, these videos are usually captured with cameras positioned at high places in large and crowded environments such as airports, metro stations, malls, etc. The videos may suffer from severe occlusions. Also recognizing activities when several activities are performed by a person at a time is also a challenge. Applications such as daily life monitoring involve challenges such as privacy concerns, social acceptance, costs and other side effects. Implementing HAR systems on people's smartphones [14] where their own device is used to store the captured data would address this issue to an extent. However, the memory and battery constraints of smartphones limit the effectiveness of this implementation. Also, differentiating between intentional and involuntary actions and the overlap between beginning and finishing times of an activity are challenges that need to be addressed.

5.6 Datasets available for activity detection research

The acquisition of a good human activity database for training and testing the model is the first stage in building an HAR system. The following are the criteria for an ideal HAR database [38]:
- The data should contain still images or video sequences.
- A sufficient quantity of high-quality data should be available to train the model.
- The data should include numerous subjects performing the same action.
- There should be several classes of activities.
- There need to be variations in illumination.
- The data must have large variations among the classes (interclass).
- Videos should include sequences with partial occlusion of the subject.
- The videos should have complex backgrounds.

There are many publicly available benchmark datasets for HAR to compare the performance of different approaches. We have reviewed several such datasets. However, we have narrowed it down to the most relevant and widely utilized, and organized them into activity categories as described by Zhang *et al* [42]: atomic action level, behavior level, interaction level and group activities level.

The following are some of the benchmark datasets available for related research classified into different categories based on their activity type.

5.6.1 Action-level dataset

According to Zhang *et al* [42], 'action/activity is middle-level human activity without any human–human or human–object interactions'. In this category of datasets, the majority of the human actions are captured video sequences of activities carried out by a single individual with no interaction between humans and objects:

- *KTH Human Action Dataset* [43]: This was created in 2004 by the Royal Institute of Technology of Sweden and is frequently cited. The latest KTH database includes 2391 clips grouped into six classes of actions (walking, boxing, running, jogging, hand clapping, waving) carried out multiple times in four types of scenarios by 25 individuals. These include indoors, outdoors, outdoors with different clothes and outdoors with scale variation scenarios. All sequences are four seconds long on average and were captured at 25 fps using a static camera over homogeneous backgrounds. The high intraclass variation of the dataset due to a variety of scenarios, viewpoints and actors' appearances is a large factor in its success

- *Weizmann Human Action Dataset* [44]: This was created in 2005 by the Weizmann Institute of Science. It includes videos of nine subjects performing ten natural actions (running, jumping-jacks, skipping, jumping forward/in place on both legs, walking, sideways galloping, waving one/both hands, etc). These activities are performed against a simple background using a fixed camera and at a resolution of 180×144 and 50 fps. To make the dataset more robust, ten sequences of people walking in diverse and complex conditions and non-uniform backdrops were also collected.

- *INRIA Xmas Motion Acquisition Sequences (IXMAS) Dataset* [45]: This is a multi-view for view-invariant HAR dataset created by Weinland *et al* in 2006. It contains video sequences of 11 individuals performing 13 daily life human actions, such as looking at a wristwatch, crossing their arms, scratching their head, sitting, walking, punching, standing up, kicking, pointing and so on. Each of these actions were captured three times from each person using five cameras with a fixed viewpoint, static background and illumination settings.

5.6.2 Interaction-level dataset

The video sequences in these datasets involve human–human or human–object interactions which makes it more realistic. Although these datasets are relatively challenging, they represent various real-life scenarios such as sports events, video surveillance, etc:

- *MSRDaily Activity 3D Dataset*: This dataset was created by Jiang Wang at Microsoft Research, Redmond. This dataset is more challenging than MSR Action3D due to the human–object interaction video sequences that are included in it. This dataset contains three channels, namely depth maps, RGB video and skeleton joint positions. Each of the channels contains 320 video sequences.

A Kinect depth camera was used to capture ten subjects performing 16 classes of daily activities such as sitting, using a laptop, walking, playing the guitar, eating and so on.

- *UCF50 Dataset* [46]: This was created in 2012 by the Center for Research in Computer Vision, the University of Central Florida, as an extension for the YouTube Action dataset (UCF11). Unlike most HAR datasets which are performed by actors in a staged environment, UCF50 contains 50 categories of actions gathered from YouTube videos with realistic scenarios. These videos are divided into 25 groups, each featuring at least four clips that share some similar characteristics, such as the same person, viewpoint, or background, etc. It also contains large interclass variations due to diversity in parameters such as appearance of the object, camera motion, scale and pose, camera viewpoint, illumination conditions, cluttered backgrounds, etc, which makes it a very challenging dataset. Some examples of the activity classes in this dataset are: shooting a basketball, baseball pitch, bench press, drumming, biking, diving, etc.

- *UCF Sports Action Dataset*: This was constructed in 2008 by the Center for Research in Computer Vision at the University of Central Florida. It contains 150 videos of 11 action categories of different sports activities taken from television broadcasts at a 720×480 resolution. It includes sports activities such swinging a bat, running, golf, diving, lifting, horse riding, kicking, skating and walking. The complex environment and intraclass variability make it a challenging dataset for HAR.

5.6.3 Group activities level dataset

- *ActivityNet*: This is a large-scale benchmark that covers a wide variety of complex daily life human activities, making it currently the largest dataset for temporal activity detection. The latest version of the ActivityNet dataset contains 19 994 untrimmed videos from 203 different activity classes, totaling up to 849 h of video. The videos were collected from video-sharing websites such as Youtube and contain 1.41 activity instances per video annotated with temporal boundaries. Each of the videos are 5–10 min long with most of them having HD resolution (1280×720) and 30 fps. Half of the video sequences are reserved for training, one quarter for validation and the other quarter for testing purposes. The activities are organized in a hierarchical structure depending on where they usually occur. A few examples of activity classes are household, eating, sports, drinking, personal care and social activities.

- *Kinetics (Kinetics Human Action Video Dataset)*: This is a large size, high-quality dataset created in 2017 by the DeepMind team for HAR. The three versions of this dataset are: Kinetics 400, Kinetics 600 and Kinetics 700. The videos for all these versions are provided in the form of different YouTube video URLs. This dataset is being used as a benchmark in several HAR papers and hence is quickly becoming a standard for HAR and a baseline for video processing deep learning systems:

- Kinetics 400: This was the initial version which contains 400 classes of human actions with >400 sequences of videos in each class.
- Kinetics 600: This is a high-quality dataset which contains 600 classes of human actions with >600 sequences of videos in each class totaling a diverse range of 500 000 videos. The clips are of 10 s in length on average and are labeled with a single class.
- Kinetics 700: This is the latest version which contains 700 classes of human actions with >600 sequences of videos in each class totaling a diverse range of 650 000 videos. The dataset includes both human–object and human–human interactions.

- *UCF-101 Action Recognition Dataset* [47]: This is a HAR dataset in realistic scenarios created in 2012 by the Centre for Research in Computer Vision, the University of Central Florida, extending the previous UCF50 dataset. It includes 27 h of video footage in the form of 13 320 video clips of 101 realistic action categories. These categories can be divided into the five classes shown in table 5.1.

  The dataset also provides a large degree of diversity as the videos are recorded with diverse backgrounds, objects, camera movement, illumination, angle of camera, etc. This, combined with the fact that the videos were taken from realistic YouTube scenarios, makes it a good dataset for HAR applications.

5.6.4 Behavior-level dataset

The behavior-level datasets are as follows:

- *VISOR dataset* [48]: This dataset was created by the University of Modena and Reggio Emilia's Imagelab Laboratory in 2005 to compare and exchange the results of many problems in the field of video surveillance. It contains videos in a wide variety of categories. For HAR we can use the 130 video sequences available in the 'HAR in video surveillance' category.
- *Caviar dataset*: Created in 2004 this comprises several videos of subjects performing nine different activities. The camera used was equipped with a wide-angle lens and the footage was captured in two different places:
  - Entrance lobby, INRIA Labs, Grenoble, France.
  - A shopping center's hallway in the city of Lisbon, Portugal.

Table 5.1. Details of the UCF-101 Action Recognition Dataset.

Class	Number of categories
Human–object interaction	20
Body motion	16
Human–human interaction	5
Playing musical instruments	10
Playing sports	50

- *Multi-Camera Action Dataset (MCAD)* [49]: This was made by The National University of Singapore. They used five cameras to record 20 subjects performing 18 daily life actions borrowed from the KTH, IXMAS and TRECVID datasets. Each activity is performed by an actor a total of eight times (four in a daylight setting and four in an evening setting) for each camera.

5.7 Scope for further research in this domain

Due to its large number of applications in different fields, the research efforts in HAR have grown rapidly in the past few decades and will most likely continue to do so in the following years as technology also progresses. We can expect the following future developments and research exploration in activity recognition:

- Since smartphones have emerged as such an important and widely accepted part of everyone's lives, we can expect HAR systems to be integrated into smart devices since this approach overcomes the privacy barriers faced by standard HAR systems. However, limited battery life, memory constraints and limited processing power are some of the big challenges to be addressed.
- With the rise in better hardware, such as better sensors, embedded devices and microchips, and also more efficient descriptors for feature extraction and better classification algorithms, we can expect the currently well-performing approaches to be integrated into smaller devices such as smartphones and smartwatches and achieve comparable performances to offline approaches.
- Human activities often tend to be complex, spontaneous and interleaved. Thus instead of concentrating solely on one activity at a time, HAR systems in the future ought to be able to effectively recognize complex and simultaneously occurring activities. They should also be able to distinguish between voluntary and unintended activities to avoid false alarms. To be future-proof, HAR systems also need to be able to handle uncertainty to avoid ambiguous behavior interpretations, as different activities can look similar.
- HAR systems for modern applications have been experiencing growing demand lately. They are quite useful, effective and convenient for solving a variety of problems faced in several fields. An HAR is immensely time-saving, cost-effective and less prone to human bias and errors as it automates processes and reduces the need for human involvement. Hence more research efforts need to be put into the advancement of this field.

5.8 Conclusion

In this chapter we have discussed the basics of HAR, recently proposed approaches in this domain and various applications of HAR. We provided a brief overview of various kinds of sensory devices used to gather data, their advantages and limitations, and also the general steps to recognize human activities using visual approaches. We also highlighted the importance of this research topic by discussing its applications in a wide variety of fields. We then examined the challenges involved in human activity recognition. We mentioned the ideal characteristics of a HAR dataset, discussed several existing human activity recognition benchmarks, and classified them according to their type of activity. The future scope of the research in this domain is also listed at the end of the chapter.

References

[1] Leo M, D'Orazio T and Spagnolo P 2004 Human activity recognition for automatic visual surveillance of wide areas *Proc. of the ACM 2nd Int. Workshop on Video Surveillance and Sensor Networks* (New York: Association for Computing Machinery) pp 124–30

[2] Gonzàlez J, Roca F X and Villanueva J 2007 HERMES: a research project on human sequence evaluation *ECCOMAS Thematic Conf. on Computational Vision and Medical Image Processing (VipIMAGE)*

[3] Jarray R, Snoun A, Bouchrika T and Jemai O 2020 Deep human action recognition system for assistance of Alzheimer's patients *Int. Conf. on Hybrid Intelligent Systems* pp 484–93

[4] Chaaraoui A A, Padilla-López J R, Climent-Pérez P and Flórez-Revuelta F 2014 Evolutionary joint selection to improve human action recognition with RGB-D devices *Expert Syst. Appl.* **41** 786–94

[5] Sagayam K M and Hemanth D J 2017 Hand posture and gesture recognition techniques for virtual reality applications: a survey *Virtual Real.* **21** 91–107

[6] Ann O C and Theng L B 2014 Human activity recognition: a review *IEEE Int. Conf. on Control System, Computing and Engineering* pp 389–93

[7] Pareek P and Thakkar A 2021 A survey on video-based human action recognition: recent updates, datasets, challenges, and applications *Artific. Intell. Rev.* **54** 2259–322

[8] Leontev A N 1978 *Activity, Consciousness, and Personality* (Englewood Cliffs, NJ: Prentice Hall)

[9] Rautaray S S and Agrawal A 2015 Vision based hand gesture recognition for human computer interaction: a survey *Artif. Intell. Rev.* **43** 1

[10] Vemulapalli R, Arrate F and Chellappa R 2014 Human action recognition by representing 3D skeletons as points in a Lie group *Proc. of the 2014 IEEE Conf. on Computer Vision and Pattern Recognition* pp 588–95

[11] Zhu C and Sheng W 2011 Wearable sensor-based hand gesture and daily activity recognition for robot-assisted living *IEEE Trans. Syst. Man Cybern.* A **41** 569–73

[12] Paulson B, Cummings D and Hammond T 2011 Object interaction detection using hand posture cues in an office setting *Int. J. Hum.-Comput. Stud.* **69** 19

[13] Cvetković B, Szeklicki R, Janko V, Lutomski P and Luštrek M 2018 Real-time activity monitoring with a wristband and a smartphone *Inf. Fusion* **43** 77–93

[14] Lu Y *et al* 2017 Towards unsupervised physical activity recognition using smartphone accelerometers *Multimed. Tools Appl.* **76** 10701–19

[15] Brémond F, Thonnat M and Zuniga M 2006 Video-understanding framework for automatic behavior recognition *Behav. Res. Methods* **38** 416–26

[16] Chang M-C, Krahnstoever N and Lim S 2010 Group level activity recognition in crowded environments across multiple cameras *Seventh IEEE Int. Conf. Advanced Video and Signal based Surveillance (Boston, MA, 29 August–1 September)* (New York: IEEE) pp 56–63

[17] Fusier F, Valentin V and Bremond F 2007 Video understanding for complex activity recognition *Mach. Vision Appl.* **18** 167–88

[18] Frontoni E, Raspa P, Mancini A, Zingaretti P and Placidi V 2013 Customers' activity recognition in intelligent retail environments *New Trends in Image Analysis and Processing*

(Lecture Notes in Computer Science vol 8158) ed A Petrosino, L Maddalena and P Pala (Berlin: Springer)

[19] Chang Y-J, Chen S-F and Huang J-D 2011 A kinect-based system for physical rehabilitation: a pilot study for young adults with motor disabilities *Res. Dev. Disabil.* **32** 2566–70

[20] Nikishina V B, Petrash E A and Nikishin I I 2019 Application of a hardware and software system of computer vision for rehabilitation training of post-stroke patients *Biomed. Eng.* **53** 44–51

[21] Zhu C and Sheng W 2011 Wearable sensor-based hand gesture and daily activity recognition for robot-assisted living *IEEE Trans. Syst. Man Cybern.* A **41** 569–73

[22] Vacher M, Istrate D and Portet F 2011 The Sweet-Home project: audio technology in smart homes to improve well-being and reliance *Conf. Proc. IEEE Eng. Med. Biol. Soc.* **2011** 5291–4

[23] Gerling K, Livingston I, Nacke L and Mandryk R 2012 Fullbody motion-based game interaction for older adults *Proc. of the 2012 ACM Annual Conf. on Human Factors in Computing Systems* p 1873

[24] Han J, Shao L, Xu D and Shotton J 2013 Enhanced computer vision with Microsoft Kinect sensor: a review *IEEE Trans. Cybern.* **43** 1318–34

[25] Schuldt C, Laptev I and Caputo B 2004 Recognizing human actions: a local SVM approach *Proc. of the 17th Int. Conf. on Pattern Recognition*

[26] Donahue J, Hendricks L A, Rohrbach M, Venugopalan S, Guadarrama S, Saenko K and Darrell T 2017 Long-term recurrent convolutional networks for visual recognition and description *IEEE Trans. Pattern Anal. Mach. Intell.* **39** 677–91

[27] Simonyan K and Zisserman A 2014 Two-stream convolutional networks for action recognition in videos *Proceedings of the 27th International Conference on Neural Information Processing Systems - Volume 1 (NIPS'14)* (Cambridge, MA: MIT Press) pp 568–76

[28] Karpathy A, Toderici G, Shetty S, Leung T, Sukthankar R and Fei-Fei L 2014 Large-scale video classification with convolutional neural networks *2014 IEEE Conf. on Computer Vision and Pattern Recognition* pp 1725–32 http://doi.org/10.1109/CVPR.2014.223

[29] Gaglio S, Re G L and Morana M 2015 Human activity recognition process using 3-D posture data *IEEE Trans. Hum.-Mach. Syst.* **45** 586–97

[30] Kumari S and Mitra S K 2011 Human action recognition using DFT *Third National Conf. on Computer Vision, Pattern Recognition, Image Processing and Graphics*

[31] Ngọc L Q, Viet V, Son T and Hoang P M 2016 A robust approach for action recognition based on spatio-temporal features in RGB-D sequences *Int. J. Adv. Comp. Sci. Appl.* **7** 070526

[32] Feichtenhofer C, Fan H, Malik J and He K 2019 SlowFast networks for video recognition *IEEE/CVF Int. Conf. on Computer Vision* pp 6201–10

[33] Ji S, Xu W, Yang M and Yu K 2013 3D convolutional neural networks for human action recognition *IEEE Trans. Pattern Anal. Mach. Intell.* **35** 221–31

[34] Wei L and Shah S 2017 Human activity recognition using deep neural network with contextual information *Proceedings of the 12th International Joint Conference on Computer Vision, Imaging and Computer Graphics Theory and Applications - Volume 5: VISAPP, (VISIGRAPP 2017)* (Mambridge, AM: MIT Press) pp 34–43 http://doi.org/10.5220/0006099500340043

[35] Kumar S S and John M 2016 Human activity recognition using optical flow based feature set *IEEE Int. Carnahan Conf. on Security Technology*

[36] Xu W, Miao Z, Zhang X-P and Tian Y 2017 Learning a hierarchical spatio-temporal model for human activity recognition *2017 IEEE Int. Conf. on Acoustics, Speech and Signal Processing (ICASSP)* http://doi.org/10.1109/icassp.2017.7952428

[37] Vrigkas M, Nikou C and Kakadiaris I A 2015 A review of human activity recognition methods *Front. Robot. AI* **2** 28

[38] Ikizler N and Duygulu P 2007 Human action recognition using distribution of oriented rectangular patches *Human Motion—Understanding Modelling Capture and Animation* (Rio de Janeiro: Springer) pp 271–84

[39] Natarajan P and Nevatia R 2008 Online, real-time tracking and recognition of human actions *IEEE Workshop on Motion and Video Computing (Copper Mountain, CO)* pp 1–8

[40] Krahnstoever N, Rittscher J, Tu P, Chean K and Tomlinson T 2005 Activity recognition using visual tracking and RFID *Seventh IEEE Workshops on Applications of Computer Vision* **1** 494–500

[41] Beddiar D R *et al* 2020 Vision-based human activity recognition: a survey *Multimed. Tools Appl.* **79** 30509–55

[42] Zhang S, Wei Z, Nie J, Huang L, Wang S and Li Z 2017 A review on human activity recognition using vision-based method *J. Healthc. Eng.* **2017** 3090343

[43] Schuldt C, Laptev I and Caputo B 2004 Recognizing human actions: a local SVM approach *Proc. of the 17th Int. Conf. on Pattern Recognition*

[44] Blank M, Gorelick L, Shechtman E, Irani M and Basri R 2005 Actions as space-time shapes in *Tenth IEEE Int. Conf. on Computer Vision* 1 *(Beijing, China)* pp 1395–402

[45] Weinland D, Ronfard R and Boyer E 2006 Free viewpoint action recognition using motion history volumes *Comput. Vis. Image Underst.* **104** 249–57

[46] Reddy K K and Shah M 2013 Recognizing 50 human action categories of web videos *Mach. Vis. Appl.* **24** 971

[47] Soomro K, Zamir A R and Shah M 2012 Ucf101: a dataset of 101 human actions classes from videos in the wild, arXiv:1212.0402

[48] Ballan L, Bertini M, Del Bimbo A, Seidenari L and Serra G 2009 Effective codebooks for human action categorization *12th Int. Conf. on Computer Vision Workshops* (Piscataway, NJ: IEEE) pp 506–13

[49] Li W, Wong Y, Liu A A, Li Y, Su Y T and Kankanhalli M 2016 Multi-camera action dataset for cross-camera action recognition benchmarking 2017 IEEE Winter Conf. on Applications of Computer Vision (WACV) pp 187–96

[50] Ghadiyaram D, Feiszli M, Tran D, Yan X, Wang H and Mahajan D 2019 Large-scale weakly-supervised pre-training for video action recognition *IEEE/CVF Conf. on Computer Vision and Pattern Recognition* pp 12038–47

[51] Abdul-Azim H A and Hemayed E E 2015 Human action recognition using trajectory-based representation *Egypt. Inform. J.* **16** 187–98

IOP Publishing

Computational Intelligence Based Solutions for Vision Systems

Varun Bajaj and Irshad Ahmad Ansari

Chapter 6

A deep learning-based food detection and classification system

Bhan Singh, Divyanshu, Mayur Kashyap, Himanshu Gupta and Om Prakash Verma

Nutrition is a basic necessity and is an essential part of the survival and development of every species. Conventional nutrition level measuring methods have various drawbacks, such as complexity and being time-consuming. These can be overcome by using convolutional neural network-based food detection techniques. Food-based industries require inventory management and sensor-based control systems as counters. Control systems that emit radiation and suffering from component decay can cause various losses as well as harmful effects. Furthermore, these systems are often not cheap. However, a simple deep learning-based food detector can help solve the aforementioned issues. Therefore the primary aim of the proposed approach is to determine the accuracy and efficiency of three deep learning-based object detection models, namely YOLOv3, YOLOv4 and SSD based on mAP, and draw useful conclusions from the results. To carry out the detection process, a dataset of fast food items is chosen which includes various types of commonly consumed food items. Due to the large pool of fast food items, ten categories have been selected to ease the research. The research yields a 74.55% mAP for YOLOv3 and 71.26% mAP for YOLOv4, compared to 13.59% mAP for an old model of SSD.

Abbreviations

AP	Average precision
BoF	Bag of freebies
BoS	Bag of specials
CIoU	Complete intersection over union
CNN	Convolutional neural network
CSP	Cross-stage partial connections
F_1-score	Harmonic mean of precision and recall
FN	False negative
FP	False positive

IoU	Intersection over union
mAP	Mean average precision
NLP	Natural language processing
NMS	Non-maximal suppression
PANet	Path aggregation network
PASCAL	Pattern analysis, statistical modeling and computational learning visual
VOC	object classes
RCNN	Region-based convolutional neural networks
SGD	Stochastic gradient descent
SPM	Spatial pyramid match
SPP	Spatial pyramid pooling
SSD	Single-shot detection
TN	True negative
TP	True positive
VGG	Visual geometry group
YOLO	You only look once

6.1 Introduction

Nutrition is an essential part of human health. It not only helps in reducing the risk of non-communicable diseases and improves the immune system, but is also directly associated with safer pregnancy and longevity. People with adequate nutrition tend to be more productive, creating better chances for progress and breaking cycles of hunger and poverty. Further, malnutrition and its co-morbidities are considered as the most prominent causes of mortality, particularly in children below five years old among which malnutrition accounts for 45% of total deaths [1]. Keeping track of nutrition intake has become a necessary measure to prevent the negative effects of malnutrition. Previous methods of nutrition checking mostly focused on clinical and growth change methods which are fairly complex, time-consuming, and usually require specialist equipment handled by professionals. Lately, AI-based object detection methods have gained popularity and are being used for similar objectives. Standard nutritional values can be displayed for the food studied and an appropriate application can be developed.

Another food-related issue is related to inventory. Food chain industries such as restaurants, street vendors, etc, need to keep track of different food items in storage, after preparation, and for delivery or takeout purposes. Assigning people to keep track of such tasks results in errors and is a major cause of losses in the long run. Conventionally, sensor-based control systems have been used to replace people. Such control systems consist of simple IR, UV, or electric pulse-based control systems that can be scaled to the required size. These methods often result in the emission of radiation or component deterioration which can be harmful to food items, in particular cooked food [2]. These methods are also highly expensive. A simple camera-based application running on a food detecting algorithm can solve the aforementioned issues.

Deep learning (DL) in artificial intelligence is a technique imitating the functions of the human brain in detection and data processing. Neural networks came into play in the 1940s. Neural networks aim at solving problems related to learning ethically and efficiently. DL models have been employed to solve the problems related to prediction and complex object detection [3–6]. Convolutional neural networks (CNNs) are frequently used in such models. This set of rules takes input snapshots and assigns learnable weights and biases for diverse targets in a photograph and makes them different from each other. Furthermore, a low-resolution image with low complexity may be used with convolutional neural networks, giving an efficient output. These strategies assign a bounding container over the items and associate the perfect item class for every container. This can be performed using various DL algorithms such as region-based CNN, YOLOv3 [7], YOLOv4 [8] and single-shot detectors (SSDs) [9]. Therefore in this work three DL-based object detection models (YOLOv3, YOLOv4 and SSD) have been employed to develop a food detection system.

The key contributions of the present proposed work can be summarized as follows:

- Trained models for various food detection applications such as nutrition checks and food item counting.
- Inferences on YOLOv3, YOLOv4 and SSD that deflect from the norm using an imbalanced dataset.

The rest of this chapter is divided into five main sections. Section 6.2 presents a literature review and section 6.3 introduces the theory behind YOLOv3, YOLOv4 and SSD. The dataset operated upon for training and testing is presented briefly in the methodology/experiments section (section 6.4). It explains the software and hardware used for training the models along with a brief description of the implementation of all three models. Section 6.5 presents and discusses the results obtained from the experiments. Lastly, section 6.6 provides concluding remarks and the scope for future research.

6.2 Literature review

Redmon *et al* introduced a new system to detect an object in 2016 [10]. In this paper, the system needs to look only once (YOLO) at an image to predict the class and position of an object. The architecture of YOLO is shown in figure 6.1. Before YOLO, the system took a classifier to detect an object with different positions and scales in a test image. The YOLO algorithm achieved a 57.9% precision on the PASCAL VOC 2012 dataset. In 2016 the same authors came up with an improved YOLO algorithm called YOLOv2. This algorithm outperformed their previous work. YOLOv2 achieved a precision of 73.4% on the same PASCAL VOC 2012 dataset [11]. YOLOv3 [7], published in 2018, achieved 57.5% AP (50) in 51 ms whereas RetinaNet achieved 57.9% AP (50) in 198 ms, a similar performance but 3.8 times faster. YOLOv3 was three times faster than an SSD with similar performance in terms of efficiency. YOLOv4 [8], introduced by Alexey in 2020, was more efficient than YOLOv3 by 12%. Its accuracy was 10% better than YOLOv3. The SSD, [9] published in 2016 by Liu, uses a single neural network for object detection in snapshots. Guneet [12] identified that the SSD performed well on a dataset of

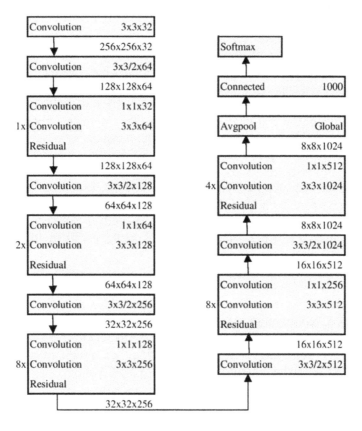

Figure 6.1. YOLOv3 architecture.

aircraft images which had a wide range, scale and orientation of objects in an image. The SSD gives a 0.916 accuracy on the validation dataset of aircraft images. It outperforms YOLOv3 (0.88) and RCNN (0.63). Asjad *et al* [13] compared YOLOv3 and YOLOv4 on a vehicle dataset. They showed that both these algorithms are fast but YOLOv4 gives 0.81 precision and YOLOv3 gives 0.76 when training of the final weight on vehicle dataset is complete. Similarly, Gupta *et al* employed faster RCNN, SSD, YOLOv3 and YOLOv4 for vehicle detection using an aerial image dataset and identified that even with a birds-eye view of the dataset, YOLOv4 outperforms the others [14].

6.3 Theory

The primary aim for any object detection algorithm is to be able to recognize a wide variety of objects with acceptable accuracy at a reasonable speed. The performance of different models should be measured to achieve the stated goals. The following sections describe the YOLOv3, YOLOv4 and SSD models along with their architectures.

6.3.1 YOLOv3

YOLOv3 employs dimension clusters as anchor boxes to predict bounding boxes. Utilizing logistic regression, it predicts the objectness score for each bounding box, which is closer to one if more overlapping is observed between the ground truth and bounding box prior compared to any other bounding box priors. Unlike classification or coordinates, objectness is lost if the bounding box prior is not allocated to the ground truth. The entire topmost feature map is employed for forecasting both confidences for multiple categories as well as bounding boxes. With the increase in the intersection over union (IoU) threshold, the performance of YOLOv3 decreases significantly [7]. Further, during training it utilizes the binary cross-entropy loss for making class predictions. In complex domains such as Open Image Dataset (OID), these loss and independent logistic classifiers are really helpful. Data augmentation, multi-scale training and batch normalization are used for training [15]. YOLOv3 adds a fully connected layer for prediction, unlike SSD which uses a convolutional predictor with multiple aspect ratios.

Architecture
The network in YOLOv3 takes a hybrid approach between the YOLOv2 network and Darknet19 [16]. It is structured as successive 3×3 and 1×1 convolutional layers totaling 53 convolutional layers, along with some skip connections, and is thus called Darknet53, as shown in figure 6.1. It predicts four coordinates t_x, t_y, t_w and t_z for every bounding box. The bounding box predictions are calculated according to the following equations:

$$b_x = \sigma(t_x) + c_x \qquad (6.1)$$

$$b_y = \sigma(t_y) + c_y \qquad (6.2)$$

$$b_z = \sigma(t_z) + c_z \qquad (6.3)$$

$$b_w = p_w e^{t_w} \qquad (6.4)$$

$$b_h = p_h e^{t_h}, \qquad (6.5)$$

where p_w and p_h indicate the width and height of the bounding box prior, whereas c_x and c_y represents the offsets for a cell in the top-left coordinate of the image. Ground truth values can be evaluated by backtracking equations (6.1)–(6.5).

The last convolutional layer predicts a 3D tensor for the encoding box class along objectness. Feature layers are concatenated with feature maps from previous layers. Therefore it is able to provide rich semantic and spatial information from upsampled features and earlier feature maps, respectively [7]. The bounding box prior is determined using k-means clustering.

6.3.2 YOLOv4

YOLOv4 achieves a fast operating, real-time high-object detector with the introduction of two bags, i.e. the bag of freebies (BoF) and bag of specials (BoS).

BoF: This bag involves methods to receive better accuracy by changing the training strategy without increasing the inference cost. For the backbone of YOLOv4 the freebies are cut mix, mosaic data augmentation, drop block regularization and class label smoothing. For detectors, the freebies include complete intersection over union (CIoU) loss and self-adversarial training [17, 18]. In addition to data augmentation, the B0F solves the problem of semantic distribution bias in the dataset.

BoS: This bag involves methods that enhance the object detection accuracy significantly at the cost of a small increase in inference cost. For backbone, specials are mish activation and cross-stage partial connection. For the detector, the BoSs have spatial pyramid pooling (SPP) and a path aggregation network (PANet) [19]. Knowledge distillation is used for better smoothing of the label. Class label smoothing makes the model more robust [8].

IoU loss is used directly to find the coordinate value of each corner of the bounding box. Spatial pyramid match (SPM) splits the feature map into $d \times d$ identical blocks with $d = 1, 2, \ldots$ forming a spatial pyramid. $k \times k$ max-pooling increases the susceptible field of the feature map as it is relatively large [20]. Activation statistics from four contrasting figures are evaluated on every individual layer using batch normalization, diminishing the need for a larger mini-batch size. The addition of the BoF and BoS training strategies makes detector performance independent of mini-batch size.

Architecture

The YOLOv4 architecture is divided into three parts, as shown in figure 6.2, i.e. the backbone, head and some layers inserted between them called the neck.

It uses CSPDarknet53 as its backbone, containing 29 convolutional layers 3×3, 725×725 receptive fields and 27.6 million parameters. The influence of receptive fields with different sizes depends on the object size, i.e. the entire viewing of the object and network size, i.e. the context around the object. An SPP block is added over CSPDarknet53 to increase the receptive field significantly. PANet is used as the neck, consisting of path aggregation from different backbone levels from different level detectors and the head is structured by implementing YOLOv3 (anchor-based).

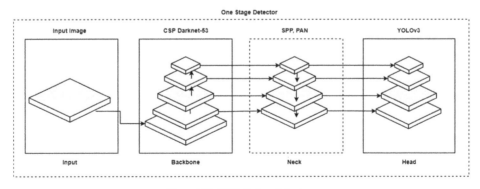

Figure 6.2. YOLOv4 architecture.

6.3.3 SSD

SSD discretizes the output area of the bounding box, utilizing several combinations of disparate aspect ratios and scales as per feature map location into default boxes. These default boxes are almost similar to the anchor boxes as employed by earlier techniques, except that now they are applied on many feature maps with different resolutions. This is centered on a feedforward convolutional network that provides a set number of bounding boxes and scores for the attendance of an object in the class accompanied by non-maximal suppression. This network mixes forecasts from a myriad of feature maps to automatically handle objects of different sizes. Lower layers of the network give fine details of the detected object. Feature maps from these layers enhance the semantic segmentation value. SSD is more sensitive to the bounding box which causes poor performance in detecting small objects compared to large objects [9].

Architecture

The VGG-16 network is used as the base in SSD 300. The default boxes combine the feature maps in such a way that the relative position of each box with the corresponding cell remains unchanged. These generated default boxes are illustrated in figure 6.3 for better visualization. Further, for every box of M from a given locality, it estimates the c class score and four offsets relative to the default box [21]. The gross objective loss can be computed by the following equation which is the weighted aggregate of localization loss and confidence loss:

$$L(x, c, l, g) = \frac{1}{N}(L_{\text{conf}}(x, c) + \alpha L_{\text{loc}}(x, l, g)). \qquad (6.6)$$

If N (number of matched default boxes) = 0, then the loss will also be 0. After matching of the default boxes, most of them being negative, they are sorted using the highest confidence loss for each with the ratio being at most 3:1. This leads to faster optimization and stable training. The top 200 detections per image can be kept after applying non-maximal suppression with the Jaccard overlap 0.45 class [9]. Non-maximal suppression (NMS) is a post-processing method used to filter out that bounding box which predicts the same object badly but retains those with a higher response.

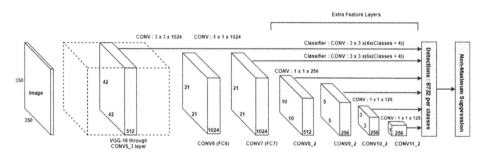

Figure 6.3. SSD architecture.

6.4 Methodology/experiments

This experiment is an attempt to train an object detection model based on single-shot detectors with decent mAP that can be used for real-world applications. The following sections contain details about the dataset, its preparation and implementation of three single-state detection algorithms, namely YOLOv3, YOLOv4 and SSD.

6.4.1 Dataset

The dataset consists of images from the open source Open Image Dataset (OID) [22] by Google, containing masks for segmentation and labels for classification, along with bounding box annotations for more than 600 categories. Given the large size of the dataset, the OIDv4 Toolkit for downloading a smaller number of images from ten classes is used for the experiment. The dataset's uneven distribution in table 6.1 is due to the lower number of images of particular classes, such as burritos and hot dogs, available on the Google Open Image Dataset and a large number of images of fast food, pizza and pasta. Moreover, this distribution helps us to analyze the model performance when the dataset is rich and also when it is weak. Figure 6.4 represents the graphical distribution of the dataset.

Table 6.1. Dataset division for each class.

Class	Bread	Burrito	Candy	Fast food	French fries	Hamburger	Hot dog	Pasta	Pizza	Snack	Total
Training	508	46	210	1064	331	372	98	268	404	750	4051
Validation	197	15	63	250	66	65	8	113	76	250	1103
Test	50	50	50	50	50	50	50	50	50	50	500
Total	755	111	323	1364	447	487	156	431	530	1050	5654

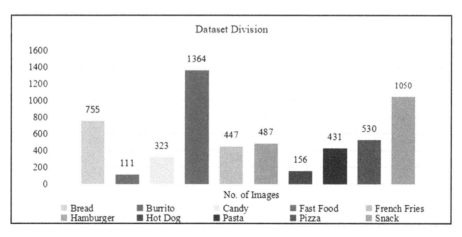

Figure 6.4. Dataset division.

6.4.2 Data augmentation

As the DL models are data-driven and there is not in an adequate amount of images, training with these images can result in low accuracy of the model. Thus to increase the volume of images, a data augmentation technique is used. For each image six transformations, namely horizontal flip, vertical flip, horizontal and vertical flip, blur, hue and rotation, are applied using the CloDSA toolkit [23] for bringing in more variation into the training dataset, hence increasing the robustness of the detector. A summary of images before and after the augmentation is shown in table 6.2.

The fast food dataset has the largest number of images (7448) while burrito has the lowest number of images (322), as shown in table 6.2.

6.4.3 Implementation

The dataset is split into training, validation and testing datasets, occupying 71.65% (20 314), 19.51% (5531) and 8.84% (2507) of 28 352 images in total, respectively. All the models have been trained end-to-end with the weights of the corresponding backbones trained on ImageNet used as initial weights.

YOLOv3: To train our YOLOv3 model, the text annotations with bounding boxes (class, leftX, topY, rightX, bottomY) were converted into YOLO format with bounding boxes (class, x-center, y-center, width, height). The training was performed with a batch size of 16 for 20 000 epochs with the model architecture built with Darknet53 as the backbone, Adam as the optimizer and initializing the remaining parameters as per [7]. Training took around 26 h to complete.

YOLOv4: This was trained with similar parameters, i.e. training data fed into a model with a batch size of 16 for 20 000 epochs as for YOLOv3, with bounding box annotations the same as for the latter. The model used a modified version of Darknet53 known as CSPDarknet53 as its backbone, keeping the optimizer, Adam, the same. Other parameters have been set as per [8] resulting in a training time similar to YOLOv3, i.e. 26 h.

SSD: For training our custom dataset on SSD, the text file annotations with bounding boxes (class, leftX, topY, rightX, bottomY) were converted to xml files for Pascal VOC with bounding boxes (x_{min}—top left, y_{min}—top left, x_{max}—bottom right, y_{max}—bottom right). Using VGG-16 as the backbone and SGD as the optimizer, this model was trained with a batch size of eight for 120 epochs with

Table 6.2. Dataset before and after augmentation.

Class	Bread	Burrito	Candy	Fast food	French fries	Hamburger	Hot dog	Pasta	Pizza	Snack	Total
Before aug.	755	111	323	1364	447	487	156	431	530	1050	5654
After aug.	3556	322	1470	7448	2312	2604	686	1876	2828	5250	28352

1000 steps per epoch at a decreasing learning rate. The rest of the parameters were according to [9]. The total training time taken was 10 h.

6.4.4 Software and hardware

Google Colaboratory, a notebook environment supporting Python execution through remote servers on Linux platforms, is worked on for training and testing the custom dataset. Google Colab provides a remote platform with a memory of nearly 100 GB out of which 33 GB is available for the user, 2 Intel(R) Xeon(R) CPU @ 2.20 GHz CPUs, a RAM of 13 GB and a Tesla K80 GPU with 2496 CUDA cores and 12 GB GDDR5 VRAM. The free version has a maximum allocation per user time limit of 12 h per server with an idle cut-off time of 90 min to make server allocation more efficient.

6.4.5 Performance parameters

The developed DL-based food detection models are evaluated against the most commonly employed evaluation metrics, namely accuracy, precision, recall, F_1-score, IoU and mAP. These metrics are defined as follows.

Accuracy: This is a measure of the percentage of correctly predicted images. Mathematically, it is defined as

$$\text{accuracy} = \frac{\text{TP} + \text{TN}}{\text{TP} + \text{TN} + \text{FP} + \text{FN}}. \tag{6.7}$$

Precision: Precision indicates the number of true positive predicted objects that actually belong to the true positive class in the dataset. Mathematically, it is represented by the ratio of the number of images that were predicted correctly to the number of images that were predicted to belong to a category irrespective of correctness:

$$\text{precision} = \frac{\text{TP}}{\text{TP} + \text{FP}}. \tag{6.8}$$

Recall: Recall signifies the fraction of the number of images that were predicted correctly to the total number of images that belonged to the category:

$$\text{recall} = \frac{\text{TP}}{\text{TP} + \text{FN}}. \tag{6.9}$$

F_1-score: The harmonic mean of precision and recall of the model is represented by the F_1-score. It is defined as

$$F_1\text{-score} = \frac{2 \times (\text{precision} \times \text{recall})}{\text{precision} + \text{recall}}. \tag{6.10}$$

IoU: This is a measure that evaluates the resemblance of the predicted bounding box with the ground truth bounding box. An IoU of value of 1, or 100%, depicts that the predicted bounding box is completely overlapping the ground truth bounding box. It can be mathematically denoted by

$$\text{IoU} = \frac{\text{area(predicted bounding box)} \cap \text{area(ground truth bounding box)}}{\text{area(predicted bounding box)} \cup \text{area(ground truth bounding box)}}. \quad (6.11)$$

mAP: Mean average precision is the mean of the AP values of all different classes as represented by

$$\text{mAP} = \frac{\sum_{i=1}^{n} \text{AP}_i}{n}, \quad (6.12)$$

where true positive (TP) indicates the total number of images that belonged to the same category and were predicted in the same category. True negative (TN) denotes the total number of images which did not belong to the specific category and were not predicted in that category. False positive (FP) signifies the total number of images that did not belong to a category but were predicted in the category. False negative (FN) represents the total number of images that belonged to a category but were not predicted in that category.

6.5 Results

YOLOv3 showed the best out of three results giving an mAP of 74.6%, an average IoU of 56.85%, a precision of 0.70, a recall of 0.67 and an F_1-score of 0.69. YOLOv4 was just slightly behind YOLOv3, achieving an mAP of 71.3%, an average IoU of 52.78% and an F_1-score of 0.67. SSD was the weakest of the three models, giving an mAP of 13.6% with no detection for the burrito and hot dog classes on the validation dataset. Relative to YOLOv4, YOLOv3 achieved a greater mAP by 4.61%. The results in figure 6.5 and table 6.3 show that YOLOv3 and YOLOv4 performed much better than SSD. YOLOv3 performed slightly better than YOLOv4, mainly due to YOLOv3's very high accuracy in classifying burritos, 25.6% more relative to YOLOv4. Both these models were indifferent to the number of images in each class, as YOLOv3 classified burrito with the highest precision of 93.6% and the largest class, fast food, with 58.9% precision, as can be verified in table 6.3.

The cause can be inferred from the intuition that YOLOv4 focuses on providing better accuracies on large sample sizes with better speed. The class burrito only had 322 samples, even after augmentation, a sample size towards the lower end of the size spectrum, thus nullifying the edge of YOLOv4 over YOLOv3 in the class. SSD performed poorly on weak classes such as burrito and hot dog. It did not perform comparatively well on a strong dataset because it gives only 9.1% accuracy on the fast food dataset, which is the strongest among all the datasets, as can be seen in figure 6.5 and table 6.3. This can happen due to confusion between similar object categories, such as pasta and pizza, because multiple categories share locations.

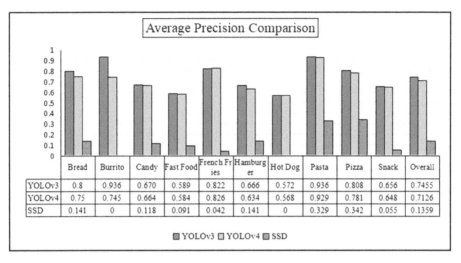

Figure 6.5. Comparison of average precision.

For the ten classes bread, burrito, candy, fast food, French fries, hamburger, hot dog, pasta, pizza and snack classes YOLOv3 achieved an AP of 80.0%, 93.6%, 67%, 58.9%, 82.2%, 66.6%, 57.2%, 93.6%, 80.8% and 65.6%, respectively. YOLOv4 followed closely behind resulting in 75%, 74.5%, 66.4%, 58.4%, 82.6%, 63.4%, 56.8%, 92.9%, 78.1% and 64.8% of AP for the respective classes compared to 14.1%, 0%, 1.8%, 9.1%, 4.2%, 14.1%, 0%, 32.9%, 34.2% and 5.5% of AP for SSD. Furthermore, table 6.4 displays the normalized confusion matrices obtained for each class based on the three experimented models YOLOv3, YOLOv4 and SSD. The test results for YOLOv3, YOLOv4 and SSD on one of the test images are shown in figure 6.6. For the tested image of pizza, YOLOv3 predicted correctly with an accuracy of 94% and YOLOv4 followed behind with 86% accuracy. In contrast, SSD gave correct prediction with lowest accuracy of 37%.

6.6 Conclusion and future scope

This research resulted in the successful training of three models for food detection on ten different food classes that can be readily applied in various applications. YOLOv3 achieved an mAP as high as 93.6% on the classes burrito and pasta, giving the best results, and is suitable for use as a common food detector for local vendors as well as food chains. Real-time inference speed was achieved for all three models. Applications based on these detectors to measure nutritional levels could be developed to avoid malnutrition. YOLOv3 and YOLOv4 were able to detect all images even though they failed at classifying some of them correctly. A simple multiple item counter application can be created using these two models to overcome the drawbacks of conventional

Table 6.3. Detection results of models on the augmented dataset.

Class	Total images	Model	Precision	Recall	Average precision(AP)	F_1 score
Bread	3556	YOLOv3	0.73	0.78	0.800	0.75
		YOLOv4	0.66	0.72	0.75	0.69
		SSD	0.28	0.19	0.14	0.23
Burrito	**322**	YOLOv3	0.89	0.55	0.93	0.68
		YOLOv4	0.66	0.25	0.74	0.36
		SSD	0	0	**0**	0
Candy	1470	YOLOv3	0.87	0.6	0.67	0.71
		YOLOv4	0.81	0.61	0.66	0.7
		SSD	0.26	0.1	0.12	0.14
Fast food	**7448**	YOLOv3	0.61	0.72	0.59	0.66
		YOLOv4	0.55	0.85	0.58	0.67
		SSD	0.16	0.06	0.09	0.09
French fries	2312	YOLOv3	0.76	0.55	0.82	0.64
		YOLOv4	0.76	0.52	0.82	0.62
		SSD	0.16	0.66	0.04	0.26
Hamburger	2604	YOLOv3	0.58	0.43	0.66	0.49
		YOLOv4	0.58	0.39	0.63	0.47
		SSD	0.28	0.19	0.14	0.23
Hot dog	686	YOLOv3	0.77	0.31	0.57	0.44
		YOLOv4	0.71	0.3	0.56	0.42
		SSD	0	0	0	0
Pasta	1876	YOLOv3	0.93	0.78	0.93	0.85
		YOLOv4	0.91	0.7	0.93	0.79
		SSD	0.37	0.46	0.33	0.41
Pizza	2828	YOLOv3	0.88	0.63	0.81	0.73
		YOLOv4	0.83	0.6	0.78	0.7
		SSD	0.42	0.42	0.34	0.42
Snack	5250	YOLOv3	0.72	0.73	0.65	0.72
		YOLOv4	0.66	0.78	0.65	0.72
		SSD	0.07	0.5	0.05	0.12
Overall	**28 352**	YOLOv3	**0.7**	**0.67**	**0.74**	**0.68**
		YOLOv4	**0.64**	**0.69**	**0.71**	**0.66**
		SSD	**0.26**	**0.21**	**0.13**	**0.23**

sensor-based counters used in industries. Moreover, food detection can become an essential daily utility for people requiring visual aids. This can be realized by combining trained detection techniques with NLP modules. Furthermore, these results will help future researchers working on similar projects.

Table 6.4. Resultant normalized confusion matrices.

Class	Model	Actual	Predicted: negative	Predicted: positive
Hamburger	YOLOv3	Actual: Others	0.49	0.12
		Actual: Hamburger	0.22	0.17
	YOLOv4	Actual: Others	0.44	0.12
		Actual: Hamburger	0.27	0.17
	SSD	Actual: Others	0.01	0.32
		Actual: Hamburger	0.54	0.13
Pizza	YOLOv3	Actual: Others	0.53	0.04
		Actual: Pizza	0.16	0.28
	YOLOv4	Actual: Others	0.48	0.06
		Actual: Pizza	0.18	0.28
	SSD	Actual: Others	0.1	0.33
		Actual: Pizza	0.33	0.24
Pasta	YOLOv3	Actual: Others	**0.72**	0.02
		Actual: Pasta	0.06	0.21
	YOLOv4	Actual: Others	0.69	0.02
		Actual: Pasta	0.09	0.21
	SSD	Actual: Others	0.24	0.4
		Actual: Pasta	0.27	0.23
Candy	YOLOv3	Actual: Others	0.24	0.06
		Actual: Candy	0.28	0.41
	YOLOv4	Actual: Others	0.2	0.1
		Actual: Candy	0.27	0.43
	SSD	Actual: Others	0.04	0.21
		Actual: Candy	0.67	0.07
Burrito	YOLOv3	Actual: Others	0.75	0.02
		Actual: Burrito	0.11	0.13
	YOLOv4	Actual: Others	0.45	0.06
		Actual: Burrito	0.36	0.12
	SSD	Actual: Others	0	0
		Actual: Burrito	0	0
Snack	YOLOv3	Actual: Others	0.19	0.18
		Actual: Snack	0.17	0.46
	YOLOv4	Actual: Others	0.16	0.24
		Actual: Snack	0.13	**0.47**
	SSD	Actual: Others	0.04	0.27
		Actual: Snack	0.02	0.02
Bread	YOLOv3	Actual: Others	0.48	0.12
		Actual: Bread	0.09	0.31
	YOLOv4	Actual: Others	0.42	0.16
		Actual: Bread	0.12	0.3
	SSD	Actual: Others	0.06	0.27
		Actual: Bread	0.49	0.18

French fries	YOLOv3	Actual: Others	0.65	0.05
		Actual: French fries	0.13	0.16
	YOLOv4	Actual: Others	0.63	0.05
		Actual: French fries	0.15	0.16
	SSD	Actual: Others	0.46	0.42
		Actual: French fries	0.04	0.08
Hot dog	YOLOv3	Actual: Others	0.36	0.05
		Actual: Hot dog	0.4	0.18
	YOLOv4	Actual: Others	0.29	0.08
		Actual: Hot dog	0.44	0.19
	SSD	Actual: Others	0	0
		Actual: Hot dog	0	0
Fast food	YOLOv3	Actual: Others	0.18	0.26
		Actual: Fast food	0.16	0.4
	YOLOv4	Actual: Others	0.29	0.08
		Actual: Fast food	0.44	0.19
	SSD	Actual: Others	0.14	0.35
		Actual: Fast food	0.07	0.43

Figure 6.6. (a) Test image, (b) prediction for YOLOv3, (c) prediction for YOLOv4 and (d) prediction for SSD.

6-15

Author contributions: conceptualization, HG and OPV; methodology, BS, MK and D; software, BS, MK and D; formal analysis, BS, MK and D; validation, HG and OPV; investigation, BS, MK and D; data curation, BS, MK and D; writing-original draft preparation, BS, MK and D; visualization, HG and OPV; writing review and editing, HG and OPV; supervision, HG and OPV. All authors have read and agreed to the published version of the manuscript.

References

[1] World Health Organisation 2012 Comprehensive implementation plan on maternal, infant, and young child nutrition https://www.who.int/publications/i/item/WHO-NMH-NHD-14.1

[2] Earman A M 2016 Eye safety for proximity sensing using infrared light-emitting diodes *Renesas* (Accessed 13 November 2021) https://www.renesas.com/us/en/document/apn/an1737-eye-safety-proximity-sensing-using-infrared-light-emitting-diodes

[3] Kumar S, Yadav D, Gupta H, Verma O P, Ansari I A and Ahn C W 2021 A novel YOLOv3 algorithm-based deep learning approach for waste segregation: towards smart waste management *Electronics* **10** 1

[4] Song H, Liang H, Li H, Dai Z and Yun X 2019 Vision-based vehicle detection and counting system using deep learning in highway scenes *Eur. Transp. Res. Rev.* **11** 51

[5] Gupta H, Varshney H, Sharma T K, Pachauri N and Verma O P 2021 Comparative performance analysis of quantum machine learning with deep learning for diabetes prediction *Complex Intell. Syst.* 1–15

[6] Lawal O M 2021 YOLOMuskmelon: quest for fruit detection speed and accuracy using deep learning *IEEE Access* **9** 15221–7

[7] Redmon J and Farhadi A 2018 YOLOv3: an incremental improvement arXiv:1804.02767

[8] Bochkovskiy A, Wang C Y and Liao H-Y M 2020 YOLOv4: optimal speed and accuracy of object detection arXiv:2004.10934

[9] Liu W, Anguelov D, Erhan D, Szegedy C, Reed S, Fu C Y and Berg A C 2016 SSD: single shot multibox detector arXiv:1512.02325

[10] Redmon J, Divvala S, Girshick R and Farhadi A 2016 You only look once: unified real-time object detection arXiv:1506.02640

[11] Everingham M, Gool L V, Williams C K I, Winn J and Zisserman A 2010 The PASCAL visual object classes (VOC) challenge *Int. J. Comput. Vision* **88** 303–38

[12] Mutreja G, Aggarwal A, Thakur R, Tiwari S S and Deshpande S 2020 Comparative assessment of different deep learning models for aircraft detection *2020 Int. Conf. for Emerging Technology (INCET)* **6** O15

[13] Khan A M 2021 Vehicle and pedestrian detection using YOLOv3 and YOLOv4 for self driving cars *PhD Thesis* California State University, San Marcos, CA https://scholarworks.calstate.edu/downloads/t435gk20h

[14] Gupta H and Verma O P 2021 Monitoring and surveillance of urban road traffic using low altitude drone images: a deep learning approach *Multimedia Tools Appl.* 1–21

[15] Zhao Z-Q, Zheng P, Xu S-T and Wu X 2019 Object detection with deep learning: a review *IEEE Trans Neural Netw. Learn. Syst.* **30** 3212–32

[16] Redmon J 2013 DarkNet: open source neural networks http://pjreddie.com/darknet/

[17] Yun S, Han D, Oh S J, Chun S and Yoo Y 2019 CutMix: regularization strategy to train strong classifiers with localizable features arXiv: 1905.04899

[18] Zhaohui Z, Wang P, Liu W, Li J, Ye R and Ren D 2019 Distance-IoU loss: faster and better learning for bounding box regression arXiv:1911.08287

[19] He K, Zhang X, Ren S and Sun J 2014 Spatial pyramid pooling in deep convolutional networks for visual recognition *European Conference on Computer Vision* (Berlin: Springer) pp 346–61

[20] Lazebnik S, Schmid C and Ponce J 2006 Beyond bags of features: spatial pyramid matching for recognizing natural scene categories *IEEE Computer Society Conf. on Computer Vision and Pattern Recognition* vol 2 (Piscataway, NJ: IEEE) pp 2169–78

[21] Simonyan K and Zisserman A 2015 Very deep convolutional networks for large-scale image recognition arXiv:1409.1556

[22] Kuznetsova A *et al* 2020 The open images dataset V4: unified image classification, object detection, and visual relationship detection at scale *Int. J. Comput. Vision* **128** 1956–81

[23] Heras J 2018 CLoDSA, GitHub repository (https://github.com/joheras/CLoDSA)

Chapter 7

The detection of images recaptured through screenshots based on spatial rich model analysis

Areesha Anjum and Saiful Islam

With the technological advancement in imaging devices, recapturing of a tampered image is become a common process to hide the tampering artifacts. Reacquisition of an image from a monitor screen requires a proper set-up. Better image displays render high quality images, and little effort is required to forge an image from the display screen, i.e. taking a screenshot. High quality screenshots avoid visible aliasing, making them difficult to detect. The reacquisition process poses a threat to security systems, since criminals can evade them by wiping out some necessary tampering fingerprints from the images. In this chapter a forensic method is utilized to extract rich features from different noise residuals on multiple quantization values. Out of 106 rich models, selected models were chosen to acquire prominent features in the spatial domain to classify the Original and Screenshots taken from light emitting diode (LED) monitors. Model selection reduces the complexity while maintaining the accuracy, providing good results compared to state-of-the-art methods. For proper distinction, a Screenshot database is constructed and LED monitors with four different screen sizes are utilized to capture different resolution Screenshots.

7.1 Introduction

In the era of digitalization, technology is involved in almost every sphere of life. Digital images play an extensive role in almost every field, such as entertainment, politics, academia, social media, business, medicine, forensics, the military and and variety of other fields [1, 2]. A large number of images is distributed publicly over the Internet every day [3] without verification of being authentic. The availability of a wide range of high definition cameras makes it easier to capture moments of life in the form of high resolution images. Even smart phones are equipped with high resolution cameras, which are now a common gadget used by most people [4].

On the other hand, various third party editing tools allow consumers to edit their pictures as they like, therefore the veracity of the image is at risk [1, 3]. The originality of an image plays an important role in many everyday life events, such as original evidence required to settle cases in a courtroom, e.g. a picture of a crime scene must be original in order to identify criminals. Forged images sometime causes chaos, and tampered images can even be used to destroy someone's life [1]. Hence, the images must be identified by their truthfulness, i.e. whether they are authentic or not.

Digital image forensics (DIF) is the field of study that utilizes various techniques to check the credibility and authenticity of images. It works in two domains: (i) content authentication and (ii) source identification [5]. In the first, forensics algorithms are used to detect whether the content of an image (i.e. what is shown in the image) is original or forged. It works based on the history of the images and tries to find fingerprints that are left behind due to tampering [6]. Various intelligent authentication algorithms exist at present to identify different kinds of forgeries, such as copy–move, copy–paste, inpainting, splicing, filtering and many others [6, 7]. It also aims to localize the forgery by checking sub-areas in the images [8]. In the second sub-field of DIF, forensics methods are used to discover the correct source of images. That is, whether the source is similar to what has been claimed. It works based on the camera model dependent features that are left behind during the image acquisition process [1].

In order to hide tampering footprints in images, cyber criminals recapture images in different possible ways. Recapturing is a process that removes the tampering evidence from the forged images and makes the image more like an original, making the manipulations undetectable to the human visual system [9–11]. The recaptured images even fool tampering detection systems, leading to the failure of existing authentication algorithms. There are various ways to recapture an images, such as Screen-Captured images, Printed-Captured images, Screenshots and Printed-Scanned images [12]. Original images displayed on a monitor screen and reacquired by a camera, are categorized as Screen-Captured images. Images printed on paper and recaptured by a camera are known as Printed-Captured images. The Printed-Scanned images are those which were originally captured by a camera and printed, then reacquired by a scanner through scanning. To recapture an image easily without requiring much equipment one can take a Screenshot of the Original image displayed on a monitor. Screenshots are more suitable to hide tampering as they do not contain any visible aliasing present in the images, which is ascertained when recaptured by a camera from a monitor screen without a proper set-up [9]. Therefore not much effort is needed to set up an environment for the recapturing process and a even a novice in the field of computers is capable of performing the task. The Screenshot process produces an image identical to the Original that cannot be distinguished using the naked eye.

Despite the fact that the process of recapturing eliminates the tampering footprints, it leaves behind other fingerprints of their own that can be used to trace the images as recaptured. The different artifacts that are present in Screen-Captured images are aliasing, blurriness, noise, color, contrast and double JPEG traces [9, 13].

Printed-Captured images contain various fingerprints such as specularity, blurriness and color dissimilarity [11, 14]. On the other hand, recapturing via Screenshot does not involve a camera while reacquiring, however due to the low monitor resolution the image properties are affected. The impact on the image attributes does not make any difference in the image content visually but it alters them statistically. Therefore Screenshots are assumed to have blurriness, aliasing and texture manipulations. They do not show visible aliasing pattern like Screen-Captured images, which makes them more difficult to detect.

The process of recapturing is a type of anti-forensic manipulation technique which aims to dodge the tampering detection methods. It is performed by forgers to eradicate tampering footprints so that manipulations cannot be detected by forensic methods. Thereby countering such anti-forensics is required to eliminate those types of attacks, through finding artifacts that have been left by anti-forensic techniques [1, 3]. The image statistics are altered during the recapturing process when the Original image is recaptured as a Screenshot. In this chapter, to find out the differences in the image properties, a counter anti-forensic method is proposed that looks for neighborhood pixel dependencies in the spatial domain. Rich model analysis is carried out to obtain well-performing neighborhood descriptors based on high-pass residuals. Edge and texture modifications are extracted through descriptors to discriminate Original images and Screenshots. Diverse residual information is obtained using the different high-pass filters with larger quantization values. High-pass quantized residuals provide significant pixel dependencies for proper distinction. The aggregated features obtained from all 106 descriptors provide plenty of different features which are very difficult to compute. To reduce the complexity of these rich features, selective neighborhood descriptors are considered, which make a concise feature vector. A Screenshot dataset is constructed to examine the performance of the proposed method. The dataset contains 4800 Original images and 19,200 Screenshots captured during a recapturing process. The Screenshots were taken from four light emitting diode (LED) monitors whereas the Original images were captured by 48 different high resolution cameras.

This chapter is organized as follows. The next section discusses the state-of-the-art techniques related to the field. Section 7.3 discusses briefly the spatial rich model that helps in extracting the feature descriptors. The proposed method is explained in detail in section 7.4. The experimental results are demonstrated and discussed in section 7.5, where the details of the dataset are also given. Section 7.6 concludes the paper and section 7.7 provides recommendations for the future.

7.2 Literature review

The recapturing process is not new; it has been exploited by forgers from more than a decade. Researchers have developed various methods to detect image recapturing that has been done in different ways. In the early 2000s when biometric systems began to receive recognition, they were also susceptible to attacks. For example, a photograph of a person can be shown to a face recognition system instead of a real person's face. Researchers worked on the image statistics of Printed-Scanned images to detect this type of attack in [15]. A statistical model containing the mean, variance, kurtosis and skewness was computed from the sub-band coefficients by employing wavelet decomposition. It was observed that dithering occurred due to printing effects and the image statistics were obtained in the horizontal, vertical and diagonal directions for different scales. The images were classified using the Fisher linear discriminant (FLD), showing promising results.

The field of recapture detection had a boost when a set of recaptured images of a South-China tiger surfaced [16], which was considered an extinct species. To distinguish the Original and Printed-Captured images, a method working on planar surface identification was given in [14]. Spatial differences in the high frequency domain were observed due to the specular component present in the recaptured images. The specularity was modeled using a dichromatic reflectance model. For difference computations, the image's gradient ratio independent of intensity scaling was obtained. It was observed that the Original images show a Laplacian type distribution while recaptured images show a Rayleigh type distribution. JPEG format based Printed-Captured images were analyzed in [11]. Since there is a difference in the image statistics and color between Original and Printed-Captured images, Markov-based features were extracted. Both the Y and R components from YC_bC_r and RGB, respectively, were considered and DCT coefficients were computed. To model the differences, the Markov process was utilized based on a threshold value. The extracted features were classified using a support vector machine (SVM) classifier and it was found that features from the R component are better than those from the Y component. A physics-based feature, set including blurriness, specularity, color, contrasts and gradient information, for printed-captured images was extracted in [17]. They created a dataset and tested the extracted features and found that they performed well. Research on the loss of image quality occurring during the recapturing process when printed images were recaptured can be found in [18]. It was modeled by utilizing the LBPV method and the contrast information was also computed. The extracted features were tested on the publicly available Institute for Infocomm Research (I^2R) open dataset for smartphone recaptured images [19]. This dataset contains low resolution images since they were captured through smartphone cameras.

More focus has been given to Screen-Captured images in the recent years. Researchers have developed various techniques based on the characteristics found in Screen-Captured images to differentiate them from Originals. It comprises different characteristics, including aliasing, blurriness, texture patterns, double JPEG artifacts, color and contrast. In [20] a technique was developed based on the footprints found in the images recaptured from LCD monitors. First a dataset is built [4, 21] in a controllable environment by determining the proper setting of the camera–LCD distance and color-brightness of both devices that leads to less quality loss in a recaptured image. The dataset was used for experiments to differentiate between Original and Screen-Captured images by human beings and a higher misclassification was obtained for the recaptured images. To distinguish both images correctly, statistical features were computed that involved blurriness, texture, structure and color. The texture pattern was calculated in 80 features using a multi-scale local binary pattern with four operators. To analyze the blurriness in the images, local variation was computed using a multi-scale wavelet for three levels on every channel of the RGB image and 54 features were obtained. It is observed that the color of recaptured images is a little different to the Original, therefore 21 color features were obtained. A total of 155 features was tested by training the probabilistic support vector machine (PSVM) and the results show that the method has a low error rate.

Images are often saved in JPEG format by cameras, therefore when the image is recaptured from the LCD screen by the camera it is again saved in JPEG. Hence, these types of recaptured images are compressed twice, thus they contain double JPEG compression artifacts. The authors, exploiting this characteristic along with others, found recaptured images in [22] and [23]. Mode based first digit feature (MBFDF) were utilized in [22] to capture the statistical structural difference between the first and second compression and obtained 180 features. Along with this, the noise characteristic was analyzed with three denoising methods, i.e. separable 2D discrete wavelet transform (DWT), real 2D dual-tree DWT and complex 2D dual-tree DWT. The four statistical attributes (mean, variance, skewness and kurtosis) were computed from these three denoising algorithms and made out 12 features. An SVM was trained with these feature sets and tested on their own high quality recaptured image dataset for two different image sizes and performed well. In [23], before extracting the features, aliasing characteristics were enhanced using Gamma correction under pre-processing steps. After this, interference information was obtained by computing the wavelet transform. The mean and standard deviation were evaluated for each sub-band to extract the sub-band variation. Double JPEG traces were analyzed as block effects and blurriness in LCD recaptures. Different block effects were evaluated by the first and second compression that occurred due to independent block quantization. This caused different high frequency information loss during the JPEG compression process, causing the effect of blurriness in the Screen-Captured images. The blurriness and block features are extracted by computing the discontinuity of adjacent blocks, pixel correlation and average deviation of adjacent pixels for each color channel in YC_bC_r color space. To evaluate the feature effectiveness, a high quality Screen-Captured image dataset was built. The experiments carried out on the build dataset show that the extracted features performed well compared to previously existing algorithms as well as containing less feature dimensionality.

The two content independent characteristics, aliasing and blurriness, were analyzed in [9]. Aliasing occurs in Screen-Captured images during the recapturing process due to the LCD monitor's grid structure. Therefore images were captured by determining certain parameters for the recapture environmental settings to eliminate the visible aliasing pattern in the Screen-Captured images. They constructed a publicly available dataset [9] in which the recaptured images are alias-free. Blurriness occurs at the edges at the time of image capture due to lens imperfections in the camera. This is increased by a certain level due to low monitor resolution when the images are reacquired, and therefore can be used as a feature. Line spread profile (LSF) differences were evaluated from the two over-complete dictionaries that were constructed for the Original and Screen-Captured images, respectively, by employing the K-SVD method [24]. The method contains few features for classification, which takes less classification time, however, the dictionary training process is complicated which increases the overall computational complexity. The method outperforms the existing techniques by giving higher classification accuracy. An edge profile based method is given in [10], in which Screen-Captured images are differentiated from Original images according to the existence of a number of different edge types. The method acted to compute the edge blurriness observed when the images were recaptured. The edge information was in the high frequency domain, therefore a stationary wavelet transform (SWT) with Daubechies (db15) were utilized to evaluate edge differences. Along with blurriness, aliasing was also introduced when the images were captured from an LCD screen. Aliasing was eliminated from the images in the pre-processing step using the anti-aliasing methods, including median and Butterworth filters. The method was constructed with few features and was tested for two datasets, ICL [9] and ROSE [21]. It was found that the features work well for an alias-free dataset, i.e. ICL, even when comparing the method with recent deep learning methods. Also, the median filter works better to avoid aliasing.

Various other methods based on image statistics have also been formulated to distinguish Screen-Captured and Original images. A simple method based on image statistics is given in [25] which works in the spatial domain. The differences were evaluated in the high frequency component, since it contains more differential information and is independent of image content. Two image residuals were obtained to get the high frequency information using two different low pass filters. Residuals provide the better description of edges and noise differences in the images, which provide information regarding blurriness and aliasing, respectively. Pixel correlation coefficients have been computed from noise residuals and considered as features. To test the method performance, two high resolution image datasets, i.e. ICL [9] and ROSE [21], were used and tested for different image resolutions. This method provided a low misclassification error compared to previously described methods along with a smaller number of features. Screen-captured images were classified in [26] using a combination of local dense descriptors obtained using a spatial rich model [27]. Based on the performance of individual sub-models, the features of ten sub-models were combined, which created a feature vector of 3,276 dimensions. These features were trained on an ensemble classifier and the results of testing show good accuracy for screen-captured image detection, but falls short for Original images. The feature dimension is high compared to other methods, which increases the computational complexity for this technique.

It was observed in [13] that the image properties are changed during the recapturing operation. Therefore, to compute the change in image quality, the generalized Gaussian distribution (GGD) and zero mode asymmetric generalized Gaussian distribution (AGGD) were used. Features related to the change in image quality were extracted based on selective patches. In addition, the authors also captured the features for double JPEG artifacts found in Screen-Captured images. For this, the difference of quantized DCT coefficients was evaluated in four directions, i.e. horizontal, vertical, diagonal and counter-diagonal. The features were computed from the histogram of these difference matrices. The method was tested on the dataset given in [23] and classified using an SVM with ten-fold cross-validation. It achieved good accuracy, however, the method is limited to JPEG images.

The techniques discussed above are related to machine learning in which features are designed manually. In recent years deep learning has received more attention due to its potential for performing better in various problem solving task and automatic feature extraction capabilities. Various techniques have been developed based on deep networks to correctly classify images as Original or recaptured. Most of the methods discussed used high resolution images, however, it is also essential to classify low resolution images. To classify low resolution images a convolutional neural network (CNN) was constructed in [28]. The images were pre-processed before by applying a Laplacian filter to enhance the noise details, and then the network learned the features for the image sizes 64×64, 128×128, 256×256 and 512×512 separately. The CNN consist of five convolutional layers and each layer was batch normalized and pooled, and the feature maps were extracted based on the parameters used. It was found that network achieved good accuracy for the 512×512 image size. To enhance the recapturing traces, in [29] a learnable filter layer was employed before the two convolutional layer CNN that helps in extracting the better discriminative features. The extracted features were then used to determine the block dependencies by utilizing an RNN. The models were used for testing on three different datasets and obtained optimal accuracy for the ICL dataset, however, these models have higher hardware requirements. HLReCapNet was proposed in [12] to classify high as well as low resolution images. It does not use any filter to enhance the image distortions while capturing the required features with three-dual convolutional layer CNN to distinguish Original and Screen-Captured images. The model was tested and works well for alias-free datasets and achieved good accuracy for high as well low resolution images.

The main objective of a spatial rich model (SRM) is to construct a method to perform steganalysis in digital images [27]. With its growing popularity and promising capabilities, SRM has been used widely in image forensics for various applications. Such scenarios include utilization of dense noise residuals for forgery detection and localization [30–32], identification of the source camera [33], image sharpening identification [34], multiple image processing operator detection [35], and edge-operator identification for Cloud trust enhancement [36]. Since the recapturing process alters the image properties, it is better to work on the neighboring pixel relationship in the spatial domain. Therefore neighborhood descriptors have been utilized in building the proposed features for the identification of Original images and screenshots.

7.3 Spatial rich model

The SRM works in the spatial domain, and different sub-models were established based on a variety of high-pass residuals. The rich feature set that constitutes 34,671 features, formed by combining a total of 106 sub-models that contain different features of the image for detection. The model diversity enhances the detection performance by extracting different valuable features. The various steps involved in this method are described briefly below. For more details regarding the method, see the original publication in [27].

7.3.1 Computing noise residuals

Noise residual based modeling suppresses the image content but provides a sufficient amount of data to unveil the statistical differences. Hence, it reduces the computational complexity and helps build a robust feature extractor. The SRM works directly in the spatial domain but instead of exploiting image content it extracts the noise residuals. A variety of residuals are constructed using linear filters with the combination of min and max operators. These operators are used to enhance the diversity of the model by introducing non-linearity. The residuals belong to six different classes (first order, second order, third order, SQUARE, EDGE3×3 and EDGE5×5) and help build the sub-models. The noise residual can be represented as

$$N_r = (r_{ij}) \in N_r^{n_1 \times n_2}, \tag{7.1}$$

where N_r is the noise residuals obtained by estimating the high-pass descriptors, r_{ij} is found by utilizing the following equation:

$$r_{ij} = \hat{P}_{ij}\left(N_{ij}\right) - fP_{ij}, \tag{7.2}$$

where N_{ij} forms the neighborhood of the central pixel P_{ij} and $P_{ij} \notin N_{ij}$. $\hat{P}_{ij}$ is central pixel predictor depending on cN_{ij}. f is the residual order which describes the number filters used depending on the type of residual (i.e. spam, minimum or maximum).

7.3.2 Residual truncation and quantization

To make the noise residuals more sensitive to spatial discontinuities for better sub-model construction, they are quantized. The truncation helps to narrow down the dynamic range of the residuals. Thus both operations quantization and truncation are performed on the residual and it can be obtained using the following equation:

$$r_{ij} = \text{truncate}_T\left(\text{round}\left(\frac{r_{ij}}{q}\right)\right). \tag{7.3}$$

The truncated and quantized residuals with quantization step (q) and small threshold value (T) are further represented as co-occurrence matrices. The different values of the quantization step include different versions of the sub-model which helps extract distinct features. The value of the quantization step is experimentally determined as

$$q \in = \begin{cases} \{f,\ 1.5f,\ 2f\}, \text{ for } f > 1 \\ \{1,\ 2\}, \text{ for } f = 1 \end{cases}. \tag{7.4}$$

Thus the quantization step is taken based on the residual order (f). Therefore only two versions of the sub-model were built with the residual when $f = 1$ and three versions were constructed for the rest of the values of f.

7.3.3 Formation of a sub-model with co-occurrence matrices

For the selection of sub-model parameters, the average correlation of the central pixel with its neighbors was computed for different directions, i.e. horizontal, vertical, diagonal and minor diagonal. It was observed that the correlation value decreased on increasing the pixel distance. Thus this occurred more when considering diagonal directions. Therefore the co-occurrence of noise residuals was computed for the horizontal and vertical directions. The threshold value was considered smaller (i.e. $T = 2$) to maintain the statistical difference.

The sub-models were constructed by computing the co-occurrence of residuals for threshold values from -2 to 2 for the horizontal and vertical directions. Therefore four-dimensional co-occurrence matrices were obtained, each of which contained 625 elements and a total of 78 sub-models was constructed. Symmetrization helps to reduce the dimensionality of the sub-models while maintaining the performance. Both the sign and directional symmetry used were based on the residual type. The type spam used both symmetries and dimensionality reduced based on the defined rules and therefore only 169 elements persisted. However, min–max type residuals have only directional symmetry and hence reduced the dimensionality of the sub-models from twice 625 (the min and max both have 625 dimensions each) to 325. The spam type sub-models of the horizontal and vertical directions were combined to form a single model of dimension 338. The total sub-models reduced from 78 to 39. These 39 sub-models formed 106 sub-models when different quantization values were included. All the sub-models of different classes with different quantized values combined to create a feature vector of 34,671 dimensions.

7.4 Proposed work

The process of recapturing an image as a screenshot has the capability of providing a recaptured image identical to the Original image. It does not leave a visible trace on the recaptured image that can be detectable by the human eye. During recaptures, the image statistics go through changes and these changes happen to be in the pixel domain. Therefore to find the descriptive changes more precisely, the proposed method worked in the spatial domain. The images reacquired as screenshots do not show a visible aliasing pattern as seen in Screen-Captured images, since no other camera is involved to capture the monitor periodic pattern and images are captured directly on screen. However, modifications such as aliasing, blurriness and texture changes take place in screenshots due to the low monitor resolution compared to the high quality cameras used. The image properties were examined to determine the statistical modifications.

To carry out statistical analysis, neighborhood descriptors are computed by utilizing a spatial rich model and selected based on the detection performance. The computation of the feature descriptor of the proposed method is shown in figure 7.1.

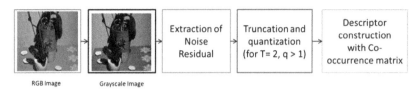

RGB Image   Grayscale Image

Figure 7.1. Feature descriptor evaluation.

The RGB Original or screenshot image is first converted to a grayscale image to make the pixel values ranges from 0 to 255 and reduce the complexity of computing different channels. The high frequency component seems to have more information regarding the changes that have taken place while recapturing. The residual based modeling extracts information about the edge alterations and modified noise differences that are associated with blurriness and aliasing, respectively. To investigate the modifications present in screenshot images, high-pass residuals were constructed, as discussed in section 7.3.1, with linear and non-linear filters. Noise residuals extract information based on complex neighboring pixel dependencies and are constructed with different filter type to obtain diverse information. Also, it suppresses the image information greatly and curbs the computation time by providing the less information to examine. It provides the crucial content that helps in extracting robust and densely packed features. Residuals are then quantized in the next step with a larger quantization value ($q > 1$). A large quantization value aids in obtaining more prominent edge and texture changes as it makes the high-pass residual sensitive to pixel discontinuities. The quantized image is then truncated to trim the residual's range by the value of the threshold (T). In the next step, local feature descriptors are constructed using quantized and truncated residuals by computing co-occurrence matrices in the horizontal and vertical directions.

7.4.1 Selection of the neighborhood descriptor

Considering the combined features extracted by all the neighborhood descriptors makes an extensive feature vector which takes a longer time in the classification phase. Therefore to reduce the computational complexity, it is important to consider a smaller number of features that are able to classify Original images and screenshots correctly. Hence the descriptor selection strategy was carried out as shown in figure 7.2. The features extracted by each descriptor were considered and the images were classified based on these features. Therefore the descriptors were selected based on the individual descriptor performance.

7.5 Experimental results

7.5.1 Screenshot dataset

To test the proposed method a screenshot dataset was built. The screenshot dataset contain 4,800 Original images and 19,200 screenshots of Original images in PNG format that were captured from different monitors. The Original images were captured from 48 different high resolution cameras, each of which was used to

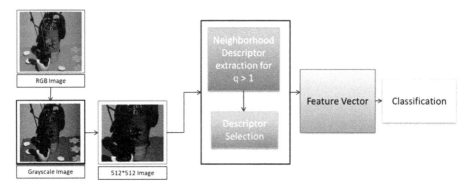

Figure 7.2. Schematic diagram of the proposed work.

take 100 high quality images. These were taken from three different databases, namely the ICL dataset [9], ROSE Recaptured dataset [21] and Dresden dataset [37]. These datasets are publicly available on the Internet for forensic purposes. The ICL dataset contained 900 Original images taken by nine different cameras namely Kodak V550 (Silver), Kodak V550 (Black), Kodak V610, Nikon D40, Nikon D70s, Panasonic TZ7, Canon600D, Olympus E-PM2 and Sony RX100, each of which captured 100 high quality images. The ROSE Recaptured dataset contains 2000 Original images captured by five different brands of high-end cameras, namely Casio, Lumix, Canon, Nikon and Sony. The rest of the 1900 images were taken from the Dresden dataset, downloaded from 19 different randomly selected camera images, including AfgaPhoto DC-504, AgfaPhoto DC-733s, AgfaPhoto DC-830i, AgfaPhoto Sensor 505-X, AgfaPhoto Sensor530s, Canon lxus 55, Canon lxus 70, Canon Powershot, FujiFilm, Kodak, Nikon CoolPix S710, Nikon D70, Nikon D70s, Nikon D200, Panasonic, Praktica, Ricoh, Rollei and Sony.

The Original images collected from three different datasets were displayed on four different LED displays, namely 22″ Lenovo, 18.5″ Lenovo, 27″ HP and 20″ HP. A screenshot of the displayed Original image is captured from each monitor separately. Therefore the dataset contained 4800 screenshots for each monitor. Therefore, from four monitors, $4 \times 4800 = 19,200$ total screenshots were captured. The Original image's resolutions ranged from 1704×2272 to 5184×3456 whereas the resolution of the screenshots ranged from 1024×768 to 1624×1084. The Original images were in JPG and PNG formats while screenshots were saved in PNG format. The recaptured images in this dataset do not contain the double JPEG fingerprint, which makes them even more difficult to detect. Hence a robust feature set can be extracted for the dataset. The screenshots contain a black area on the sides other than the image content. Since this area does not benefit the performance of the classification method it is removed manually from the screenshots.

The Original images taken from the Dresden [37], ICL [9] and ROSE [21] databases are shown in figures 7.3(a), 7.4(a) and 7.5(a), respectively. These images were displayed on four LED monitors and screenshots were captured from each. These screenshots of each Original image are presented in figures 7.3(b)–(e), 7.4(b)–(e) and figure 7.5(b)–(e), respectively. After acquiring the screenshots, the black area

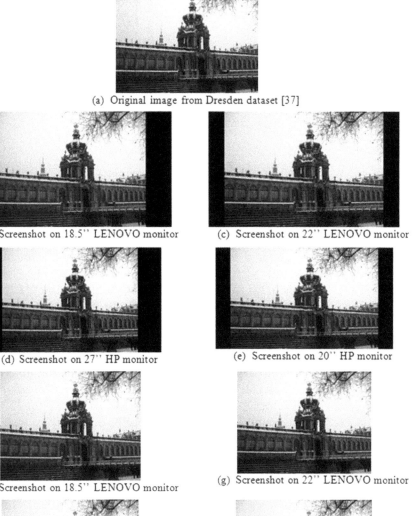

Figure 7.3. The Original image (a) taken from the Dresden dataset [37], and its screenshot captured on four monitors in (b) (c), and (d). The black area of the screenshots was removed in (e), (f), (g) and (h). Reprinted with permission from the Dresden Image Databse.

(a) Original image from ICL dataset [9]

(b) Screenshot on 18.5'' LENOVO monitor

(c) Screenshot on 22'' LENOVO monitor

(d) Screenshot on 27'' HP monitor

(e) Screenshot on 20'' HP monitor

(f) Screenshot on 18.5'' LENOVO monitor

(g) Screenshot on 22'' LENOVO monitor

(h) Screenshot on 27''monitor

(i) Screenshot on 20'' HP monitor

Figure 7.4. The Original image (a) taken from the ICL dataset [9], and its screenshot captured on four monitors in (b), (c) and (d). The black area of the screenshots was removed in (e), (f), (g) and (h). Copyright 2015 IEEE. Reprinted with permission from [9].

(a) Original image from ROSE dataset [21]

(b) Screenshot on 18.5" LENOVO monitor

(c) Screenshot on 22" LENOVO monitor

(d) Screenshot on 27" HP monitor

(e) Screenshot on 20" HP monitor

(f) Screenshot on 18.5" LENOVO monitor

(g) Screenshot on 22" LENOVO monitor

(h) Screenshot on 27" HP monitor

(i) Screenshot on 20" HP monitor

Figure 7.5. The Original image (a) taken from the ROSE dataset [21], and its screenshot captured on four monitors in (b), (c) and (d). The black area of the screenshots was removed in (e), (f), (g) and (h). The images were reprunted frim the ROSE Recaptured Image Dataset made available by the ROSE Lab at the Nanyang Technological University, Singapore [21].

was cropped manually and the final screenshots are shown in figures 7.3 (f)–(i), 7.4 (f)–(i) and 7.5 (f)–(i), respectively. It has been observed that from the figure one cannot detect the difference between Original images and screenshots with the naked eye.

The method extracted the desired features using MATLAB R2014a on a 64 bit operating system with an Intel Xeon-processor and 32 GB RAM. For the performance evaluation of the proposed method, the ensemble classifier and an SVM with PolyKernel is used.

7.5.2 Detection performance of the neighborhood descriptors

To examine the performance of the individual neighborhood descriptors, the screenshot dataset was balanced. For this 4800 images of both Original images and screenshots were taken. To equalize the dataset, only 25 screenshots out of 100 for each camera were chosen for all four monitors. Thus a total of $25 \times 4 \times 48 = 4800$ screenshots were selected. The screenshots were chosen randomly during the feature extraction process to extract robust descriptors. Therefore to analyze the detection accuracy of the features extracted by neighborhood descriptors the dataset contained 4800 Original images and 4800 screenshots.

The images were pre-processed before constructing the feature vector. During the pre-processing, the images were cropped to 512×512 resolution and RGB images were converted to grayscale as shown in figure 7.2. Individual neighborhood descriptors extracted features, where each spam type descriptor contained 338 features whereas the min–max type descriptors contained 325 features. The detection performances of all 106 descriptors are demonstrated in the graph in figure 7.6. The horizontal axis in the graph represents descriptors and the vertical axis shows their corresponding detection error. It is observed that around 70 models obtained error levels less than 0.01, i.e. they have achieved a detection accuracy around 99%.

7.5.3 The detection performance of neighborhood descriptors with an ensemble classifier

The top five descriptors which were evaluated using the ensemble classifier [38] are presented in table 7.1 with their overall accuracy and testing error. It is observed that the EDGE3×3 descriptor achieved good accuracy compared to the other

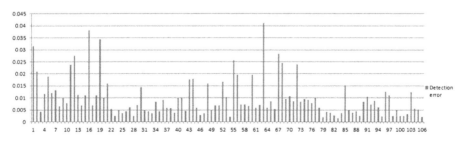

Figure 7.6. The detection error for 106 neighborhood descriptors.

Table 7.1. Detection accuracies for the top five descriptors using an ensemble classifier.

Descriptor no.	Model name	No. of features	Overall accuracy (%)	Testing error
83	**S3x3_spam14hv-q1.5 (EDGE3×3)**	**338**	**99.8438**	**0.001563**
79	S3×3_minmax24-q1.5 (EDGE3×3)	325	99.7958	0.002042
106	S5×5_spam14hv-q2 (EDGE5×5)	338	99.7813	0.002188
54	S3_minmax24-q1.5 (third order)	325	99.7729	0.002271
95	S5×5_minmax24-q1.5 (EDGE5×5)	325	99.7542	0.002458

Table 7.2. Detection accuracies for the top three descriptors using an SVM.

Descriptor no.	Model name	No. of features	Accuracy (%)		Overall accuracy (%)
			Original	Screenshots	
83	**S3×3_spam14hv-q1.5 (EDGE3×3)**	**338**	**99.56**	**99.81**	**99.68**
79	S3×3_minmax24-q1.5 (EDGE3×3)	325	99.33	99.83	99.58
106	S5×5_spam14hv-q2 (EDGE5×5)	338	98.18	99.27	98.72

descriptors, although all five descriptors exhibited more than 99.70% accuracy. The majority of the descriptors in the top five are EDGE3×3 or EDGE5×5, which used filters of 3 × 3 and 5 × 5 type, respectively. Thus the descriptors effectively calculated the neighborhood dependences containing edges and the 3 × 3 filter showed little improvement in detection. The descriptors with larger quantization values, i.e. greater than 1, are better at classifying images into the correct class, since they estimate the feature values in regions containing edges and texture better. The value $q = 1.5$ shows little improvement in performance compared to $q = 2$. The linear descriptors work comparatively better than non-linear descriptors, whereas the spam type descriptors have a few more features than the min–max type.

7.5.4 Detection performance of neighborhood descriptors with an SVM

The top three descriptors were evaluated using an SVM to obtain the detection accuracy for the Original images and screenshots, as presented in table 7.2. We found that both classifiers provided more than 99% overall detection accuracy.

The screenshots achieved a better accuracy of 99.81% compared to the Original images, of which 99.56% were classified correctly. The results were obtained by utilizing an SVM classifier with ten cross-folds accompanied by the PolyKernel. The ten cross-fold means the dataset was divided into ten subsets with an equal number of both Original images and screenshots. Each subset of images was taken as training data while the rest of the subsets was considered for testing. In this way ten separate models were trained and tested with the rest of the data and achieved a good detection accuracy each time. The final result was computed by taking the average of the accuracy of all ten models. Hence the model learned well from the training.

7.5.5 Performance comparison of the neighborhood descriptors

The results computed from the proposed method are compared to state-of-the-art algorithms that have achieved high detection accuracies in the field of image recapture. The computed results of various algorithms along with the proposed method are demonstrated in table 7.3. The authors were unable to find any existing method that was formulated only for classifying Original images and screenshots. Therefore the algorithms work for Screen-Captured images taken into consideration for comparison purposes. All the methods presented in table 7.3 computed the features for the dataset built in this chapter. The evaluated feature vectors were then classified with an SVM classifier in the same environment as the proposed method.

From table 7.3, it is observed that the proposed method outperforms the existing algorithms. Both existing methods computed features for larger resolutions but were used here for comparison; they obtained features for 512×512 resolution images. This may be one of the reasons for their low overall detection performance. It is observed from the table that the image statistics-based approach in [25] had low detection accuracy for screenshots compared to Original images. The edge-type method formulated in [10] was unable to classify most of the screenshots, whereas it performed well for Original images. The reason behind this is the low resolution of the screenshots, as this method is based on image content. Despite having a smaller amount of content in which to look for features, the proposed method computed more prominent features to correctly classify images as screenshots and Original images. The proposed method has a higher number of features compared to the other techniques, but also achieved good accuracy. The method proposed in this chapter achieved a

Table 7.3. Detection comparison of Original images and screenshots.

Method no.	Method	No. of features	Accuracy (%) Original	Screenshots	Overall accuracy (%)
1	Image statistics-based approach [25]	28	77.58	67.77	72.67
2	Edge-type method [10]	2	92.50	27.87	60.19
3	**Proposed method**	**338**	**99.56**	**99.81**	**99.68**

0.004 classification error for Original images whereas it achieved 0.0019 for screenshots. Therefore it achieved quite good accuracy and classified most of the images into the correct class. The bold entries in the table are to highlight the better results.

7.6 Conclusion

Image recapture is an anti-forensic method adopted by cyber criminals to hide tampering artifacts left by a particular forgery. The objective of their method is to eliminate the forgery footprints and make a tampered image undetectable by existing forgery detection techniques. Even though the tampering fingerprints are wiped out, recaptured images can still be detected by the artifacts left during the recapturing process. This paper proposes a simple method to differentiate Original images from the images recaptured via screenshots. Due to low monitor resolution, screenshots contain certain artifacts such as aliasing, blurriness and texture differences that can be explored. For the evaluation of features, rich model analysis is performed. Neighborhood pixel dependencies are computed by extracting the various neighborhood descriptors from high-pass residuals for larger quantization values. Higher quantization values help in finding out the more prominent edge and texture differences. The noise residuals for the horizontal and vertical directions were obtained by utilizing different linear and non-linear filters to extract the diverse information. The feature vector was constructed based on the individual descriptor performance.

It was observed that the proposed method outperforms the existing detection algorithms, but there is a trade-off between accuracy and the number of features. Our method contain a higher number of features, but performs well compared to the other methods. The method was evaluated on low resolution images and is expected to also perform well on high resolution images. A dataset is also constructed in this chapter for performance evaluation. The dataset contained 4800 Original images and 19,200 screenshots. The Original images were taken from three different datasets which were captured using 48 different high resolution cameras. To capture the screenshots, the Original images were displayed on four different LED monitors.

7.7 Future work

The proposed method performs well, but it still has room for improvements. The obtained feature vector can be used to classify images of different formats, since they are format independent features. The extracted feature set is robust, however, it contains a large number of features. This can be reduced by exploring the other characteristics presented by images recaptured through screenshots. The constructed dataset can also be improved by adding more screenshot data taken from other brands of LED monitors to enhance the diversity in the dataset.

Acknowledgements

(Portions of) the research in this paper used the ROSE Recaptured Image Dataset [21] made available by the ROSE Lab at Nanyang Technological University, Singapore.

References

[1] Walia S and Kumar K 2019 Digital image forgery detection: a systematic scrutiny *Aust. J. Forensic Sci.* **51** 488–526

[2] Mushtaq S and Mir A H 2014 Digital image forgeries and passive image authentication techniques: a survey *Int. J. Adv. Sci. Technol.* **73** 15–32

[3] Qureshi M A and Deriche M 2015 A bibliography of pixel-based blind image forgery detection techniques *Signal Process. Image Commun.* **39** 46–74

[4] Cao H 2010 Statistical image source model identification and forgery detection *PhD Thesis* Nanyang Technological University, Singapore

[5] Redi J A, Taktak W and Dugelay J L 2011 Digital image forensics: a booklet for beginners *Multimed. Tools Appl.* **51** 133–62

[6] Korus P 2017 Digital image integrity—a survey of protection and verification techniques *Digit. Signal Process.* **71** 1–26

[7] Piva A 2013 An overview on image forensics *ISRN Signal Process.* **2013** 1–22

[8] Birajdar G K and Mankar V H 2013 Digital image forgery detection using passive techniques: a survey *Digit. Investig.* **10** 226–45

[9] Thongkamwitoon T, Muammar H and Dragotti P L 2015 An image recapture detection algorithm based on learning dictionaries of edge profiles *IEEE Trans. Inf. Forensics Secur.* **10** 953–68

[10] Anjum A and Islam S 2020 Recapture detection technique based on edge-types by analysing high-frequency components in digital images acquired through LCD screens *Multimed. Tools Appl.* **79** 6965–85

[11] Yin J and Fang Y 2012 Markov-based image forensics for photographic copying from printed picture *Proc. 20th ACM Int. Conf. Multimedia* pp 1113–6

[12] Anjum A and Islam S 2019 Hlrecapnet: Convnet to detect high and low-resolution screen captured images *ICT for Competitive Strategies: Proc. of 4th Int. Conf. on Information and Communication Technology for Competitive Strategies (ICTCS 2019)* (Boca Raton, FL: CRC Press) pp 257–64

[13] Yang P, Li R, Ni R and Zhao Y 2017 Recaptured image forensics based on quality aware and histogram feature *Digital Forensics and Watermarking—16th Int. Workshop (IWDW)* pp 31–41

[14] Yu H, Ng T T and Sun Q 2008 Recaptured photo detection using specularity distribution *15th IEEE Int. Conf. Image Processing* pp 3140–3

[15] Farid H and Lyu S 2003 Higher-order wavelet statistics and their application to digital forensics *IEEE Comput. Soc. Conf. Comput. Vis. Pattern Recognit. Work.* 8 1–8

[16] American Association for the Advancement of Science 2007 Rare-tiger photo flap makes fur fly in China *Science* **318** 893

[17] Gao X, Ng T T, Qiu B and Chang S F 2010 Single-view recaptured image detection based on physics-based features *Multimedia and Expo (ICME) 2010 IEEE Int. Conf.* pp 1469–74

[18] Zhai X, Ni R and Zhao Y 2013 Recaptured image detection based on texture features *Ninth Int. Conf. Intelligent Information Hiding and Multimedia Signal Processing* pp 234–7

[19] Gao X, Qiu B, Shen J, Ng T T and Shi Y Q 2011 A smart phone image database for single image recapture detection *International Workshop on Digital Watermarking* (Lecture Notes on Computer Science vol 6526) (Berlin : Springer) pp 90–104

[20] Cao H and Kot A C 2010 Identification of recaptured photographs on LCD screens *IEEE Int. Conf. on Acoustics, Speech and Signal Processing* pp 1790–3

[21] Cao H and Kot A C 2010 ROSE recaptured image dataset https://rose1.ntu.edu.sg/dataset/recapturedImages/

[22] Yin J and Fang Y 2012 Digital image forensics for photographic copying *Proc. SPIE* **8303** 83030F

[23] Li R, Ni R and Zhao Y 2015 An effective detection method based on physical traits of recaptured images on LCD screens *Int. Workshop on Digital Watermarking* pp 107–16

[24] Aharon M, Elad M and Bruckstein A 2006 RMK-SVD: an algorithm for designing overcomplete dictionaries for sparse representation *IEEE Trans. Signal Process.* **54** 4311–22

[25] Wang K 2017 A simple and effective image-statistics-based approach to detecting recaptured images from LCD screens *Digit. Investig.* **23** 75–87

[26] Li J and Wu G 2017 Image recapture detection through residual-based local descriptors and machine learning *Third Int. Conf. Cloud Computing and Security* pp 653–60

[27] Fridrich J J and Kodovský J 2012 Rich models for steganalysis of digital images *IEEE Trans. Inf. Forensics Secur.* **7** 868–82

[28] Yang P, Ni R and Zhao Y 2016 Recapture image forensics based on Laplacian convolutional neural networks *Int. Workshop on Digital Watermarking* pp 119–28

[29] Li H, Wang S and Kot A C 2017 Image recapture detection with convolutional and recurrent neural networks *Electron. Imaging* **7** 87–91

[30] Liu Y, Guan Q, Zhao X and Cao Y 2018 Image forgery localization based on multi-scale convolutional neural networks *Proc. 6th ACM Workshop on Information Hiding and Multimedia Security, (Innsbruck, Austria)* pp 85–90

[31] Cozzolino D, Gragnaniello D and Verdoliva L 2014 Image forgery detection through residual-based local descriptors and block-matching *IEEE Int. Conf. on Image Processing (ICIP)* pp 5297–301

[32] Zhang R and Ni J 2020 A dense U-Net with cross-layer intersection for detection and localization of image forgery *IEEE Int. Conf. on Acoustics, Speech and Signal Processing (ICASSP)* pp 2982–6

[33] Marra F, Poggi G, Sansone C and Verdoliva L 2015 Evaluation of residual-based local features for camera model identification *International Conference on Image Analysis and Processing* (Lecture Notes in Computer Science vol 9281) (Berlin: Springer) pp 11–8

[34] Ding F, Zhu G and Shi Y Q 2013 A novel method for detecting image sharpening based on local binary pattern *International Workshop on Digital Watermarking* (Lecture Notes in Computer Science vol 8389) (Berlin: Springer) pp 180–91

[35] Li H, Luo W, Qiu X and Huang J 2018 Identification of various image operations using residual-based features *IEEE Trans. Circuits Syst. Video Technol.* **28** 31–45

[36] Saleem M, Warsi M R and Islam S 2019 Feature evaluation for learning underlying data-processing to enhance cloud trust through rich models *Proc. 4th Int. Conf. on Information and Communication Technology for Competitive Strategies* (Boca Raton, FL: CRC Press) pp 539–44

[37] Gloe T and Böhme R 2010 The 'Dresden Image Database' for benchmarking digital image forensics *Proc. 2010 ACM Symp. on Applied Computing (SAC), Sierre, Switzerland* pp 1584–90

[38] Kodovsky J, Fridrich J and Holub V 2012 Ensemble classifiers for steganalysis of digital media *IEEE Trans. Inf. Forensics Secur.* **7** 432–44

Chapter 8

Data augmentation for deep ensembles in polyp segmentation

Loris Nanni, Daniela Cuza, Alessandra Lumini and Sheryl Brahnam

The last few years have witnessed a growing interest in semantic segmentation among computer vision researchers. Semantic segmentation in general, learns low-level features and the semantics of an image via an encoder–decoder structure. In brief the task of the encoder is to extract features by exploiting convolutional layers; the job of the decoder is to generate the same image by applying skip connections in the first layer. This chapter aims to test different data augmentation approaches for boosting segmentation performance by taking DeepLabv3+ as the architecture and ResNet18/ResNet50 as the backbone. The proposed set of data augmentation approaches is coupled with an ensemble of networks obtained by randomly changing the activation functions inside the network multiple times. Moreover, the proposed approach is combined with HardNet-SEG, a recent architecture for semantic segmentation, for a further boost of the performance.

8.1 Introduction

Semantic segmentation applies class labels to pixels within an image containing different objects, such as people, trees, chairs and dogs. This technique has proven highly useful in many tasks, such as autonomous driving [1] and medical diagnosis from medical images [2]. As is the case in many fields, contemporary research in semantic segmentation has begun exploring the possibilities offered by deep learning. The architectural design of one of the earliest semantic segmentation networks (U-Net [3]) included what is now a widely used encoder–decoder structure. A drawback of U-Net is its inability to classify the borders of objects, a problem that was fixed by applying skip connections in the decoder. Most contemporary segmentation networks are now modeled on the encoder–decoder architecture [4–6] because of their success in advancing the field across many computer vision tasks.

In this chapter we explore semantic segmentation using DeepLabv3+ and test our system on the critical problem of colorectal cancer segmentation. Early detection of colorectal cancer is essential for good outcomes. Because there is a strong correlation between polyps and the eventual development of colorectal cancer, polyps need to be detected and removed as early as possible [7]. The detection of polyps is difficult, however, even for seasoned experts, primarily because the edges of polyps are often occluded and highly similar to the surrounding mucosa. Moreover, without being able to detect polyps, classifying them is impossible. There are five common types of polyps: (i) adenomatous, (ii) serrated, (iii) hyperplastic, (iv) tubulovillous adenoma and (v) inflammatory. Adenomas and serrated polyps are the most dangerous and challenging to detect. Automatic polyp detection could augment recognition.

Segmentators based on traditional classifiers succeeded in matching human experts in polyp segmentation long ago [2, 8–10]. In [11] the authors compared convolutional neural networks (CNNs) to the performance of classical classifiers, demonstrating the superiority of CNNs. The power of deep learning in segmentation was illustrated in a system proposed in [12] that used CNNs. This segmentator placed first and second in the 2017 and 2018 Gastrointestinal Image ANAlysis (GIANA) contests. It is well known that deep learners, such as CNNs, require large datasets to generalize well. Only recently have large datasets for colorectal cancer detection become available to researchers [2, 8]. For example, Jha *et al* [13] recently proposed a new public polyp dataset called Kvasir-SEG that contains 1000 polyp images annotated at the pixel level by expert endoscopists at Oslo University Hospital. Jha *et al* [13] also trained a segmentator based on ResNet and U-Net on this novel dataset that produced some very promising results.

A very recent revolution in the field of deep learning is given by transformers. The transformer was originally developed in 2017 for natural language processing [14], and it has also attracted enormous interest recently in the computer vision field. The network employs an encoder–decoder structure such as RNN, the difference is that the input sequence can be passed in parallel. A transformer is a self-attention-based architecture, where the attention mechanism allows it to focus in 'high resolution' on a certain part of the input while the rest of the input is in 'low resolution'. These models usually consist of a two-step training procedure: pre-training on a large dataset and then fine-tuning on a smaller dataset, specific for the application [15]. The application of transformers to image computer vision tasks is based on image splitting into patches [16] to better deal with the large number of pixels of which the image is composed and the fact that the attention is a quadratic operation. Then a linear transformation is applied and position embeddings are added. The vectors obtained in this way are the input to a standard transformer encoder. The model TransFuse [17] combines CNNs and transformers, where a CNN uses kernels to aggregate local information in each layer, while a transformer captures global context information. A new method for image segmentation is UACANet [18], which uses U-Net as backbone, a parallel axial attention encoder, and a decoder to obtain both local and global information and a self-attention mechanism.

In this work the aim is to improve the performance of a segmentation approach based on DeepLabV3+ using ResNet18 and ResNet50 as a backbone. We increase the training data size using different data augmentation approaches. These augmented training sets are fed into an ensemble of networks whose activation functions are randomly selected from a pool of ReLU variants. To increase diversity, each network is stochastically designed by varying the activation layers. A collection of the most diverse networks is selected to be trained on the augmented training sets, with the best performing networks chosen for inclusion in the final ensemble. For computational reasons, the selection procedure has been carried out for the lighter ResNet18 architecture, while pure random generation has been performed for ResNet50. Empirical results using two different testing protocols and five datasets (Kvasir-SEG, CVC-ColonDB, EndoScene, ETIS-Larib Polyp DB and CVCClinic DB) show that the proposed ensemble gains performance which is better than all models based on CNN and is almost comparable with the actual state-of-the-art transformer approaches.

8.2 Deep learning for semantic image segmentation

As stated in the introduction, semantic segmentation is the process whereby class labels of objects represented in an image are applied to each of the pixels composing the objects. One of the first applications of deep learning to the problem of semantic image segmentation employed a fully convolutional network (FCN), which replaces the last fully connected layers of a network with a fully convolutional layer so that the network can classify an image on the pixel level [6]. A significant advancement in semantic segmentation was the insertion of an encoder–decoder unit [3] into the FCN architecture that enabled a multi-layer deconvolution network to be learned. U-Net, so named because it is a U-shape network, is another architecture that has proven successful in semantic image segmentation. The function of the decoder in U-Net is to downsample the image and increase the number of features; the task of the encoder is to increase the image resolution to match the input size [19]. Another encoder–decoder architecture that produces excellent results is SegNet [4], which uses VGG [20] as a backbone encoder; the decoder utilizes max-pooling indices from the corresponding encoder layer rather than concatenating them as is the case with U-Net. As a result, SegNet requires less memory while producing better boundary reconstructions.

Another step in advancing image segmentation is the semantic segmentation model designed by Google called DeepLab [21]. This model attains dense prediction by up-sampling the output of the last convolution layer with atrous convolution and by computing pixel-wise loss. Atrous convolution applies a dilation rate to enlarge the field of view of filters without adding parameters that increase computational resources. The superiority of the DeepLab family of segmentators [21–24] is the result of three key features: (i) dilated convolutions that avoid the decrease in resolution caused by the pooling layers and large strides, (ii) atrous spatial pyramid pooling, which uses filters with multiple sampling rates to retrieve information from the image at different scales, and (iii) a better method for localizing object boundaries that couples convolutional networks with probabilistic graphical models. DeepLabV3 enhanced previous versions of DeepLab by combining cascade and parallel modules of dilated convolutions and by modifying the atrous spatial pyramid pooling with the addition of batch normalization and a 1×1 convolution. The output is given by a final layer that is also a 1×1 convolution; DeepLabV3 outputs the probability distribution of the classes over every pixel. Finally, DeepLabV3+ [24], the architecture used in this work, extends DeepLabV3 by combining cascaded and parallel modules of dilated convolutions. DeepLabV3+ includes (i) a decoder with point-wise convolutions that operate on the same channel but at different locations and (ii) depth-wise convolutions that operate at the same location but on different channels.

Many other architectures have also been proposed for image segmentation, with the most popular based on recurrent neural networks, attention models and generative models. For a recent survey of the literature see [25].

Aside from architectural considerations, segmentation performance is affected by other design choices, such as the selection of the pretrained backbone used for the encoder. Among the many CNN [26] architectures widely used for transfer learning, in this work we explore ResNet18 and ResNet50 [27]. These CNNs use residual blocks whose intermediate layers learn a residual function concerning the block input.

In addition, different loss functions affect how a network is trained. For image segmentation, the most popular is pixel-wise cross-entropy loss, which treats classification as a multi-label problem where the prediction of each pixel is individually compared with the actual class label. Pixel-wise cross-entropy is calculated as the log loss summed over each class and averaged over each pixel. Unfortunately, in the case where classes are unbalanced, training with this loss function can favor the most prevalent class. One method for handling this problem is to apply counterweights to offset any imbalance in the dataset [6].

Dice loss [28], based on the Sørensen–Dice similarity coefficient for measuring the overlap between two segmented images, is yet another common loss function and one that is explored here. Dice loss ranges from 0 to 1, with 1 indicating perfect overlap. The reader is referred to [28] for an overview of other popular loss functions for image segmentation.

Finally, activation functions have a significant impact on the performance of CNN. ReLU is one of the most powerful nonlinearities, but there is a growing body of literature demonstrating improved performance using ReLU variants [29]. We take advantage of these performance differences to add diversity to an ensemble of networks. Our proposed method for replacing activation layers is detailed in the next section.

8.3 Stochastic activation selection

Introduced in [29], stochastic activation selection takes a specific neural network topology and generates a diverse set of them by randomly selecting different activation functions for each network. The random selection is iterated multiple times to generate a large number of networks with maximum diversity. After training each network on the same training set, the results are combined by the sum rule (i.e. by averaging the softmax outputs of each network composing the ensemble).

Given DeeplabV3+ [24] as the neural network architecture, the pool of activation functions is composed of classic ReLU [30] and some of the best ReLU variants including Leaky ReLU [31], ELU [32], PReLU [33], S-Shaped ReLU (SReLU) [34] and many others. The interested reader can find the whole set of activation functions with a detailed mathematical explanation in [35] (see the code on GitHub for more details).

8.4 Data augmentation

This section describes some image augmentation techniques, created with the aim of increasing the size of the starting dataset and therefore increasing the performance of the classification system. We use both shape-based and color-based transformation: in the first case, the augmentation technique is applied to both the training images and their labels. No test set augmentation is performed.

8.4.1 Spatial stretch

The transformation consists of stretching the original image. The stretching direction is randomly chosen from the four possible options: left/up, right/up, left/down and right/down. The stretching is applied to the columns first, then the empty spaces are interpolated with a weighted nearest neighbor method, and the same procedure is repeated for the rows. The stretching of the original image is obtained by changing the position of the rows/columns according to the following equations:

$$\lambda = U(2, 17)$$

$$k[i] = \frac{\frac{1}{\lambda} - \lambda}{s - 1} t[i] + \lambda, \ i \in [1, s]$$

$$k[i] = \frac{\lambda - \frac{1}{\lambda}}{s - 1} t[i] + \frac{1}{\lambda}, \ i \in [1, s]$$

$$a = a + k(j), \ j \in (2, s)$$

$$y[j] = \begin{cases} 1 & j = 1 \\ \mathrm{round}(a*5) & j \in [2, s] \end{cases},$$

where s is the number of columns and rows (in this work both equal 224), $t[i]$ is a vector containing the numbers $[0, s-1]$, $k[i]$ is the distance between the row/column of the original image and the final image, while $y[j]$ is the final row/column which varies according to j, the original position. The function $U(a, b)$ returns a random number in the range a, b. An example of the application of the spatial stretch technique to an image of the training set and its mask is shown in figure 8.1.

8.4.2 Shadows

The final image is obtained by applying a shadow [36] to the left or the right of the original image, as shown in figure 8.2. In particular, the intensities of the columns are multiplied by the following equation:

$$
y = \begin{cases} \min\left\{0.2 + 0.8\sqrt{\frac{x}{0.5}}, \ 1\right\} \text{direction} = 1 \\ \min\left\{0.2 + 0.8\sqrt{\frac{1-x}{0.5}}, \ 1\right\} \text{direction} = 0 \end{cases}.
$$

8.4.3 Contrast and motion blur

This transformation [36] is the composite of two alterations: first, it is necessary to modify the contrast of the original image, increasing or decreasing it, then a filter that simulates the movement of the camera is applied. Two functions to modify the contrast are implemented, but only one randomly chosen between the two is applied to the image.

The first contrast function (figure 8.3) is based on the following equation:

$$
y = \frac{\left(x - \frac{1}{2}\right)\sqrt{1 - \frac{k}{4}}}{\sqrt{1 - k(x - \frac{1}{2})^2}} + 0.5, \ k \leqslant 4.
$$

The parameter k controls the contrast, there is an increase in contrast if $k < 0$, a decrease in contrast if $0 < k \leqslant 4$, the image remains the same when $k = 0$.

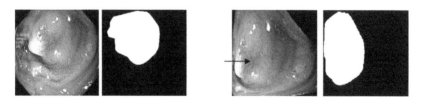

Figure 8.1. Example of application of the spatial stretch technique.

Figure 8.2. Example of application of the shadows technique (no changes are needed in the mask).

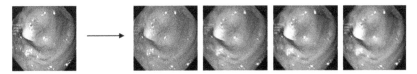

Figure 8.3. Example of application of the contrast function 1 for decreasing values of k and subsequent use of the motion blur filter.

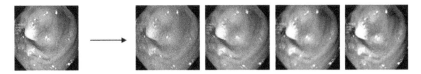

Figure 8.4. Example of application of the contrast function 2 for increasing values of α and subsequent use of the motion blur filter.

In the code k is chosen randomly from a specific range, among the following four:
- $U(2.8, 3.8) \rightarrow$ Hard decrease in contrast.
- $U(1.5, 2.5) \rightarrow$ Soft decrease in contrast.
- $U(-2, -1) \rightarrow$ Soft increase in contrast.
- $U(-5, -3) \rightarrow$ Hard increase in contrast.

The second contrast function (figure 8.4) is based on the following equation:

$$y = \begin{cases} \frac{1}{2}\left(\frac{x}{0.5}\right)\alpha & 0 \leqslant x < \frac{1}{2} \\ 1 - \frac{1}{2}\left(\frac{1-x}{0.5}\right)\alpha & \frac{1}{2} \leqslant x \leqslant 1 \end{cases}.$$

The parameter α controls the contrast, there is an increase in contrast if $\alpha > 1$, a decrease in contrast if $0 < \alpha < 1$ and the image remains the same when $\alpha = 1$. This parameter is chosen randomly from four possible ranges:
- $U(0.25, 0.5) \rightarrow$ Hard decrease in contrast.
- $U(0.6, 0.9) \rightarrow$ Soft decrease in contrast.
- $U(1.2, 1.7) \rightarrow$ Soft increase in contrast.
- $U(1.8, 2.3) \rightarrow$ Hard increase in contrast.

8.4.4 Color change and rotation

This technique consists of three color operations (color adjusting, blurring and adding Gaussian noise) and a spatial operator (image rotation). The *jitterColorHSV (I, Name, Value)* function is used for color adjusting by randomly changing saturation, contrast and brightness levels within a random range:
- Saturation $\rightarrow$ [−0.3–0.1].
- Contrast $\rightarrow$ [−0.3–0.1].
- Brightness $\rightarrow$ [1.2 1.4].

The *imgaussfilt* function is used for blurring and the *imnoise* function is used for adding Gaussian noise. The image is finally rotated by an angle in the interval [−90° 90°] (figure 8.5).

8.4.5 Segmentation

This technique consists of the segmentation of the image based on three different colors. The image obtained in this way is divided into three images, each of these containing a different color. The two images with the highest number of black pixels are selected, then the third image with the highest brightness is added to these. The images are combined and rotated by an angle selected from the range [−90°, 90°] (figure 8.6).

8.4.6 Rand augment

This approach consists of the random selection of two transformations (one color-based and one shape-based) among a set of 21 [37].

Thirteen transformations belong to the color category:
- Create a composite image from two images A and B, by using the function *imfuse.*
- Add Gaussian noise.
- Adjust the saturation.
- Adjust the brightness.
- Control the contrast.
- Adjust the sharpness by using the function *imsharpen.*
- Application of the *motion* filter to blur the image.
- Histogram equalization.
- Conversion from RGB to YUV and histogram equalization.

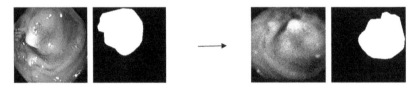

Figure 8.5. Result of the application of the 'color change and rotation' transformation.

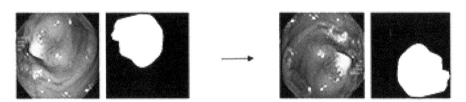

Figure 8.6. Example of the segmentation technique.

- Application of the *disk* filter to blur the image.
- Add salt-and-pepper noise by using the function *imnoise*.
- Convert from **RGB** to HSV and adjust the hue by using the function *jitterColorHSV(I,Name,Value)*.
- Adjust the local contrast by using the function *localcontrast*.

Eight transformations belong to the shape category:
- Rotation of an angle selected from the range [−40°, 40°].
- Vertical flip.
- Horizontal shear by using the function *randomAffine2d*.
- Vertical shear by using the function *randomAffine2d*.
- Horizontal translation by using the function *randomAffine2d*.
- Vertical translation by using the function *randomAffine2d*.
- Uniform scaling.
- Cutout by using the function *imcrop*.

The Rand augment technique (figure 8.7) consists of the application of a transformation from the color category with probability 1 and the subsequent application of a technique from the shape category with a probability of 0.3.

8.4.7 RICAP

The RICAP transformation [38] consists of three steps:
Four images are randomly selected from the training set.
The selected images are cropped.
The cropped images are patched together to construct a new image (figure 8.8).

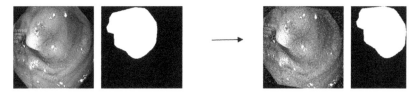

Figure 8.7. Example of the Rand augment technique.

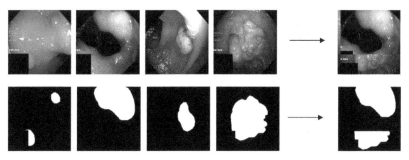

Figure 8.8. Example of the RICAP technique.

8.4.8 Color and shape change

Ten artificial images are created (figure 8.9) for each image in the dataset [39]. The operations performed are:

- The image is displaced to the right or the left.
- The image is displaced up or down.
- The image is rotated by an angle randomly selected from the range [0°, 180°].
- Horizontal or vertical shear is applied by using the function *randomAffine2d*.
- A horizontal or vertical flip is applied.
- Change the brightness levels by adding the same value to each RGB channel.
- Change the brightness levels by adding different values to each RGB channel.
- Add speckle noise by using the function *imnoise*.
- Application of the technique 'contrast and motion blur', described previously.
- Application of the technique 'shadows', described previously.

8.4.9 Occlusion 1

Three occlusion methods are used. The first technique consists in selecting some rows (or columns) and replacing them with black lines (figure 8.10). The distance between the lines in terms of pixels is chosen randomly from the interval $U(15, 30)$.

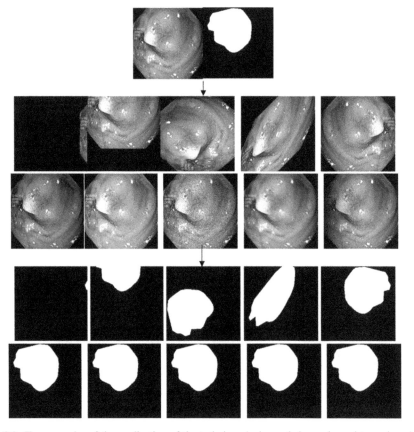

Figure 8.9. Ten examples of the application of the technique 'color and shape change' to a given image.

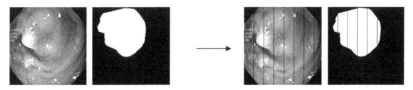

Figure 8.10. Example of the application of the occlusion 1 technique.

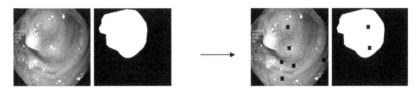

Figure 8.11. Example of the application of the occlusion 2 technique.

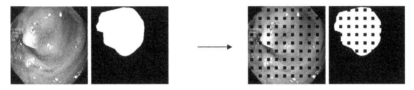

Figure 8.12. Example of the GridMask technique.

8.4.10 Occlusion 2

In the second occlusion technique the images are transformed by replacing some parts of them with black rectangles (figure 8.11). The size of the rectangles, their number and their position are chosen randomly from the following intervals:
- Length of the rectangle $n \rightarrow U(4, 14)$.
- Height of the rectangle $m \rightarrow U(4, 14)$.
- Number of rectangles $\rightarrow U(7, 14)$.
- Coordinate $x \rightarrow U(1, 224 - n)$.
- Coordinate $y \rightarrow U(1, 224 - m)$.

8.4.11 GridMask

Given an input image, some of its pixels are removed, as shown in figure 8.12. The equation used is $y = x \times M$, where x is the input image, M is a binary mask that stores pixels to be removed, while y is the final image.

8.4.12 AttentiveCutMix

For each image x_1 of the training set an image x_2 from the original dataset is chosen randomly. The image x_2 is divided into a 7×7 grid, and N elements are cut from this grid. The elements cut from the second image are pasted on top of the first in their original position, as in figure 8.13. The equation used [40] is

$$y = B \times x2 + (1 - B) \times x1,$$

where y is the result of the algorithm, while B is a binary mask (figure 8.13).

8.4.13 Modified ResizeMix

For each image A of the training set, a second image B is selected randomly, resized and pasted over image A [41]. Then the technique 'color change and rotation' is applied (figure 8.14).

8.4.14 Color mapping

This technique consists of randomly selecting an image B from the training set for each original image A. Three methods of color normalization of image A versus image B are applied (figure 8.15), using the Stain Normalization toolbox by Nicholas Trahearn and Adnan Khan [42]:

- RGB histogram specification.
- Reinhard.
- Macenko.

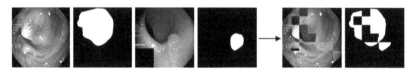

Figure 8.13. Example of application of the AttentiveCutMix technique.

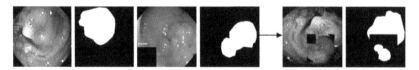

Figure 8.14. Example of the 'modified ResizeMix' technique.

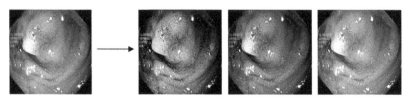

Figure 8.15. Example of application of the 'color mapping' technique.

8.5 Results on colorectal cancer segmentation

8.5.1 Datasets, testing protocol and metrics

We have performed the experiments following two different protocols, which are used widely in the literature.

The first testing protocol [13, 43] uses the Kvasir-SEG dataset [44] partitioned into 880 images for training and the remaining 120 for testing. The Kvasir-SEG dataset includes 1000 polyp images acquired using a high-resolution electromagnetic imaging system (the image sizes vary between 332×487 and 1920×1072 pixels), with a ground-truth consisting of bounding boxes and segmentation masks.

The second testing protocol exploits five polyp datasets, namely Kvasir-SEG, CVC-ColonDB, EndoScene, ETIS-Larib Polyp DB and CVCClinic DB. The CVC-ClinicDB [45] and ETIS-Larib [46] datasets consist of frames extracted from colonoscopy videos, annotated by expert video endoscopists, and include 612 images (384×288) and 196 high-resolution images (1225×966), respectively. The CVC-ColonDB [47] dataset contains 380 images (574×500) representing 15 different polyps. EndoScene is a combination of CVC-ClinicDB and CVC300. The training set for the second testing protocol includes 900 images from Kvasir-SEG and 550 images from CVC-ClinicDB. The testing set is made up of the remaining images from the above-cited datasets: 100 images from Kvasir-SEG, 62 images from CVC-ClinicalDB, 380 from CVC-ColonDB, 196 from ETIS-Larib and 60 from CVC-T, which is the testing set for EndoScene. Note that only a small set of images are taken from EndoScene to avoid the inclusion of images already seen in the training stage.

All the datasets for both protocols can be downloaded from the GitHub of [43].

In all experiments, even when the images are resized to the input size of a CNN model, the predicted masks are resized back to the original dimensions before performance evaluation.We do not include other approaches in the comparison that evaluated the performance on the resized version of the images.

In accordance with most of the works on polyp segmentation we use pixel-wise metrics as performance indicators: accuracy, precision, recall, F_1-score, F_2-score, intersection over union (IoU) and Dice. A mathematical definition of each indicator for a bi-class problem (foreground/background), starting from the confusion matrix (TP, TN, FP and FN refer to the true positives, true negatives, false positives and false negatives, respectively), is the following:

$$\text{accuracy} = \frac{TP + TN}{TP + FP + FN + TN},$$

which is the number of pixels correctly classified over the total number of pixels in the image,

$$\text{precision} = \frac{TP}{TP + FP},$$

which is the fraction of the polyps that are correctly classified,

$$\text{recall} = \frac{TP}{TP + FN},$$

which is the fraction of the predicted mask that is actually polyp pixels,

$$F_1\text{-score} = \frac{2 \times TP}{2 \times TP + FP + FN},$$

$$F_2\text{-score} = \frac{5 \times \text{precision} \times \text{recall}}{4 \times \text{precision} + \text{recall}},$$

which are two measures that try to average precision and recall,

$$IoU = \frac{|A \cap B|}{|A \cup B|} = \frac{TP}{TP + FP + FN},$$

which is defined as the area of intersection between the predicted mask A and the ground-truth map B, divided by the area of the union between the two maps, and

$$Dice = \frac{|A \cap B|}{|A| + |B|} = \frac{2 \times TP}{2 \times TP + FP + FN},$$

which is defined as twice the overlap area of the predicted and ground-truth masks divided by the total number of pixels (it coincides with the F_1-score for binary masks)

All the above metrics range in [0,1] and must be maximized. The final performance is obtained by averaging on the test set the performance obtained for each test image.

8.5.2 Experiments

The first experiment in table 8.1 is aimed at comparing the two different backbone networks: ResNet18 and ResNet50. Since the size of images in the Kvasir dataset is quite large we also evaluate versions of the ResNet with larger input size, i.e. 299 × 299 (ResNet18–299/ResNet50–299) and 352 × 352 (ResNet18–352/ResNet50–352). Clearly, a larger input size improves the performance.

The training of all the models has been performed with the SGD optimizer for 20 epochs, with an initial learning rate of 10e-2, a learning rate drop period of 5 epochs and a drop factor of 0.2. In this experiment we use the same 'base' data augmentation of our previous paper [48], i.e. horizontal and vertical flip, 90° rotation.

The second experiment (table 8.2) is aimed at comparing the different data augmentation approaches proposed in this work. For the sake of computation time

Table 8.1. Experiments with different backbones (first protocol).

Backbone	IoU	Dice	F_2	Prec.	Rec.	Acc.
ResNet18	0.759	0.844	0.845	0.882	0.856	0.952
ResNet50	0.751	0.837	0.836	0.883	0.845	0.952
ResNet18–299	0.782	0.863	0.870	0.881	0.883	0.959
ResNet50–299	0.798	0.872	0.876	0.898	0.886	0.962
ResNet18–352	0.787	0.865	0.871	0.891	0.884	0.960
ResNet50–352	0.801	0.872	0.884	0.881	0.900	0.964

Table 8.2. Performance of the different data augmentation approaches (first protocol).

Data augmentation	IoU	Dice	F_2	Prec.	Rec.	Acc.
ResNet18	0.759	0.844	0.845	0.882	0.856	0.952
Spatial stretch	0.732	0.822	0.824	0.868	0.838	0.948
Shadows	0.748	0.836	0.842	0.868	0.858	0.952
Contrast and motion blur	0.749	0.836	0.843	0.857	0.860	0.952
Color change and rotation	0.761	0.849	0.852	0.874	0.863	0.953
Segmentation	0.758	0.846	0.861	0.854	0.883	0.953
Rand augment	0.754	0.841	0.846	0.870	0.858	0.952
RICAP	0.745	0.834	0.835	0.876	0.847	0.949
Color and shape change	0.803	0.874	0.883	0.885	0.900	0.961
Occlusions 1	0.747	0.834	0.846	0.855	0.867	0.954
Occlusions 2	0.737	0.825	0.830	0.852	0.847	0.951
GridMask	0.746	0.836	0.841	0.869	0.855	0.949
AttentiveCutMix	0.735	0.826	0.830	0.869	0.843	0.945
Modified ResizeMix	0.757	0.846	0.846	0.882	0.855	0.952
Color mapping	0.760	0.841	0.854	0.853	0.877	0.954
Comb_1	0.802	0.875	0.886	0.886	0.904	0.959
Comb_2	0.805	0.875	0.882	0.891	0.893	0.962
Comb_3	0.799	0.870	0.877	0.894	0.889	0.962

all the tests are performed using ResNet18 with an input size of 224 and compared to the 'base' data augmentation reported in the first rows of tables 8.1 and 8.2. The other rows of table 8.2 include the performance obtained using the different data augmentation approaches described in section 8.4 and the last three rows report the performance obtained by evaluating a combination of several data augmentation approaches.

Comb_1 → 'color and shape change' and 'color mapping';

Comb_2 → 'color and shape change' and 'color change and rotation';

Comb_3 → 'color and shape change' and 'color mapping' and 'color change and rotation'.

Clearly, the combination of different data augmentation approaches boosts the performance.

The third experiment (table 8.3) is aimed at designing effective ensembles by varying the activation functions. Each ensemble is the fusion by the sum rule of 14 models (since we use, in [48], 14 activation functions). For sake of computation time, this test is performed only in the Kvasir-SEG dataset augmented by the same method as table 8.1 (base data augmentation, first testing protocol). The ensemble name is the concatenation of the name of the backbone network and a string to identify the creation approach:

- act: each of the 14 networks of the ensemble is obtained by substituting its activation layers by one of the activation functions used in [48] (the same function for all the layers, but a different function for each network).

Table 8.3. Experiments on ensembles (first protocol).

Ensemble name	IoU	Dice	F_2	Prec.	Rec.	Acc.
ResNet18_act	0.774	0.856	0.856	0.888	0.867	0.955
ResNet18_relu	0.774	0.858	0.858	0.892	0.867	0.955
ResNet18_sto	0.780	0.860	0.857	0.898	0.864	0.956
ResNet50_act	0.779	0.858	0.859	0.894	0.869	0.957
ResNet50_relu	0.772	0.855	0.858	0.889	0.870	0.955
ResNet50_sto	0.779	0.859	0.864	0.891	0.877	0.957
ResNet50–352_sto	0.820	0.885	0.888	0.915	0.896	0.966
ResNet50–352_sel	0.825	0.888	0.892	0.915	0.902	0.967

- sto: 14 stochastic models are generated, repricing the activation layers by randomly selected activation function used in [48] (which may be different for each layer).
- sel: ensembles of 'selected' stochastic models. The network selection is performed using three cross-validations on the training set among 100 stochastic models. The selection procedure is aimed at picking the most performing/independent classifiers to be added to the ensemble. For a fair comparison with other ensembles, we selected a set of 14 networks, which are finally fine-tuned on the whole augmented training set at a larger resolution.
- relu: 14 networks with standard architecture. All the starting models in the ensemble are the same, except for the initialization.

According to the results reported in table 8.3, it is clear that stochastic variation of activation functions (sto) allows a performance improvement with respect to a simple fusion of networks sharing the same architecture (relu) or a set of networks differing by the activation function (act). Such improvement is also noticeable if a selection procedure (sel) is used to include only the most performing architecture. Unfortunately, the selection process is computationally heavy, because it is performed among a pool of 100 networks. The best performance among the ensembles is obtained by ResNet50–352_sel, showing that the input size is critical in this problem.

Finally, in tables 8.4 and 8.5 a comparison with some state-of-the-art results is reported according to the above-cited first and second testing protocols, respectively.

In these final experiments, for sake of computational time, ResNet50 is trained using only the base data augmentation consisting of horizontal and vertical flip, and 90° rotation, while ResNet18 is trained using the here-proposed data augmentation 'color and shape change' and 'color mapping'.

The methods named HarDNet_SGD and HarDNet_Adam are our experiments using HardNet [43] trained by SGD and Adam optimizers (using the code shared by the authors). The reason for this choice is that the authors of [43] proposed a different optimizer for the two protocols.

Table 8.4. State-of-the-art approaches using the first testing protocol.

Method	IoU	Dice	F_2	Prec.	Rec.	Acc.
ResNet18_352_sel	0.819	0.886	0.890	0.910	0.899	0.966
ResNet50_352_sel	0.823	0.887	0.890	0.916	0.899	0.966
ResNet18&50	0.831	0.893	0.896	0.920	0.904	0.967
HarDNet_SGD	0.847	0.906	0.914	0.916	0.924	0.971
HarDNet_Adam	0.829	0.888	0.893	0.916	0.904	0.963
HardNet_SGD⊕ResNet18&50	0.851	0.908	0.914	0.922	0.922	0.972
HardNet_Adam⊕ ResNet18&50	0.834	0.892	0.896	0.919	0.905	0.964
HardNet_SGD⊕HardNet_Adam⊕ ResNet18&50	0.846	0.902	0.906	0.924	0.914	0.970
U-Net [13]	0.471	0.597	0.598	0.672	0.617	0.894
ResUNet [13]	0.572	0.69	0.699	0.745	0.725	0.917
ResUNet++ [13]	0.613	0.714	0.72	0.784	0.742	0.917
FCN8 [13]	0.737	0.831	0.825	0.882	0.835	0.952
HRNet [13]	0.759	0.845	0.847	0.878	0.859	0.952
DoubleUNet [13]	0.733	0.813	0.82	0.861	0.84	0.949
PSPNet [13]	0.744	0.841	0.831	0.890	0.836	0.953
DeepLabV3+ResNet50 [13]	0.776	0.857	0.855	0.891	0.861	0.961
DeepLabV3+ResNet101 [13]	0.786	0.864	0.857	0.906	0.859	0.961
U-Net ResNet34 [13]	0.810	0.876	0.862	0.944	0.86	0.968
ColonSegNet [13]	0.724	0.821	0.821	0.843	0.850	0.949
DDANet [49]	0.78	0.858	—	0.864	0.888	—
HarDNet-MSEG [43]	0.848	0.904	0.915	0.907	0.923	0.969
U-Net ResNet34 [13]	0.81	0.876	0.862	0.944	0.860	0.968

In table 8.4, in addition to the methods presented in the above tables, we also report the performance of the following fusions by average rule (symbol ⊕):

- Res18&50 = ResNet18_352_sel ⊕ ResNet50_352_sel.
- HardNet_SGD/Adam ⊕ Res18&50, which is the fusion of HardNet (SGD or ADAM version) with the ensemble above.
- HardNet_SGD⊕HardNet_Adam⊕ Res18&50, which is the fusion of both HardNet (SGD and ADAM version) with our ensemble.

As far the latter protocol is concerned, since the training set is larger, to reduce computation time we have run the following methods without supervised selection:

- ResNet18_352, a stand-alone ResNet18 trained using the base data augmentation approach (only horizontal/vertical flip and 90° rotation).
- ResNet18_352_a, a stand-alone ResNet18 trained using the data augmentation 'color and shape change' and 'color mapping'.
- ResNet50_352, a stand-alone ResNet50 trained using base data augmentation.
- ResNet18_352_relu_a, an ensemble of ten standard ResNet18 networks trained using the data augmentation 'color and shape change' and 'color mapping'.

Table 8.5. State-of-the-art approaches using the second testing protocol. For each test set the number of images is enclosed in parenthesis. The last three columns are the average of IoU and Dice and the rank (on IoU).

Method	Kvasir (100)		ClinicalDB (62)		ColonDB (380)		ETIS (196)		CVC-T (60)		Average		
	IoU	Dice	IoU	Dice	IoU	Dice	IoU	Dice	IoU	Dice	IoU	Dice	Rank
ResNet18_352	0.832	0.893	0.842	0.89	0.646	0.721	0.582	0.652	0.796	0.871	0.740	0.805	15
ResNet18_352_a	0.82	0.888	0.861	0.914	0.653	0.74	0.555	0.631	0.772	0.844	0.732	0.803	18
ResNet50_352	0.839	0.895	0.845	0.898	0.637	0.716	0.523	0.591	0.819	0.892	0.733	0.798	17
ResNet18_352_relu_a	0.835	0.898	0.876	0.924	0.685	0.768	0.591	0.66	0.783	0.857	0.754	0.821	10
ResNet50_352_relu	0.85	0.904	0.865	0.911	0.635	0.712	0.554	0.615	0.821	0.891	0.745	0.807	14
ResNet18_352_sto_a	0.834	0.896	0.871	0.921	0.685	0.763	0.573	0.642	0.785	0.851	0.750	0.815	12
ResNet50_352_sto	0.853	0.909	0.859	0.906	0.655	0.729	0.561	0.617	0.82	0.891	0.750	0.810	13
Res18&50sto	0.849	0.906	0.877	0.924	0.678	0.75	0.586	0.647	0.813	0.882	0.761	0.822	9
HarDNet_SGD	0.857	0.908	0.864	0.911	0.677	0.752	0.562	0.639	0.799	0.868	0.752	0.816	11
HarDNet_Adam	0.854	0.906	0.875	0.924	0.678	0.751	0.625	0.716	0.831	0.903	0.773	0.840	7
HN1&R	0.861	0.912	0.882	0.929	0.684	0.757	0.644	0.727	0.833	0.904	0.781	0.846	5
HN2&R	0.87	0.918	0.884	0.929	0.695	0.768	0.635	0.710	0.830	0.900	0.783	0.845	4
HarDNet-MSEG [43]	0.857	0.912	0.882	0.932	0.66	0.731	0.613	0.677	0.821	0.887	0.767	0.828	8
PraNet [43]	0.84	0.898	0.849	0.899	0.64	0.709	0.567	0.628	0.797	0.871	0.739	0.801	16
SFA [43]	0.611	0.723	0.607	0.700	0.347	0.469	0.217	0.297	0.329	0.467	0.422	0.531	21
U-Net++ [43]	0.743	0.821	0.729	0.794	0.41	0.483	0.344	0.401	0.624	0.707	0.570	0.641	20
U-Net [43]	0.746	0.818	0.755	0.823	0.444	0.512	0.335	0.398	0.627	0.710	0.581	0.652	19
SETR [50]	0.854	0.911	0.885	0.934	0.69	0.773	0.646	0.726	0.814	0.889	0.778	0.847	6
TransUnet [51]	0.857	0.913	0.887	0.935	0.699	0.781	0.66	0.731	0.824	0.893	0.785	0.851	3
TransFuse [17]	0.870	0.92	0.897	0.942	0.706	0.781	0.663	0.737	0.826	0.894	0.792	0.855	1
UACANet [18]	0.859	0.912	0.88	0.926	0.678	0.751	0.678	0.751	0.849	0.910	0.789	0.850	2

- ResNet50_352_relu, an ensemble of ten standard ResNet50 networks trained using base data augmentation.
- ResNet18_352_sto_a, an ensemble of ten stochastic ResNet18 networks trained using the data augmentation 'color and shape change' and 'color mapping'.
- ResNet50_352_sto, an ensemble of ten stochastic ResNet50 networks trained using base data augmentation.

Moreover, in table 8.5 the performance of the following fusions by the average rule are reported:

- Res18&50sto = ResNet18_352_sto_a $\oplus$ ResNet50_352_sto.
- HN1&R = HardNet_Adam$\oplus$ Res18&50sto, which is the fusion of HardNet_Adam with the ensemble above.
- HN2&R = HardNet_SGD$\oplus$HardNet_Adam$\oplus$Res18&50sto, which is the fusion of both HardNet (SGD and ADAM version) with our ensemble.

Finally, for the sake of comparison in table 8.5, we report the performance of several state-of-the-art approaches: only methods following the second protocol exactly are included.

The following conclusions can be obtained from tables 8.4 and 8.5:

- From the comparison of ResNet18_352 (or ResNet18_352_a) and the ensembles ResNet18_352_relu_a (or ResNet18_352_sto_a) we can observe the advantage of fusing networks together.
- While in table 8.2 data augmentation granted a performance improvement for ResNet18, from the results in table 8.5 it seems that data augmentation is not helpful. The reason may be the different input sizes of the networks—by using larger input layers the performance improves reducing the need for data augmentation.
- The fusion of ensembles created from different models (ResNet18 and ResNet50) allows a performance improvement over each component.
- The best method for training the HarDNet model is Adam (considering all datasets from the second protocol).
- HarDNet_Adam has a slight advantage over our proposed ensembles (Res18&50 or Res18&50sto), nonetheless, the fusion of both approaches improves both performances.

This work shows the usefulness of ensembles. Our best method is HN2&R which is given by the fusion of HardNet_SGD, HardNet_Adam and the ensemble Res18&50sto. This method closes the gap with transformers, gaining performance almost comparable to that of transformers.

8.6 Conclusion

Semantic segmentation is a very important topic in medical image analysis. In this chapter our goal is to improve the performance of polyp segmentation during colonoscopy tests.

We tested several data augmentation approaches, then we proposed combining a set of them to increase the size of the training set. Finally, we used the augmented training set for feeding an ensemble of networks, where we randomly substitute their activation functions. Very recent methods based on transformers gain the best segmentation performance in this problem. In any case, some of the ideas proposed in this paper (i.e. stochastic ensemble generation and selection, advanced data augmentation) could be coupled advantageously to transformer-based approaches.

In future work we plan to study the feasibility of reducing the complexity of our ensemble by applying some techniques such as pruning, quantization, low-rank factorization and distillation.

The MATLAB code of all the descriptors and experiments reported in this paper will be available at https://github.com/LorisNanni.

Acknowledgments

We gratefully acknowledge the support of the NVIDIA Corporation in the form of a 'NVIDIA Hardware Donation Grant' for the Titan X used in this research.

References

[1] Feng D, Haase-Schütz C, Rosenbaum L, Hertlein H, Glaeser C, Timm F, Wiesbeck W and Dietmayer K 2020 Deep multi-modal object detection and semantic segmentation for autonomous driving: datasets, methods, and challenges *IEEE Trans. Intell. Transp. Syst.* **22** 1341–60

[2] Brandao P *et al* 2018 Towards a computed-aided diagnosis system in colonoscopy: automatic polyp segmentation using convolution neural networks *J. Med. Robot. Res.* **3** 1840002

[3] Noh H, Hong S and Han B 2015 Learning deconvolution network for semantic segmentation *Proc. of the IEEE Int. Conf. on Computer Vision* pp 1520–8

[4] Badrinarayanan V, Kendall A and Cipolla R 2017 SegNet: a deep convolutional encoder–decoder architecture for image segmentation *IEEE Trans. Pattern Anal. Mach. Intell.* **39** 2481–95

[5] Bullock J, Cuesta-Lázaro C and Quera-Bofarull A 2019 XNet: a convolutional neural network (CNN) implementation for medical x-ray image segmentation suitable for small datasets *Proc. SPIE* **10953** 109531Z

[6] Shelhamer E, Long J and Darrell T 2015 Fully convolutional networks for semantic segmentation *IEEE Trans. Pattern Anal. Mach. Intell.* **39** 640–51

[7] Roncucci L and Mariani F 2015 Prevention of colorectal cancer: how many tools do we have in our basket? *Eur. J. Intern. Med.* **26** 752–6

[8] Wang Y, Tavanapong W, Wong J, Oh J and De Groen P C 2013 Part-based multiderivative edge cross-sectional profiles for polyp detection in colonoscopy *IEEE J. Biomed. Heal. Informatics* **18** 1379–89

[9] Mori Y, Kudo S, Berzin T M, Misawa M and Takeda K 2017 Computer-aided diagnosis for colonoscopy *Endoscopy* **49** 813

[10] Wang P *et al* 2018 Development and validation of a deep-learning algorithm for the detection of polyps during colonoscopy *Nat. Biomed. Eng.* **2** 741–8

[11] Thambawita V, Jha D, Riegler M, Halvorsen P, Hammer H L, Johansen H D and Johansen D 2018 The Medico-Task 2018: disease detection in the gastrointestinal tract using global features and deep learning arXiv:1810.13278

[12] Guo Y B and Matuszewski B 2019 GIANA polyp segmentation with fully convolutional dilation neural networks *Proc. of the 14th Int. Joint Conf. on Computer Vision, Imaging and Computer Graphics Theory and Applications* pp 632–41

[13] Jha D, Ali S, Johansen H D, Johansen D, Rittscher J, Riegler M A and Halvorsen P 2020 Real-time polyp detection, localisation and segmentation in colonoscopy using deep learning arXiv:2011.07631

[14] Vaswani A, Shazeer N, Parmar N, Uszkoreit J, Jones L, Gomez A N, Kaiser Ł and Polosukhin I 2017 Attention is all you need *Advances in Neural Information Processing Systems* pp 5998–608

[15] Khan S, Naseer M, Hayat M, Zamir S W, Khan F S and Shah M 2021 Transformers in vision: a survey arXiv:2001.05566

[16] Kolesnikov A 2021 An image is worth 16×16 words arXiv:2103.13915

[17] Zhang Y, Liu H and Hu Q 2021 TransFuse: fusing transformers and CNNs for medical image segmentation arXiv:2102.08005

[18] Kim T, Lee H and Kim D 2021 UACANet: uncertainty augmented context attention for polyp segmentation arXiv:2107.02368

[19] Ronneberger O, Fischer P and Brox T 2015 U-net: convolutional networks for biomedical image segmentation *International Conference on Medical Image Computing and Computer-Assisted Intervention* (Lecture Notes in Computer Science vol 9351) (Berlin: Springer) pp 234–41

[20] Simonyan K and Zisserman A 2015 Very deep convolutional networks for large-scale image recognition *Int. Conf. on Learning Representations* pp 1–14

[21] Chen L C, Papandreou G, Kokkinos I, Murphy K and Yuille A L 2018 DeepLab: semantic image segmentation with deep convolutional nets, atrous convolution, and fully connected CRFs *IEEE Trans. Pattern Anal. Mach. Intell.* **40** 834–48

[22] Chen L-C, Papandreou G, Kokkinos I, Murphy K and Yuille A L 2014 Semantic image segmentation with deep convolutional nets and fully connected CRFS arXiv:1412.7062

[23] Chen L-C, Papandreou G, Schroff F and Adam H 2017 Rethinking atrous convolution for semantic image segmentation arXiv:1706.05587

[24] Chen L C, Zhu Y, Papandreou G, Schroff F and Adam H 2018 Encoder–decoder with atrous separable convolution for semantic image segmentation *European Conference on Computer Vision* (Lecture Notes in Computer Science vol 11211) (Berlin: Springer) pp 833–51

[25] Minaee S, Boykov Y, Porikli F, Plaza A, Kehtarnavaz N and Terzopoulos D 2020 Image segmentation using deep learning: a survey arXiv:2001.05566

[26] Khan A, Sohail A, Zahoora U and Qureshi A S 2020 A survey of the recent architectures of deep convolutional neural networks *Artif. Intell. Rev.* **53** 1–87

[27] He K, Zhang X, Ren S and Sun J 2016 Deep residual learning for image recognition *2016 IEEE Conf. on Computer Vision and Pattern Recognition (CVPR)* pp 770–8

[28] Jadon S 2020 A survey of loss functions for semantic segmentation *IEEE Conf. on Computational Intelligence in Bioinformatics and Computational Biology (CIBCB 2020)* pp 1–7

[29] Nanni L, Lumini A, Ghidoni S and Maguolo G 2020 Stochastic selection of activation layers for convolutional neural networks *Sensors* **20** 1626

[30] Glorot X, Bordes A and Bengio Y 2011 Deep sparse rectifier neural networks *J. Mach. Learn. Res.* **15** 315–23

[31] Maas A L, Hannun A Y and Ng A Y 2013 Rectifier nonlinearities improve neural network acoustic models *ICML Workshop on Deep Learning for Audio, Speech and Language Processing (Atlanta, GA)* pp 16–21

[32] Clevert D A, Unterthiner T and Hochreiter S 2016 Fast and accurate deep network learning by exponential linear units (ELUs) *4th Int. Conf. on Learning Representations, ICLR 2016—Conf. Track Proc.* arXiv:1511.07289

[33] He K, Zhang X, Ren S and Sun J 2015 Delving deep into rectifiers: surpassing human-level performance on ImageNet classification *Proc. IEEE Int. Conf. on Computer Vision* pp 1026–34

[34] Jin X, Xu C, Feng J, Wei Y, Xiong J and Yan S 2016 Deep learning with S-shaped rectified linear activation units *30th AAAI Conf. on Artificial Intelligence* pp 1737–43

[35] Nanni L, Maguolo G, Brahnam S and Paci M 2021 Comparison of different convolutional neural network activation functions and methods for building ensembles arXiv:2103.15898

[36] Varkarakis V, Bazrafkan S and Corcoran P 2020 Deep neural network and data augmentation methodology for off-axis iris segmentation in wearable headsets *Neural Netw.* **121** 101–21

[37] Yao P, Shen S, Xu M, Liu P, Zhang F, Xing J, Shao P, Kaffenberger B and Xu R X 2021 Single model deep learning on imbalanced small datasets for skin lesion classification arXiv:2102.01284

[38] Chen P, Liu S, Zhao H and Jia J 2020 GridMask data augmentation arXiv:2001.04086

[39] Sánchez-Peralta L F, Picón A, Sánchez-Margallo F M and Pagador J B 2020 Unravelling the effect of data augmentation transformations in polyp segmentation *Int. J. Comput. Assist. Radiol. Surg.* **15** 1975–88

[40] Walawalkar D, Shen Z, Liu Z and Savvides M 2020 Attentive CutMix: an enhanced data augmentation approach for deep learning based image classification *IEEE Int. Conf. on Acoustics, Speech and Signal Processing—Proc.* arXiv:2003.13048

[41] Qin J, Fang J, Zhang Q, Liu W, Wang X and Wang X 2020 ResizeMix: mixing data with preserved object information and true labels arXiv:2012.11101

[42] Khan A M, Rajpoot N, Treanor D and Magee D 2014 A nonlinear mapping approach to stain normalization in digital histopathology images using image-specific color deconvolution *IEEE Trans. Biomed. Eng.* **61** 1729–38

[43] Huang C-H, Wu H-Y and Lin Y-L 2021 HarDNet-MSEG: a simple encoder-decoder polyp segmentation neural network that achieves over 0.9 mean Dice and 86 FPS arXiv:2101.07172

[44] Jha D, Smedsrud P H, Riegler M A, Halvorsen P, de Lange T, Johansen D and Johansen H D 2020 Kvasir-SEG: a segmented polyp dataset *MultiMedia ModelingLecture Notes in Computer Science* (Berlin: Springer)

[45] Bernal J, Sánchez F J, Fernández-Esparrach G, Gil D, Rodríguez C and Vilariño F 2015 WM-DOVA maps for accurate polyp highlighting in colonoscopy: validation vs saliency maps from physicians *Comput. Med. Imaging Graph.* **43** 99–111

[46] Silva J, Histace A, Romain O, Dray X and Granado B 2014 Toward embedded detection of polyps in WCE images for early diagnosis of colorectal cancer *Int. J. Comput. Assist. Radiol. Surg.* **9** 283–93

[47] Bernal J, Sánchez J and Vilariño F 2012 Towards automatic polyp detection with a polyp appearance model *Pattern Recognit.* **45** 3166–82

[48] Lumini A, Nanni L and Maguolo G 2021 Deep ensembles based on stochastic activations for semantic segmentation *Signals* **2** 820–33

[49] Tomar N K, Jha D, Ali S, Johansen H D, Johansen D, Riegler M A and Halvorsen P 2021 DDANet: dual decoder attention network for automatic polyp segmentation arXiv:2012.15245

[50] Zheng S *et al* 2020 Rethinking semantic segmentation from a sequence-to-sequence perspective with transformers arXiv:2012.15840

[51] Chen J, Lu Y, Yu Q, Luo X, Adeli E, Wang Y, Lu L, Yuille A L and Zhou Y 2021 TransUNet: transformers make strong encoders for medical image segmentation arXiv:2102.04306

Chapter 9

Identification of the onset of Parkinson's disease through a multiscale classification deep learning model utilizing a fusion of multiple conventional features with an nDS spatially exploited symmetrical convolutional pattern

Ranita Khumukcham and Gaurav Saxena

Parkinson's disease (PD) is a chronic neuropathological disorder caused by a lack of dopaminergic neurons in specific brain cell clusters. Individuals suffering from Parkinson's disease exhibit prominent signs and symptoms such as difficulty writing, walking and unusual vocal tremors. Because vocal tremors are commonly observed at the onset of the condition, various notable research efforts that employ speech and image-based methodologies are currently of interest among academics. The efficient distinction of a voice issue caused by Parkinson's disease from those caused by abuse of laryngeal vocal folds at the initial stage where Parkinson's disease is not prominent is a challenge for researchers. This chapter intends to give an extensive assessment of existing research works that integrate speech/acoustic data with different deep learning (DL) and machine learning (ML) approaches as a forerunner to addressing deficiencies and critical gaps in this field. Aside from one-dimensional (1D) ML techniques, methods that have used the 1D DL method, such as long short-term memory (LSTM), which is a recurrent neural network used to classify, process and make predictions based on the data, and 2D DL will be explored. It has been observed that 1D-based DL algorithms outperform state-of-the-art ML methods, despite being a relatively new methodology. Scalogram-image-based CNN architectures have the potential to outperform their 1D-based DL equivalents; however, relatively little research has been conducted. In this context, the current research provides an insight into a novel multiscale object detection and location architecture which is called multiscale-multiple-feature-convolution with hybrid n-dilation (MFCHnD). The proposed model uses 540 deep learning layers to learn from a wide range of features by using two unique attributes. First, by learning features from three different sizes of the same input image, i.e. $224 \times 22 \times 3$, $168 \times 168 \times 3$ and $112 \times 112 \times 3$. Thereafter, a three-stage, deep-feature fusion procedure is employed for combining features resulting from pruning of the three inputs. This is followed by a product fusion module (PFM) and an Additive Fusion Module (AFM) used together in a unique sequence to perform three-stage fusion. Second, a base-CNN learner network is suggested which uses a symmetrical arrangement of six different dilated learning module sequence (DLMS) capsules with max-pooling followed by depth concatenation to extract and learn a diverse set of features. The fully connected layer, softmax layer and a classification layer are the network of the final layers for providing the prediction of the input test image. The architecture is handcrafted such that rich feature sets can be extracted from small datasets of samples. Therefore the above mentioned base-CNN, downsampler, PFM and AFM modules are concatenated so as to enhance the accuracy, in particular for voice pathology samples. The efficiency of the proposed MFCHnD network is demonstrated by using a revised application relevant dataset that houses healthy, laryngeal voice pathology and Parkinson's disease (PD) voice samples. Compared to previous state-of-the-art deep learning models, the current architecture provides a superior performance for standard metrics such as sensitivity (99.74%), specificity (99.77%), precision (99.72%), FPR (0.23%), F_1 score (99.74%), MCC (99.49%) and kappa (99.15%).

9.1 Introduction

Parkinson's disease (PD) is a chronic neuropathic disorder produced in some clusters of the brain by the absence of dopaminergic neurons. Dopamine acts as a communicator between the human brain neurons. It aids the brain in sending signals to other areas, specifically signals related to the body's movement and speech. The symptoms of Parkinson's disease occur when large amounts of neurons are destroyed or when the dopamine level is incorrect. It has been observed that this neurological system dysfunction in elderly people is progressive [1]. The progression of Parkinson's disease spans five phases. The first phase is the mild phase, in which patients have the least interruption to their daily activities. Tremors and other symptoms are only present on one side of the body. The second stage is the moderate phase, during which patients begin to experience symptoms such as stiffness, tremors and shaking on both sides of the body. The mid phase is the third phase in which significant changes in body motion, such as balance loss and reduced reflexes, is noticed in addition to those found in the second phase. The fourth phase is the progressive phase, in which the patient's condition worsens and movement is accomplished with the use of mechanical aids such as a walker. The final stage is the most debilitating, with leg rigidity causing freezing when standing erect. Patients at this stage may also have symptoms such as hallucinations and delusions, as well as being unable to stand without falling. Most physicians use three types of motor movement tests to determine whether a patient has Parkinson's disease. They are (a) tremor, (b) trouble beginning movement and (c) stiffness in twisting the body.

Unfortunately, these symptoms appear at a very late stage of the disease, when the condition has become incurable. It is consequently critical to recognize the disease's development at an early stage [2, 3].

Vocal tremor is a typical symptom from the start among individuals who have the condition. Several noteworthy research attempts have been undertaken to discover Parkinson's disease from speech. So far it is thought to be the simplest approach to diagnose the condition since a patient just speaks into a microphone and allows a trained artificial intelligence (AI) to detect the ailment. Vocal shakiness, inaccurate articulation, decreased vocal amplitude and breathiness are some commonly observed signs and symptoms [4]. The amount of vocal impairment can be measured using running speech or continuous vowel phonations. The diagnosis of this condition by voice impairments is highly common since the telemonitoring and telediagnostic systems based on voice signals are relatively inexpensive and simple to use, reducing physical visits to clinics and therefore the strain on medical professionals. Using machine learning, three operations are used to discover the Parkinson's disease, namely data processing, features extraction and classification [5–13].

Several speech signal processing approaches have been employed in research to extract clinically important characteristics, which were then input into various machine learning algorithms to obtain reliable categorization. The most often utilized architectures in PD classification are support vector machines (SVMs) [14, 15] and artificial neural networks (ANNs), however, random forest (RF) [16] and k-nearest neighbors (k-NN) [17] are also appropriate. The success of the aforementioned algorithms is directly dependent on the quality of the data characteristics or features utilized. Manually selecting the appropriate characteristics that capture the fundamental qualities of the voice data is tedious. Deep learning may be used to automatically learn the latent characteristics of the data. The hierarchical layers of deep neural networks (DNNs) can provide abstract representations that are analogous to machine learning features. There have also been a few studies that have used deep learning to detect Parkinson's disease [18–21]. Deep learning is well suited to the early PD diagnosis because of it ability to construct complex and non-linear correlations from data.

Despite several research studies on voice pathology, it is yet to be proven in real-time settings. This is mostly due to the fact that a vocal tremor can also be caused by a physically mistreated vocal folds or a respiratory disease. According to our knowledge, there is a dearth of studies that can identify a PD-affected voice from aberrant voices caused by vocal folds or pulmonary diseases. Because vocal tremors are often seen during the onset of the PD, a number of significant research projects that utilize speech and image-based techniques are now gaining traction among academics. It is difficult for researchers to distinguish a voice problem caused by Parkinson's disease from one produced by misuse of the laryngeal vocal folds at the initial stage when Parkinson's disease is not completely visible.

The chapter is arranged as follows. The first part presents the introduction, a comprehensive literature review and contributions from the current work. The second section describes the suggested architecture in detail. The third section discusses the implementation procedure and the findings of the current research. The fourth section is the conclusion.

9.1.1. A comprehensive literature review

Various research groups around the world have attempted to identify Parkinson's disease by utilizing methods such as EEG [22, 23], speech signals [1, 2, 24–26], magnetic resonance imaging (MRI) [27], handwriting and gait signals [28, 29]. Among these processes, speech processing and analysis is considered the most advantageous method for initial identification of Parkinson disease since vocal pathology can be discovered in an individual even before a medical diagnosis has begun [4, 30]. PD disturbs the complex layers of speech, such as phonation and articulation, which aid in the creation of pure speech and the differentiation of resonance, prosody and speech sounds. Initially, it disrupts the normal functioning of the vocal folds, resulting in aberrant air volume and pitch. The articulatory component which is connected directly to the formation or production of speech signals via respiration is therefore impacted. The acoustic voice samples of Parkinson's disease patients who exhibit vocal difficulties is known as hypokinetic dysarthria [31].

The voice of a PD patient is usually more monotonous and there are disfluencies in sentence construction. As per the report, patients often find it difficult to articulate consonants such as b, d, g, t, k and p [31, 32]. The delivery of vowels is also hampered, and substantial differences between vowels are discovered, as well as a loss in sensitivity. The phonation, pitch and strength of prolonged vowels are unstable, and the tone becomes harsh. Researchers have made use of different types of features and machine learning classifiers for detecting the presence of Parkinson's disease [2, 24, 25, 31–33].

Machine learning methods for the diagnosis of PD. The selection of suitable feature extraction and DL methods is essential as it affects the overall performance of the PD classification method directly.

Many reported research works have utilized the same dataset of 31 occurrences (23 PD patients and eight healthy persons) with 195 sound recordings which is available [7]. Another Parkinson's disease dataset has 40 sample with 20 PD patients and 20 healthy people with numerous voice recordings [25]. Both datasets contain characteristics in common, such as fundamental frequency, amplitude, etc. The features derived are commonly known as baseline features. Tunable Q-factor wavelet transform (TQWT), Mel Frequency Cepstral Coefficient (MFCC) and signal-to-noise ratio (SNR) are some key methods for feature extraction from speech in order to diagnose Parkinson's disease [34]. Most studies employ a mixture of different feature types to accomplish classification tasks.

PD patients mostly experience vocal causalities, which have a direct impact on voice loudness, instability and frequency irregularity. Other flaws that might be detected include voice breaks and poor vocal quality. Several machine learning based studies on the detection of Parkinson's disease using voice characteristics have been conducted during the last decade. Tsanas *et al* [34] suggests a technique to discover Parkinson's disease by combining voice characteristics with multiple feature selection approaches to pick the top ten features as the model's inputs. Lease absolute shrinkage and selection operator (LASSO), relief and local learning based feature selection (LLBFS) were utilized to extract features that were then used to train RF and SVM learners. Using harmonic-to-noise ratios (HNRs), shimmer and vocal fold excitation characteristics, they achieved a precision of 98.6%.

Little *et al* [7] proposed pitch period entropy (PPE), a robust measure of dysphonia that performs well in a loud and uncontrolled setting. The data for their investigation was obtained from 31 participants (23 were Parkinson's disease patients and the rest were healthy) and consisted of 195 sustained vowel phonations. They screened features first, then utilized the ten most uncorrelated measures to choose the best feasible combination of characteristics. It was discovered that four different combinations gave the best categorization result. Their model has a 91.4% accuracy rate. It was discovered that combining HNRs with non-standard techniques is quite helpful.

Tsanas *et al* [34] evaluated the performance of several classification approaches so as to properly detect Parkinson's disease. They employed the decision tree, regression, DMneural and neural network classifiers, achieving accuracies of 84.3%, 88.6%, 84.3% and 92.9%, respectively. They did, however, utilize an unusual method of dividing the training and testing samples, which is 65%:35%.

Das [35] suggested models using various prominent measures such as accuracy, specificity and sensitivity. The trained k-NN classifier performed the best, with a score of 93.82%.

Rouzbahani and Daliri [36] developed a method for differentiating between normal and Parkinson's disease individuals. The dimension of the feature vector was decreased in their study, and optimal features were produced using a genetic algorithm (GA), with k-NN utilized for classification.

Sakar *et al* [13] proposed a methodology for categorizing healthy and Parkinson's disease individuals. Data for their study were gathered from 40 participants, 20 of whom were abnormal and 20 of whom were healthy. Each participant was required to record 26 voice samples, which included words, brief phrases, numerals and sustained vowels. The values 1, 3, 5 and 7 were used for k in the k-NN classifier, while linear and radial basis function (RBF) kernels were employed in the SVM. The accuracies attained by k-NN and SVM were 82.50% and 85%, respectively.

Shirvan and Tahami [37] proposed a method to detect Parkinson's disease. To give the significance scores of the features, a multi-layer perceptron (MLP) with a customized cost function was trained. As a result, 20 features with high significance ratings were fed into a Lagrangian SVM for classification. The total implementation of the suggested hybrid MLP-LSVM was compared to other similar research, and the findings indicated a 100% accuracy rate.

The dataset [38] for their investigation included 197 voice samples from which 22 characteristics were retrieved. They employed a variety of classification models, including PLS, k-NN, LDA, SVM and ID3. The accuracy of the k-NN and LDA classifiers was greater than 90%. The random tree, on the other hand, was 100% accurate.

In another paper [39] the authors proposed techniques which employ a two-layer ANN-based MLP network. It was discovered that the SVM generated more significant findings than the MLP. Linear SVM and puk kernels were employed, yielding accuracies of 91.79% and 93.33%, respectively. An accuracy rate of 92.31% was obtained for the MLP classifier.

Gil and Manuel [40] utilized an SVM supervised machine learning technique to differentiate between Parkinson's disease and healthy individuals. They utilized Weka, a data mining tool. Before using the classification method, the dataset [38] was preprocessed. A random split was repeated several times until the highest possible accuracy on the various kernel values was obtained using libsvm.

Bhattacharya and Bhatia [41] utilized MLP and RBF techniques for classification. The network was trained with 112 phonations and tested with 24 phonations. When matched to the MLP, the RBF network produced better results. The MLP network generated an accuracy of 86.66%, whereas the RBF network delivered an efficiency of 90.12%.

Shahbakhi *et al* [15] suggested an algorithm for Parkinson's disease diagnosis in which the genetic algorithm was used to identify optimum characteristics from the [38] dataset. The optimized features were trained using a linear SVM classifier, yielding an accuracy of 94.5%.

Rani and Holi [42] proposed a technique for predicting Parkinson's disease. They also utilized the Weka tool to apply the methods suggested in [39] for pre-processing, categorization and analysis of findings in the dataset. In various combinations, they employed the MLP, Adaboost and k-NN classifiers. It has been proven that a combination of k-NN+MLP and k-NN+Adaboost yielded 91.28%.

Sakar *et al* [25] used the TQWT on voice signals to diagnose Parkinson's disease. Studies were conducted using numerous voice examples acquired from 252 persons, and various sorts of feature sets were retrieved from these cases. Furthermore, when the mRmR selection was used, the combination of MFCC and TQWT characteristics improved the classification performance.

Mathur *et al* [43] demonstrated a novel approach for detecting early indications of Parkinson's disease using speech analysis. The SVM, random forest, naive Bayes (NB) and neural network techniques were utilized. The accuracies of the SVM with a RBF kernel and neural network were 92.38% and 91.10%, respectively.

Mostafa et al [26] presented a method that identified the 11 top features in another major study. A ten-fold cross-validation technique was utilized with the NB, RF and neural network classifiers. It was discovered that random forest produced the best accuracy of 99.492%. The neural network, SVM and NB, on the other hand, achieved accuracies of 96.50%, 95.43% and 89.340%, respectively.

Braga *et al* [44] used the ensemble technique of learning for the categorization of Parkinson's disease. Min–max normalization was used to normalize the data. The necessary characteristics were chosen using mRMR and recurssive feature elimination (RFE). To complete the task, the selected characteristics were supplied to the classifiers. The XGBoost with mRMR approach obtained the best accuracy of 95.39%.

Nissar *et al* [45] used the dataset in [25] to find highly correlated features using linear discriminant analysis (LDA) and principal component analysis (PCA).

The random and grid search algorithms were used to optimize performance, and it was discovered that the grid search performed better. PCA outperformed LDA in terms of performance as well. The AdaBoost classifier attained the maximum accuracy of 94% when utilizing grid search and ten-fold cross-validation.

Anisha and Arulanand [46] utilized ANN and k-NN to separate between the samples of Parkinson's disease and healthy samples. Their samples for the ANN were split in ratios of 70:25:5, with 70% used for training, 25% used for testing and 5% maintained for validation. They had a mean accuracy of 96.7%. The samples for the k-NN were split in the ratio 70:30, i.e. 70% for training and 30% for testing. They attained 79.31% accuracy by using the cosine distance function and setting the value of k to 1.

Asmae [47] suggests a framework for the initial detection of Parkinson's disease. They used the RFE technique to pick features from the dataset in [8]. The SVM, ANN and classification and regression tree classifiers were employed. Without proper feature selection, these classifiers achieved mean accuracies of 79.98%, 80.25% and 85.23%, respectively. The mean accuracies were increased to 93.84%, 91.54% and 90.76%, respectively, after using a suitable feature selection procedure.

Deep learning methods for diagnosis of PD. There have been a few research papers that have used deep learning in PD investigations. The work by [48] presents a DNN classifier made up of a stacked autoencoder (SAE) and a softmax layer. While the SAE was used to extract data from speech characteristics, the softmax layer was utilized to evaluate the encoded data in order to categorize the patients. Several tests were carried out using two different datasets so as to clarify the performance. When the findings were compared against state-of-the-art machine learning models, the experimental results revealed that the DNN classifier offered the best diagnosis.

Another Parkinson's disease diagnosis study relies on the DNN's efficacy [49]. The data utilized in this investigation include digital biomarkers and voice records gathered from PD and non-PD patients using a smartphone application.

Because Parkinson's disease is caused by a brain malfunction, EEG signals are the most important indications for early detection of the disease. Another automated detection approach for Parkinson's disease using CNN was proposed in [50]. In their study, the EEG data of 20 Parkinson's disease patients and 20 healthy people were input into a 13-layer CNN architecture to identify Parkinson's disease. They achieved 88.25% accuracy, 91.77% specificity and 84.71% sensitivity, respectively.

For signal processing, the authors of [51] suggested a one-dimensional CNN architecture. They avoided using signal processing for the feature extraction stage, allowing them to work with raw voice data. Some modifications were made to a dataset during the network's training. The full recording was analyzed without phoneme selection, and windowing was applied, where the signal of the voice was split into 20 ms of window, each with an overlap, and each window was being used as data input individually. The final categorization was carried out using a majority vote system. The data were trained using 85% of the windows and validated with 15%. The binary categorization of illness development attained a classification accuracy of 83.63% between the succeeding phases at the window level. The binary categorization was performed utilizing the technique between the extremity levels, with 80.5% accuracy.

Frid *et al* [52] presented a diagnosis of Parkinson's disease known as deep belief network (DBN). The DBN was made up of two stacked restricted Boltzmann machines (RBMs) with an output layer. It was discovered that 8700 iterations of supervised learning were required to achieve a steady state of MSE. Their proposed approach obtained 94% accuracy.

Fatlawi *et al* [53] presented a deep learning based model for finding the extremity of Parkinson's disease. The data were obtained from 42 individuals, with 200 recordings made from each patient for a total of 5875 voice recordings. There were sixteen speech biological characteristics in the sample. Min–max normalization was used to normalize the voice data. Normalized data were utilized for training and testing in proportions of 80% and 20%, respectively.

Deep learning was used by Grover *et al* [54] to categorize data into PD and control individuals. They made use of the DNN and LSTM models. Several tests were performed on the dataset to identify the best network settings, which ultimately enhanced network performance. Their findings were compared to traditional machine learning methods. It was discovered that LSTM and DNN could give 99.03% and 97.12% accuracy, respectively.

Rizvi et al [55] presented an approach by utilizing grid search optimization to create a model of deep learning to discover Parkinson's disease in its early stages. It was discovered that after successfully fine-tuning the model, a test accuracy of 89.23% was obtained, with an average accuracy of 91.69% recorded.

9.1.2 Contributions

In this work a multiscale object detection architecture which is abbreviated as MFCHnD is presented. It can learn a wide variety of features in comparison to reported architectures. In order to extract features in MFCHnD, a base-CNN network having 280 layers is proposed, which uses six unique combinations of convolutional kernel sizes and dilation factors. The repeated use of these combination variants enlarges the field-of-reception differently each time, so that different kinds of features can be extracted from a single image. As a result of this the number of parameters involved is reduced, which leads to a speed up in the training process. It will be further shown in a later section how these unique combinations are used with max-pooling layers to further increase the training speed. It would not be sufficient to say that this mode of feature extraction is only for a single image, the current architecture concurrently extracts such features from a total of three images. The size of the second image has a 0.25% reduction in comparison to the first image and, similarly, the third image has a 0.25% reduction against the second image. Therefore this style of multiscale feature extraction results in two times more than the number of features in comparison to earlier models that use only a single input image. Needless to say this will be conducive for learning multivarient information as well. A total of $280 \times 3 = 840$ layers, which does not include the final prediction layers, thus take part in learning. On top of this, three deep-feature fusion procedures are undertaken to combine the features derived from the first, second and third image's depth-concatenation layers into a single platform.

In summary, the techniques used for combining several features are depth-wise concatenation, product and addition of features. Taking advantage of this unique architecture, and the goodness of the fully connected softmax classification layer stack, the proposed model sees a very good increase in the mean accuracy and per-class accuracy against previous state-of-the-art approaches.

9.2 Proposed methodology

The proposed framework is composed of three major stages, which are as follows. (A) *Retrieval of voice samples*—For the differentiation of Parkinson's disease speech samples from healthy and laryngeal voice samples, the speech samples will be retrieved from the research works reported earlier [56, 57]. (B) *Pre-processing*—In this phase the training samples will be split up into several segments after which all the segments will be transformed into the two-dimensional (2D) scalogram format. (C) *Training*—In this phase the scalograms will be used for training a multiscale deep learning model that will be able to distinguish healthy or laryngeal voice pathology from Parkinson's disease. These processes are discussed in detail in the following subsections.

9.2.1 Retrieval of voice samples

The current research will use speech samples from two standard sources, namely (a) the Parkinson's disease dataset [56] and (b) the Voice ICar fEDerico II (VOICED) dataset [57]. The first dataset houses healthy and Parkinson's affected voice samples, which will form two classification classes, while the second dataset houses different types of voice pathology samples which are associated with laryngeal abnormalities, and therefore its samples will be grouped under the laryngeal voice pathology class. For initial detection of Parkinson's disease, the algorithm will be trained to identify three distinct classification classes with a very high accuracy, i.e. healthy, Parkinson's disease and laryngeal pathology. A description of these datasets is provided below.

(a) *The Parkinson's disease dataset* [56]. This dataset consists of voice samples gathered from three different categories of people. The first set of samples were collected from fifteen individuals who were healthy and were aged in the range 19–29 years. There are 46 voice samples in this set, which were gathered by making everyone read three texts of average duration 44.07 s, 43.90 s and 45.90 s. The second set of samples were collected from 22 individuals who were healthy and were aged in the range 60–77 years. Similarly, this set also has 349 voice samples. However, the samples of this set have varying duration, i.e. from as low as 43.16 s to 148.83 s. The third set of samples was collected from 28 individuals suffering from Parkinson's disease (PD) aged between 40–80 years. This set has 437 voice samples of varying lengths, with the shortest being 45.35 s and the longest being 242.50 s. For each category the individuals were made to read Italian phonemically balanced text, phrases, words and sustained vowels. This dataset is quite comprehensive and has ample signal duration for performing classification.

For the current work, all the young and elderly healthy voice samples were placed in a single class, which is the healthy class. This results in the formation of healthy and Parkinson's categories with 395 and 437 voice samples, respectively

(b) *The VOICED dataset* [57]. This is a relatively new database and was jointly developed by the Institute of High-Performance Computing and Networking of the Italian National Research Council (ICAR-CNR) and the University Hospital of Naples (Federico II). This dataset is composed of 55 healthy and 151 pathological voice samples. The voice samples had 32 bit and 85 kHz resolution. The pathological speech samples were further subdivided into reflux laryngitis, hyperkinetic dysphonia and hypokinetic dysphonia. For the current work, all 151 pathological voice samples in this dataset are placed in the laryngeal pathology class.

9.2.2 Pre-processing

The samples retrieved from the above datasets are placed in three different categories (healthy, laryngeal pathology and Parkinson's disease) as mentioned in table 9.1. The lengths of the healthy and PD voice samples are quite long and distributed rather unevenly. Thus the samples residing in these two classes are segmented into small samples of length 1 s, and the samples having lengths of less than 1 s are discarded to maintain uniformity. A total of 8652 segmented healthy samples and 10 510 PD samples are obtained by applying this segmentation method. On the other hand, all the laryngeal pathology voice samples have a uniform length of 4.76 s.

These samples are segmented into four equal length samples of length roughly 1 s (approximated from the actual 1.19 s). Applying this segmentation method, a total of 604 segmented samples are obtained for this class. The number of laryngeal pathology samples is significantly less than the other two classes and may be prone to high variance or overfitting. The current study will also dwell on this aspect.

The next stage is the transformation of the segmented voice samples residing in each of these three classes into Morse scalogram 2D images. A wavelet transformation decomposes an input segmented voice sample into the time-domain by applying various resolutions instead of decomposing into the frequency domain. In this transformation, each value of the time-axis is related to a frequency band that may result if a short-time Fourier transform (STFT) is employed. A time-shifted signal is produced by applying the wavelet with a mother wavelet (m).

Table 9.1. Summary of the training and test samples.

Class	Original	Training	Testing	Total	Source
Healthy	395	6922	1730	8652	[57]
Laryngeal pathology	151	483	121	604	[57]
Parkinson's disease	437	8408	2102	10 510	[56]
Total	**983**	**15 813**	**3953**	**19 766**	

The continuous wavelet transform (CWT) of a given signal having function $f(t)$ is evaluated by using the mother wavelet through the expression

$$\mathrm{CWT}(x, y) = \frac{1}{\sqrt{x}} \int_{-\alpha}^{+\alpha} f(t)^* m\left(\frac{t - y}{x}\right) dt, \qquad (9.1)$$

where x and y are the scaling and shifting factors for the mother wavelet and $*$ signifies the convolution operation. The above expression can be translated as an integration of the summation of the input audio sample multiplied by the time scaled and shifted forms of the mother wavelet (m).

The Morse wavelet is chosen for the current work because it displays strong localization in both the frequency and temporal domains, making it ideal for studying localized discontinuities.

The Fourier transform of a Morse wavelet is expressed as

$$m_{d, \eta}(\omega) = \xi(\omega)\alpha_{d, \eta}\omega^{\frac{d^2}{\eta}}e^{-\omega^\eta}, \qquad (9.2)$$

where $\xi(\omega)$ is a unit step function, d^2 is the time–bandwidth product, $\alpha_{d, \eta}$ signifies the normalization constant and η is the symmetry parameter. Different combinations of d^2 and η can produce diverse Morse wavelets.

The current study is motivated by the need to demonstrate that a 2D image format of brief duration has enough information to categorize multiple classes when fed to a deep convolutional neural network. For each input 2D scalogram image, every layer of CNN extracts n activation maps, each of which depicts the input image in n distinct ways. Segmented voice samples have also been implemented successfully by researchers in [57, 58].

9.2.3 Proposed multiscale multiple feature convolution with hybrid n-dilations (MMFCHnD) architecture

Related works. The use of dilated convolutional layers has been hailed with enthusiasm by many researchers working in the area of computer vision. Researchers also reported a reduction of 96% in the number of parameters in the ResNet base-network with faster convergence when the non-dilated convolutions were replaced by dilated ones [59]. The above literary works, however, does not consider the gridding effect arising from repeated stacking of convolution layers, which may cause a partial loss of continuity in the image. As a remedy, the authors of [60] replaced the non-dilated convolution kernels of ResNet with dilated ones, and also completely did away with max-pooling layers. This arrangement reduced the amount of high-amplitude and high-frequency features that may propagate through the lower layers thereby reducing the gridding effect. The authors of [61] used dilated CNN for denoising images while reducing the effect. Dilated CNNs have also been employed successfully in detecting license plates by extracted multiscale features for reducing computation cost [62].

Proposed architecture. An illustration of the suggested classification architecture is shown in figure 9.1. It learns features using three different sizes and a proposed

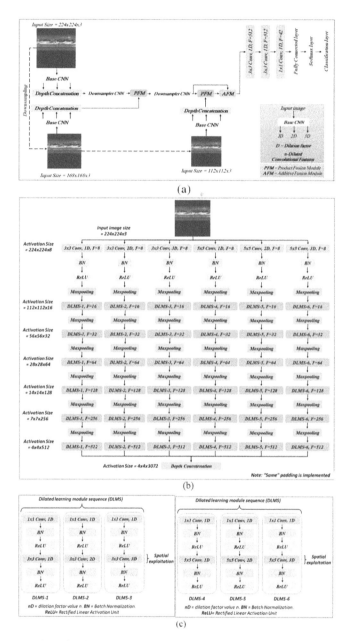

Figure 9.1. (a) Proposed multiscale-MFCHnD architecture. (b) Dilated learning multiple sequence (DLMS) capsules. (c) Proposed base-CNN network.

base-CNN architecture. It is thus multiscale, unlike popular deep CNN models such as VGG-16 and ResNet-50 which used repeated stacks of vanilla-CNN layers to learn from a single image. Semantically strong deep features are produced by repeated stacking of a combination of max-pooling layers after conventional CNN blocks, but lose out on vital discriminative features that are likely to differentiate different classes. A unique feature extraction strategy is presented in the current section. Initially, an image is downsampled into three different sizes $224 \times 224 \times 3$, $168 \times 168 \times 3$ and $112 \times 112 \times 3$. The image's width and height are scaled by a factor of 1/4 to obtain the second image size of $168 \times 168 \times 3$. Then the image with dimensions $168 \times 168 \times 3$ is again scaled by the same factor resulting in the third image of size $112 \times 112 \times 3$. The second and third sets of bounding boxes are also scaled by the same factor over two steps using the first set which is meant for the first image. It can be seen in figure 9.1(a) that the three input images are passed to a common base-CNN learner which uses multiple mixtures of non-dilated and dilated convolutional layer sequences. Due to the use of multiple combinations of kernel size (K) and dilation factor (D), the network is trained to learn a wide variety of features. Three dilation factors are used, i.e. dilation factors one (1Df), two (2Df) and three (3Df). These dilation factors are paired with three kernel sizes, i.e. 1×1, 3×3 and 5×5, to produce richer discriminative features, and hence the term 'nDs' or 'n-dilations spatial exploitation property'. Then, the extracted features, obtained after using these dilated convolutional neural networks, are concatenated depthwise. These kinds of base-CNN and depth-concatenation pairings are also implemented on the other two downsampled images. The features extracted by the three image–CNN set-ups are now fused over three stages before applying to the final bounding box prediction layers. The first fusion is carried out between the first and second image–CNN pair through a product fusion module (PFM). However, before fusing, the activation maps produced by the first image–CNN pair is downsampled to match the size of the maps produced by the second pair. The composition of this downsampler CNN is three layers—batch normalization (BN), convolutional layer and rectified linear unit (ReLU). In the second fusion process, the activation maps obtained from the first PFM block are again subjected to another downsampler CNN network having parameters different from that of the previous one. Another PFM block computes the new activation map by using the derivatives from the first fusion process and that of the third image–CNN pair. Finally, in the third stage the features derived from the second downsampler CNN network are fused with the output from the latest PFM block through an additive fusion module (AFM). The PFM and AFM are based on the product and addition of activation feature maps, respectively, and have complementary benefits, and therefore the use of the third fusion stage will provide another unique set of rich feature. The final stage includes a fully connected layer having dimensions equal to the number of classes desired for classification, a softmax layer and a classification layer.

The base-CNN architecture. The base-CNN learner network proposed in this work has multiple columns of shallow CNN layers. It is a small network which can be implemented in real-time without placing many restrictions on low resource systems. Moreover, for the current application it provided a lower latency. To be precise, a repetition of the vanilla-CNN structure with a max-pooling layer is used so as to extract the feature and the size of the activation map can be reduced to half of it. This form of arrangement results in faster learning. The loss due to halving of the feature map sizes is compensated by increasing the number of filters by a factor of 2 at each stage of the vanilla-CNN with the max-pooling stack. Two different, yet parasitic, settings are employed for extracting rich features from the proposed network. The first is the use of the 3×3 and 5×5 convolutional kernels, and the second is the use of the 1D, 2D and 3D dilation factors. The core structure of the base-CNN shown in figure 9.1(b) is used for all three input images. However, the dimensions of the activation maps will vary due to the varying input sizes. The structure is explained below.

Initially, the image is applied to six convolutional layers having different values of convolution kernel–dilation factor pair. However, all of the six layers have an initial feature size equal to 8. Starting from the left column and proceeding to the right-most column, the first convolution layer has kernel filter number (S) equal to 8 and dilation factor (D) as 1. The second layer has $S = 3$, $D = 2$; the third layer has $S = 3$, $D = 3$; the fourth layer has $S = 5$, $D = 1$; the fifth layer has $S = 5$, $D = 2$; and the sixth layer has $S = 5$, $D = 3$. The six convolutional features are followed by BN, ReLU and max-pooling layers. These six columns are arranged in a symmetrical fashion meaning that each level of every column carries out the same function. In each column a dilated learning module sequence (DLMS) which has a unique combination of S and D is used six times up to the depth-concatenation layer. For example, the left-most stack/column utilizes the DLMS-1 block six times with a max-pooling layer in between each of them. It is worth noting that all the max-pooling layers have the same parameters and this reduces the feature map by half. This can be observed from the size of the activation maps at each stage. The number of filters increases by a factor of 2 for a single increase in the number of DLMS-1 blocks, with the first block having 16 and the last having 512 filters. A similar arrangement of the DLMS modules and max-pooling layers is seen in the remaining five stacks/columns as well. Therefore, a total of six DLMS modules are implemented in our base-CNN network, which are: DLMS-1, DLMS-2, DLMS-3, DLMS-4, DLMS-5 and DLMS-6. All of the convolutional layers used in the base-network have the 'same-padding' arrangement so that for a particular row, all of the DLMS blocks will result in the same activation size. The outputs from the bottom-row DLMS blocks are combined using a depth-wise concatenation arrangement thereby resulting in the formation of $512 \times 6 = 3072$ filters. Since each of the six columns has a shallow depth feature-size reduction capability with multiple types of spatial feature extraction, the network is both speedy and more accurate.

n-dilated convolution. At the heart of our base-CNN learner network is the use of a dilated convolutional layer which is mathematically expressed by

$$y(m, n) = \sum_{i=1}^{M} \sum_{j=1}^{N} x(m + r \times i, n + r \times j)w(i, j), \tag{9.3}$$

where $y(m, n)$ is the output with respect to the input x having length m and width n, and w is a filter having dimensions i and j. Finally, r is the dilation factor which is $\geqslant 2$, if $r = 1$ then it is called normal convolution.

The use of a dilation factor greater than 2 has brought about a significant increase in accuracy.

Dilated learning module sequence (DLMS). This is a capsule consisting of two convolutional layers where one normalizes for reducing overfitting and learning undilated features, and the other extracts dilated features and also serves as an optimizer. Three dilation factors are employed, which are 1, 2 and 3. The proposed base-CNN network employs six DLMS capsules as shown in figures 9.1(c) and (d). All of them have a 1×1 convolution layer with a dilation factor equal to 1 which is followed by BN and an ReLU layer. The DLMS-1, 2 and 3 are shown together since they use the same 3×3 kernel size, but with different dilation factors 1, 2 or 3. Similarly, the DLMS-4, 5 and 6 belong to a different group since all of them use the same 5×5 kernel size. These capsules serve as the main feature extractor in our base-CNN network thus featuring as the chief factor in the class-detection process. The use of DLMS capsules followed by max-pooling layer speeds up the network while avoiding overfitting.

The product fusion module (PFM). Two feature models are introduced for fusing features arriving from the three images' input variants so that the network is trained to learn multiscale features. One of them is the PFM, and the other is the AFM as shown in figure 9.1(a). In the current work, almost all forms of fusion are considered, i.e. concatenation, element-wise product and sum. An element-wise product of features arriving from two different image inputs forms the PFM block. This is because multiplying any two different weights will provide a better result than simply adding them. A ReLu layer and a convolution layer are also used with the PFM block so that the new features are generated and normalized properly before passing into the deeper layers of the network. Supposing I is the input image from which features F_k are extracted from the kth layer. Then the features formed by fusing with another feature G_k are

$$\text{fused1}_k = \varphi(\beta(F_k) \otimes \beta(G_k)), \tag{9.4}$$

where fused_k are the new features realized after fusion, $\varphi_k(.)$ is a function denoting ReLU and $\beta_k(.)$ is the BN function. The use of the PFM has the capability for harnessing the discriminative potential of multiscale inputs.

The additive fusion module (AFM). This is another feature fusion module used in our object detection architecture shown in figure 9.1(a). Its function is to further integrate the features formed by the first PFM block with the result of the second PFM block. An element-wise addition operator is the core of the AFM block. It is followed by an ReLU operation which connects to a convolutional layer for further normalization. It is mathematically expressed by

$$\text{fused2}_k = \varphi(\phi_k(\text{fused1}_k - 1) \oplus \beta(\text{fused1}_k)), \tag{9.5}$$

where φ is the ReLU activation function, $\phi_k(.)$ is a sequential function performed by convolutional and BN layers, and $\beta(.)$ is a BN function.

9.3 Experimental results and discussion

9.3.1 Evaluation metrics

Accuracy. This is the simplest and most common metric for model evaluation. It is the ratio of the correct prediction which is the sum of true positive (TP) and true negative (TN) to the total number of predictions of the given dataset or samples, which is given by

$$\text{accuracy} = \frac{\text{TP} + \text{TN}}{\text{TP} + \text{TN} + \text{FP} + \text{FN}}. \tag{9.6}$$

Sensitivity (recall): This identifies the actual number of positive samples of all the positives samples. It is also called as the true positive rate (TPR) and is given by

$$\text{sensitivity} = \frac{\text{TP}}{\text{TP} + \text{FN}}. \tag{9.7}$$

Specificity: This identifies the actual number of negative samples of all the negative samples. Here it is more important to classify the negative than to classify the positive. So it is also called the true negative rate (TNR):

$$\text{specificity} = \frac{\text{TN}}{\text{TN} + \text{FP}}. \tag{9.8}$$

Precision: This is the ratio of the true positives to all the positives of the samples:

$$\text{precision} = \frac{\text{TP}}{\text{TP} + \text{FP}}. \tag{9.9}$$

False positive rate: This is the probability that a positive result is predicted when the true value is negative which is a false prediction:

$$\text{FPR} = \frac{\text{FP}}{\text{FP} + \text{TN}}. \tag{9.10}$$

F_1-score: This combines the precision and recall of the samples which is given by the harmonic mean of precision and recall and is known as the Dice similarity coefficient (DSC). It gives better performance for unbalanced dataset:

$$F_1 = \frac{2\text{TP}}{2\text{TP} + \text{FP} + \text{FN}}. \tag{9.11}$$

Matthews correlation coefficient: This is a measure of a binary classification's quality. It gives the best result for unbalanced classes while taking into consideration the TPs, TNs, FPs and FNs:

$$\text{MCC} = \frac{\text{TP} \times \text{TN} - \text{FP} \times \text{FN}}{\sqrt{(\text{TP} + \text{FP})(\text{TP} + \text{FN})(\text{TN} + \text{FP})(\text{TN} + \text{FN})}}. \tag{9.12}$$

Cohen's kappa index: This is used to measure the fidelity of two raters. If the values are less than zero then there is no agreement and if it is between 0.81 and 1 then there is perfect agreement:

$$\text{CKI} = \frac{p_o - p_e}{1 - p_e} = 1 - \frac{1 - p_o}{1 - p_e}. \tag{9.13}$$

9.3.2 Development of the training and testing images

The proposed multiscale-multiclass voice pathology classification model is implemented with a total of 19 766 samples (description in table 9.1). The number of samples that will undergo training and testing for each class is divided up in the ratio of 80%:20%, respectively. The training and testing samples are kept in two separate folders, thereby making the test samples unseen during the training process. The training samples are further divided up in the ratio of 85%:15% within the program to differentiate training samples from the validation samples. Following this splitting format, the healthy class houses 6922 and 1730 training and test samples, respectively. Similarly, the laryngeal pathology class houses 483 and 121 training and testing samples, respectively. Finally, the Parkinson's disease class has 8408 and 2102 training and test samples, respectively. These values are also listed in table 9.1. All of the 19 766 segmented voice samples are transformed into the Morse scalogram 2D image format by using a filter bank with using symmetry value 3 and time–bandwidth product 60. The value of 3 is chosen for the present implementation because of its ability to impart zero skewness and produce wavelets with perfect symmetry in the frequency domain. This set of parameters is employed to produce 19 766 Morse scalograms.

9.3.3 Deep learning training details

We use a straightforward approach to train the MFCHnD-net as an end-to-end structure. The stochastic gradient descent (SGD) technique is applied with a fixed learning rate of 0.001 during training. The upper limit for stopping the training is fixed as 150 epochs. The minibatch size is set as 8. The loss function is

$$L(\theta) = \frac{1}{2N} \sum_{i=1}^{N} \|Z(X_i; \theta) - Z_i^{GT}\|_2^2, \tag{9.14}$$

where N is the size of the training batch, $Z(X_i; \theta)$ is the output generated by using the model's parameters (θ), X_i is the input image and Z_i^{GT} is the ground truth result due to the input image.

The number of training and validation samples taking part in the training are summarized in table 9.2.

The training progress plot of the proposed deep learning architecture is shown in figure 9.2. It took roughly 57 min for the model's validation accuracy and validation

Table 9.2. Summarization of the number of training, validation and testing scalogram samples.

Class	Training	Validation	Testing	Total
Healthy	5833	1089	1730	8652
Laryngeal pathology	410	73	121	604
Parkinson's disease	7146	1262	2102	10 510
Total	**13 389**	**2424**	**3953**	**19 766**

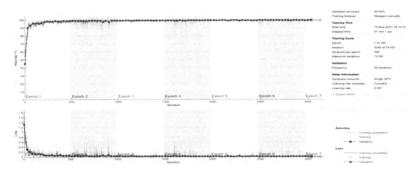

Figure 9.2. Training progress of the proposed model.

loss to completely flatten. The model starts to provide very good validation accuracy at the advent of the third epoch itself. However, for extracting the best performance, the model is trained further until the all the loss and accuracy curves flatten completely.

9.3.4 Implementation results

Standard architectures such as GoogLeNet, ImageNet and ResNet have reported an error rate of greater than 6%. Moreover, these architectures are mainly focused on image datasets consisting of large number of samples. In contrast, the proposed architecture is specifically designed for voice pathologies and works with smaller datasets as well, since accuracy is increased by employing feature extraction methods such as max-pooling, dilation, resizing of images, multiscaling, fully connected, softmax and classification layer. The test samples for each class mentioned in table 9.2 are tested against the network trained in the above subsection. The confusion matrix obtained from the test is shown in figure 9.3. It is observed that 1727 out of 1730 healthy test samples are classified correctly, thereby providing 99.8% accuracy. The remaining three healthy test samples are misclassified as Parkinson's disease. Meanwhile, all the 121 laryngeal pathology test samples are 100% correctly classified. Finally, for the third category, which is Parkinson's, 2090 out of 2102 test samples are correctly classified, thereby accounting for 99.4%. These per-class scores are recorded in table 9.3. The values of sensitivity, specificity, precision, false positive rate (FPR), F_1 score, Matthews correlation coefficient (MCC) and kappa are tabulated in table 9.4. The proposed technique obtains sensitivity and specificity values of 99.74% and 99.77%, respectively. The confusion matrices are shown in figures 9.3–9.7.

For a comprehensive evaluation, the proposed result is compared with that of other state-of-the-art deep learning techniques such as GoogleNet [63], MobileNet [64], ResNet-101 [65] and ResNet-18 [66]. Among these state-of-the-art models, MobileNet outperforms the remaining three models with an accuracy of 99.2% for the healthy class. Similarly, for the laryngeal pathology ResNet-101 delivers the best performance with an accuracy of 99.2%. Finally, for the Parkinson's test samples,

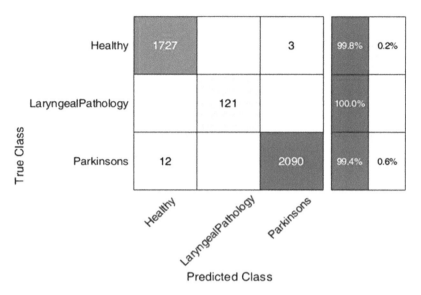

Figure 9.3. Confusion matrix of the proposed model.

Table 9.3. Per-class accuracies (%) of various deep learning models.

Method	Healthy	Laryngeal pathology	Parkinson's disease
GoogLeNet [63]	98.7	88.4	95.8
MobileNet [64]	99.2	95.0	98.6
ResNet-101 [65]	96.0	99.2	97.8
ResNet-18 [66]	98.6	98.3	97.9
Proposed	99.8	100	99.4

Table 9.4. Overall performance of various deep learning models.

Method	Sen.	Spe.	Pre.	FPR	F_1	MCC	Kappa
GoogLeNet [63]	94.30	98.06	97.45	1.94	95.75	93.86	92.89
MobileNet [64]	97.64	99.24	99.13	0.76	98.36	97.61	97.27
ResNet-101 [65]	97.67	98.07	97.48	1.93	97.57	95.67	93.40
ResNet-18 [66]	98.27	98.87	98.21	1.13	98.24	97.09	95.96
Proposed	99.74	99.77	99.72	0.23	99.74	99.49	99.15

MobileNet provides the highest accuracy of 98.6%. The performance of each of the test samples and their corresponding per-class accuracies are illustrated in the confusion matrices of figures 9.4, 9.5, 9.6 and 9.7 and tabulated in table 9.3. The mean classification scores of all seven metrics are recorded in table 9.4. It is observed

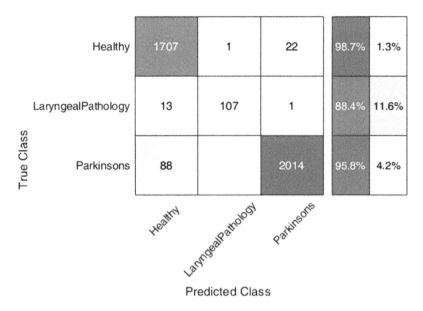

Figure 9.4. Confusion matrix of the GoogLeNet model.

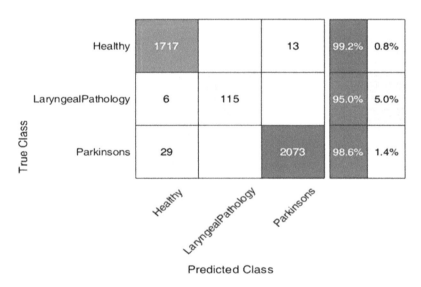

Figure 9.5. Confusion matrix of the MobileNet model.

from the sensitivity, FPR, F_1 score, MCC and kappa that GoogLeNet performs the worst for the current dataset. MobileNet, on the other hand, shows consistent values for all seven metrics. It also has the lowest value of FPR. Nevertheless, for PD detection the proposed work outperforms all the other methods.

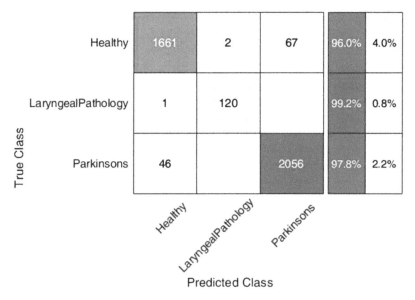

Figure 9.6. Confusion matrix of the ResNet-101 model.

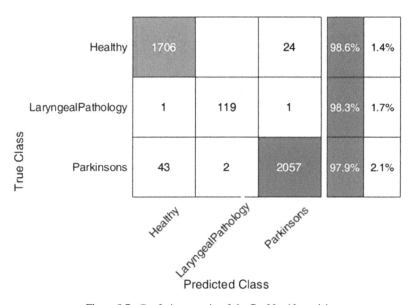

Figure 9.7. Confusion matrix of the ResNet-18 model.

9.4 Conclusion

An efficient architecture for detecting the onset of Parkinson's disease through an image-based multiscale analysis is proposed and demonstrated successfully. The six columns present in the proposed base-CNN model has made the network shallow, thereby enabling faster training, but also not at the cost of vital features. In fact, the use of base-CNN with the three input images has facilitated a two-fold increase in the number of features, and that too at varying scales. Another noteworthy aspect is the use of a three-stage deep-feature fusion, for it not only brings these multiscale features into a single platform, but also provides a rich mixing of features by using techniques such as depth concatenation, product and addition of weights. The current cross-dataset evaluation over these three classes is a tremendous success, with all the class displaying more than 99% accuracy. Among these three, the laryngeal pathological voice test samples are detected with 100% accuracy. The onset of Parkinson's disease is successfully differentiated from voice pathology associated with vocal folds with a per-class accuracy of 99.4%. The proposed method also outperformed various state-of-the-art deep learning techniques by demonstrating highly reliable values for sensitivity (99.74%), specificity (99.77%), precision (99.72%), FPR (0.23%), F_1 score (99.74%), MCC (99.49%) and kappa (99.15%).

References

[1] Tuncer T, Dogan S and Acharya U R 2020 Automated detection of Parkinson's disease using minimum average maximum tree and singular value decomposition method with vowels *Biocybern. Biomed. Eng.* **40** 211–20

[2] Gupta D, Julka A, Jain S, Aggarwal T, Khanna A, Arunkumar N and de Albuquerque V H C 2018 Optimized cuttlefish algorithm for diagnosis of Parkinson's disease *Cogn. Syst. Res.* **52** 36–48

[3] Bourouhou A, Jilbab A, Nacir C and Hammouch A 2016 Comparison of classification methods to detect the Parkinson disease *2016 Int. Conf. on Electrical and Information Technologies (ICEIT)* (Piscataway, NJ: IEEE) pp 421–4

[4] Harel B, Cannizzaro M and Snyder P J 2004 Variability in fundamental frequency during speech in prodromal and incipient Parkinson's disease: a longitudinal case study *Brain Cogn.* **56** 24–9

[5] Baken R J and Orlikoff R F 2000 *Clinical Measurement of Speech and Voice* (Boston, MA: Cengage Learning)

[6] Dejonckere P H, Bradley P, Clemente P, Cornut G, Crevier-Buchman L, Friedrich G, Van De Heyning P, Remacle M and Woisard V 2001 A basic protocol for functional assessment of voice pathology, especially for investigating the efficacy of (phonosurgical) treatments and evaluating new assessment techniques *Eur. Arch. Oto-Rhino-Laryngol.* **258** 77–82

[7] Little M, McSharry P, Hunter E, Spielman J and Ramig L 2008 Suitability of dysphonia measurements for telemonitoring of Parkinson's disease *Nat. Preced.* **2008**

[8] Little M, McSharry P, Roberts S, Costello D and Moroz I 2007 Exploiting nonlinear recurrence and fractal scaling properties for voice disorder detection *BioMed. Eng. OnLine* **6** 23

[9] Sakar B E, Isenkul M E, Sakar C O, Sertbas A, Gurgen F, Delil S, Apaydin H and Kursun O 2013 Collection and analysis of a Parkinson speech dataset with multiple types of sound recordings *IEEE J. Biomed. Health Inform.* **17** 828–34

[10] Tsanas A, Little M, McSharry P and Ramig L 2009 Accurate telemonitoring of Parkinson's disease progression by non-invasive speech tests *Nat. Preced.* **2009**

[11] Gürüler H 2017 A novel diagnosis system for Parkinson's disease using complex-valued artificial neural network with *k*-means clustering feature weighting method *Neural Comput. Appl.* **28** 1657–66

[12] Peker M 2016 A decision support system to improve medical diagnosis using a combination of k-medoids clustering based attribute weighting and SVM *J. Med. Syst.* **40** 116

[13] Erdogdu Sakar B, Serbes G and Sakar C O 2017 Analyzing the effectiveness of vocal features in early telediagnosis of Parkinson's disease *PLoS One* **12** e0182428

[14] Sharma A and Giri R N 2014 Automatic recognition of Parkinson's disease via artificial neural network and support vector machine *Int. J. Innov. Technol. Explor. Eng. (IJITEE)* **4** 2278–3075

[15] Shahbakhi M, Far D T and Tahami E 2014 Speech analysis for diagnosis of Parkinson's disease using genetic algorithm and support vector machine *J. Biomed. Sci. Eng.* **6** 147–56

[16] Kubota K J, Chen J A and Little M A 2016 Machine learning for large-scale wearable sensor data in Parkinson's disease: concepts, promises, pitfalls, and futures *Mov. Disord.* **31** 1314–26

[17] Alemami Y and Almazaydeh L 2014 Detection of Parkinson disease through voice signal features *J. Am. Sci.* **10** 44–7

[18] LeCun Y, Bengio Y and Hinton G 2015 Deep learning *Nature* **521** 436–44

[19] Oh S L, Hagiwara Y, Raghavendra U, Yuvaraj R, Arunkumar N, Murugappan M and Acharya U R 2018 A deep learning approach for Parkinson's disease diagnosis from EEG signals *Neural Comput. Appl.* 1–7

[20] Pereira C R, Weber S A, Hook C, Rosa G H and Papa J P 2016 Deep learning-aided Parkinson's disease diagnosis from handwritten dynamics *29th SIBGRAPI Conf. on Graphics, Patterns and Images (SIBGRAPI)* pp 340–6

[21] Eskofier B M *et al* 2016 Recent machine learning advancements in sensor-based mobility analysis: deep learning for Parkinson's disease assessment *38th Annual Int. Conf. of the Engineering in Medicine and Biology Society* (Piscataway, NJ: IEEE) pp 655–8

[22] Yuvaraj R, Murugappan M, Acharya U R, Adeli H, Ibrahim N M and Mesquita E 2016 Brain functional connectivity patterns for emotional state classification in Parkinson's disease patients without dementia *Behav. Brain Res.* **298** 248–60

[23] Ly Q T, Handojoseno A A, Gilat M, Chai R, Martens K A E, Georgiades M, Naik G R, Tran Y, Lewis S J and Nguyen H T 2017 Detection of turning freeze in Parkinson's disease based on S-transform decomposition of EEG signals *39th Annual Int. Conf. of the Engineering in Medicine and Biology Society* (Piscataway, NJ: IEEE) pp 3044–47

[24] Gómez-Vilda P *et al* 2017 Parkinson disease detection from speech articulation neuromechanics *Front. Neuroinform.* **11** 56

[25] Sakar C O, Serbes G, Gunduz A, Tunc H C, Nizam H, Sakar B E, Tutuncu M, Aydin T, Isenkul M E and Apaydin H 2019 A comparative analysis of speech signal processing algorithms for Parkinson's disease classification and the use of the tunable *Q*-factor wavelet transform *Appl. Soft Comput.* **74** 255–63

[26] Mostafa S A, Mustapha A, Mohammed M A, Hamed R I, Arunkumar N, Abd Ghani M K, Jaber M M and Khaleefah S H 2019 Examining multiple feature evaluation and classification methods for improving the diagnosis of Parkinson's disease *Cogn. Syst. Res.* **54** 90–9

[27] Cigdem O, Beheshti I and Demirel H 2018 Effects of different covariates and contrasts on classification of Parkinson's disease using structural MRI *Comput. Biol. Med.* **99** 173–81

[28] Joshi D, Khajuria A and Joshi P 2017 An automatic non-invasive method for Parkinson's disease classification *Comput. Methods Programs Biomed.* **145** 135–45

[29] Zeng W, Liu F, Wang Q, Wang Y, Ma L and Zhang Y 2016 Parkinson's disease classification using gait analysis via deterministic learning *Neurosci. Lett.* **633** 268–78

[30] Rusz J, Hlavnička J, Tykalová T, Bušková J, Ulmanová O, Růžička E and Šonka K 2016 Quantitative assessment of motor speech abnormalities in idiopathic rapid eye movement sleep behaviour disorder *Sleep Med.* **19** 141–7

[31] Jeancolas L, Benali H, Benkelfat B E, Mangone G, Corvol J C, Vidailhet M, Lehericy S and Petrovska-Delacrétaz D 2017 Automatic detection of early stages of Parkinson's disease through acoustic voice analysis with mel-frequency cepstral coefficients *Int. Conf. on Advanced Technologies for Signal and Image Processing (ATSIP)* (Piscataway, NJ: IEEE) pp 1–6

[32] Viswanathan R, Khojasteh P, Aliahmad B, Arjunan S P, Ragnav S, Kempster P, Wong K, Nagao J and Kumar D K 2018 Efficiency of voice features based on consonant for detection of Parkinson's disease *Life Sciences Conf.* (Piscataway, NJ: IEEE) pp 49–52

[33] Aich S, Younga K, Hui K L, Al-Absi A A and Sain M 2018 A nonlinear decision tree based classification approach to predict the Parkinson's disease using different feature sets of voice data *20th Int. Conf. on Advanced Communication Technology* (Piscataway, NJ: IEEE) pp 638–42

[34] Tsanas A, Little M A, McSharry P E, Spielman J and Ramig L O 2012 Novel speech signal processing algorithms for high-accuracy classification of Parkinson's disease *IEEE Trans. Biomed. Eng.* **59** 1264–71

[35] Das R 2010 A comparison of multiple classification methods for diagnosis of Parkinson disease *Expert Syst. Appl.* **37** 1568–72

[36] Karimi Rouzbahani H and Daliri M R 2011 Diagnosis of Parkinson's disease in human using voice signals *Basic Clin. Neurosci.* **2** 12–20

[37] Shirvan R A and Tahami E 2011 Voice analysis for detecting Parkinson's disease using genetic algorithm and KNN classification method *18th Iranian Conf. of Biomedical Engineering* (Piscataway, NJ: IEEE) pp 278–83

[38] Parisi L, RaviChandran N and Manaog M L 2018 Feature-driven machine learning to improve early diagnosis of Parkinson's disease *Expert Syst. Appl.* **110** 182–90

[39] Ho A K, Iansek R, Marigliani C, Bradshaw J L and Gates S 1998 Speech impairment in a large sample of patients with Parkinson's disease *Behav. Neurol.* **11** 131–7

[40] Gil D and Manuel D J 2009 Diagnosing Parkinson by using artificial neural networks and support vector machines *Global J. Comput. Sci. Technol.* **9** 63–71

[41] Bhattacharya I and Bhatia M P S 2010 SVM classification to distinguish Parkinson disease patients *Proc. of the First Amrita ACM-W Celebration on Women in Computing in India* pp 1–6

[42] Rani K U and Holi M S 2012 Analysis of speech characteristics of neurological diseases and their classification *Third Int. Conf. on Computing, Communication and Networking Technologies (July)* (Piscataway, NJ: IEEE) pp 1–6

[43] Mathur R, Pathak V and Bandil D 2019 Parkinson disease prediction using machine learning algorithm *Emerging Trends in Expert Applications and Security* (Berlin: Springer) pp 357–63

[44] Braga D, Madureira A M, Coelho L and Ajith R 2019 Automatic detection of Parkinson's disease based on acoustic analysis of speech *Eng. Appl. Artif. Intell.* **77** 148–58

[45] Nissar I, Rizvi D, Masood S and Mir A 2019 Voice-based detection of Parkinson's disease through ensemble machine learning approach: a performance study *EAI Endorsed Trans. Pervasive Health Technol.* **5** 1–9

[46] Anisha C D and Arulanand N 2020 Early prediction of Parkinson's disease (PD) using ensemble classifiers *Int. Conf. on Innovative Trends in Information Technology* (Piscataway, NJ: IEEE) pp 1–6

[47] Asmae O, Abdelhadi R, Bouchaib C, Sara S and Tajeddine K 2020 Parkinson's disease identification using KNN and ANN algorithms based on voice disorder *First Int. Conf. on Innovative Research in Applied Science, Engineering and Technology* (Piscataway, NJ: IEEE) pp 1–6

[48] Senturk Z K 2020 Early diagnosis of Parkinson's disease using machine learning algorithms *Med. Hypotheses* **138** 109603

[49] Caliskan A, Badem H, Basturk A and Yuksel M E 2017 Diagnosis of the Parkinson disease by using deep neural network classifier *IU-J. Elect. Electron. Eng.* **17** 3311–18

[50] Wroge T J, Özkanca Y, Demiroglu C, Si D, Atkins D C and Ghomi R H 2018 Parkinson's disease diagnosis using machine learning and voice *IEEE Signal Processing in Medicine and Biology Symp. (December)* (Piscataway, NJ: IEEE) pp 1–7

[51] Oh S L, Hagiwara Y, Raghavendra U, Yuvaraj R, Arunkumar N, Murugappan M and Acharya U R 2020 A deep learning approach for Parkinson's disease diagnosis from EEG signals *Neural Comp. Appl.* **32** 10927–33

[52] Frid A, Kantor A, Svechin D and Manevitz L M 2016 Diagnosis of Parkinson's disease from continuous speech using deep convolutional networks without manual selection of features *IEEE Int. Conf. on the Science of Electrical Engineering* (Piscataway, NJ: IEEE) pp 1–4

[53] L-Fatlawi A H, Jabardi M H and Ling S H 2016 Efficient diagnosis system for Parkinson's disease using deep belief network *IEEE Congress on Evolutionary Computation (CEC)* (Piscataway, NJ: IEEE) pp 1324–30

[54] Grover S, Bhartia S, Yadav A and Seeja K R 2018 Predicting severity of Parkinson's disease using deep learning *Procedia Comput. Sci.* **132** 1788–94

[55] Rizvi D R, Nissar I, Masood S, Ahmed M and Ahmad F 2020 An LSTM based deep learning model for voice-based detection of Parkinson's disease *Int. J. Adv. Sci. Technol* **29** 337–43

[56] Kaur S, Aggarwal H and Rani R 2020 Hyper-parameter optimization of deep learning model for prediction of Parkinson's disease *Mach. Vis. Appl.* **31** 1–15

[57] Cesari U, De Pietro G, Marciano E, Niri C, Sannino G and Verde L 2018 A new database of healthy and pathological voices *Comput. Electr. Eng.* **68** 310–21

[58] Harar P, Alonso-Hernandezy J B, Mekyska J, Galaz Z, Burget R and Smekal Z 2017 Voice pathology detection using deep learning: a preliminary study *Int. Conf. and Workshop on Bioinspired Intelligence* (Piscataway, NJ: IEEE) pp 1–4

[59] Kudo Y and Aoki Y 2017 Dilated convolutions for image classification and object localization *Fifteenth IAPR Int. Conf. on Machine Vision Applications* (Piscataway, NJ: IEEE) pp 452–5

[60] Yu F, Koltun V and Funkhouser T 2017 Dilated residual networks *Proc. of the IEEE Conf. on Computer Vision and Pattern Recognition* pp 472–80

[61] Liu C, Shang Z and Qin A 2019 A multiscale image denoising algorithm based on dilated residual convolution network *Chinese Conf. on Image and Graphics Technologies* (Singapore: Springer) pp 193–203

[62] Xiang H, Zhao Y, Yuan Y, Zhang G and Hu X 2019 Lightweight fully convolutional network for license plate detection *Optik* **178** 1185–94

[63] Zhong Y, Wang J, Peng J and Zhang L 2015 Anchor box optimization for object detection *Proc. of the IEEE/CVF Winter Conf. on Applications of Computer Vision* pp 1286–94

[64] Szegedy C, Liu W, Jia Y, Sermanet P, Reed S, Anguelov D, Erhan D, Vanhoucke V and Rabinovich A 2015 Going deeper with convolutions *Proc. of the IEEE Conf. on Computer Vision and Pattern Recognition* pp 1–9

[65] Howard A G, Zhu M, Chen B, Kalenichenko D, Wang W, Weyand T, Andreetto M and Adam H 2017 MobileNets: efficient convolutional neural networks for mobile vision applications arXiv:1704.04861

[66] He K, Zhang X, Ren S and Sun J 2019 Deep residual learning for image recognition *Proc. of the IEEE Conf. on Computer Vision and Pattern Recognition* pp 770–8

Chapter 10

Computer vision approach with deep learning for a medical intelligence system

Monali Gulhane

The use of computer vision and intelligent systems in healthcare is emerging, particularly in the field of future version. In this chapter we discuss various AI-powered developments that address several of the most critical societal health problems, including cardiovascular disease, cancer, and dermatological, neurological, pulmonary and gastrointestinal illnesses. We describe how advances in these fields have evolved through a wide variety of research methods, ranging from the augmentation, detection, classification, and categorization of anatomy and lesions, to full systems that automatically diagnose and categorize a spectrum of ailments to improve medical assessment.

Various imaging techniques, such as computerized tomography, magnetic resonance, radiography, ultrasonography, dermoscopy and microscopes, include a variety of opportunities to construct automated processes that aid in diagnosing clinical conditions by utilizing inherent physicochemical characteristics. Due to systemic features, including signal-to-noise, brightness and sensitivities in time, location, and wavelengths, such imaging technologies place significant limits on the development of automated image analysis systems for diagnostic assistance. Furthermore, we cover the upcoming opportunities and issues that computer vision and intelligent systems will encounter in the years ahead in order to generate systems that can tackle problems.

10.1 Introduction

There have long been attempts to use computer vision (CV) to allow a computer to detect visual information effectively [2]. Computer vision encompasses a wide range of activities, from low-level activities such as recognizing edges, to high-level tasks such as comprehending entire scenes [1]. Three things have contributed substantially to advancements in the past decade: (i) artificial intelligence and specifically the deep learning (DL) mechanisms, that allow for edge training of exceedingly complex algorithms from original data, are maturing [3]; (ii) advances in GPU-based concentrated computational power [4]; and (iii) the access to massive labeled datasets to train these algorithms [5].

Investigators now have access to the information they need to develop this field thanks to the confluence of these three aspects. Progress has accelerated as the research community has developed dramatically. In a wide range of scientific disciplines the expansion of digital CV had coincided with the generation of vast volumes of digital data. Modern medical advancements have indeed been abundant [7, 8], due in large part to DL's exceptional capability to learn a range of tasks from a range of data sources. CV algorithms may learn a variety of trend skills using huge datasets, ranging from health professional diagnostics [8] to medical scenario interpretation [9]. See the schematic in figure 10.1.

There are two types of models. The first is models of discrimination using multiple modalities. Neural network models can be built to simultaneously understand from picture data, often using a deep learning approach, and non-image information, typically using standard deep networks. Image data are typically used in convolutional networks, as shown in figure 10.2. Among the types of learned annotations are clinical forecasts, prognostics, illness diagnostics and number of different combinations. The second type is a model that is generative in nature. Artificial neural networks can be programmed to generate the images, which is a useful application. Image-to-picture regression (as depicted), super-resolution image augmentation, new image synthesis and other tasks are among the possible applications.

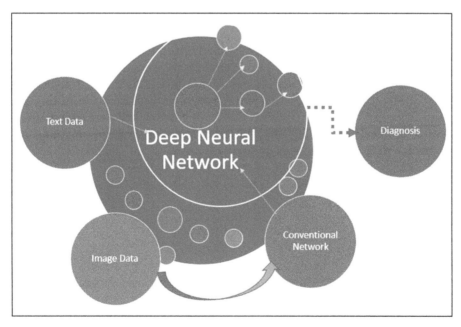

Figure 10.1. Schematic showing the tasks of medical computer vision.

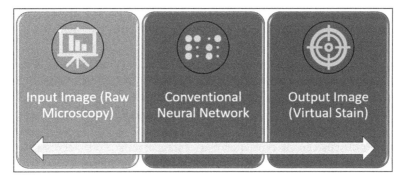

Figure 10.2. Sample flow of tasks for medical computer vision.

We look at the junction of CV and healthcare in this study, concentrating on real-world clinical applications, medical video and medical imaging. We go over the essential algorithmic capabilities that enabled these opportunities, as well as the numerous achievements of recent years. A few of the medical areas that are well-suited for CV include screening and evaluation, illness evaluation, forecasting future consequences, fragmenting diseases from tissues to cells, clinical research and monitoring disease. We look at the technology's future potential as well as the implications for medicine and healthcare altogether.

10.2 Defining computer vision

There are several terms to describe the method of establishing the categorization of objects in an image, their placement in an image and the kind of item, while also determining its location in an image. These terms include detection and recognition, classification and cognition. In fact, since its began a decade ago, the large-scale visual recognition challenge (ILSVRC) for generative adversarial networks appears to have played a significant role in the advancement of these initiatives [9]. It has sparked a sizable community of deep learning researchers who have competed and collaborated to develop methods for CV problems. The launch of the first GPU-powered deep learning technique in 2012 was a watershed moment in the community's evolution [10], ushering in a period of significant year-on-year improvements [11] all the way up to the competition's final year in 2017. During this period, the categorization accuracy increased to levels comparable to that of humans [12–14]. A wide range of illnesses have been effectively categorized and diagnosed using fine-grained variants of these algorithms in medicine [15]. When given adequate data, the accuracy of artificial intelligence often matches or exceeds that of professional doctors [16]. When it comes to challenging applications such as physiological categorization of several types of cells in microscopy [17, 18], object categorization has made considerable strides forward, particularly in recent years. The deep neural network is a deep learning technique that hardcodes longitudinal invariance, a crucial characteristic of picture data, into the network's structure [19]. Just a few of the CV activities that already have benefited from this improvement include image registrations (trying to identify equivalent locations spanning relevant pictures), information extraction (finding similar images), pattern analysis and improvement, and information extraction and registrations. Working with medical data comes with its own set of problems, necessitating the use of a variety of AI algorithms.

CNNs which have been trained to classify sickness states have been carefully evaluated and compared to professionals across a wide spectrum of conditions. When both are put through an identical image categorization challenge, the results CV are frequently comparable to those of professionals.

These techniques make substantial use of supervised learning, which uses datasets that contain both pieces of data (such as images) and data labeling (e.g. object classes). Transfer learning, which involves training an algorithm on a huge and unconnected dataset (e.g. ImageNet), then fine-tuning it on a collection of interest (e.g. medical data), has proven to be beneficial for medical data progress. Several strategies, such the basis of the data collected and generating stochastic networks (GANs), are now being developed [20, 21] in order to reduce the expense involved in gathering and categorizing data. Open-source picture annotations have even been found to be useful for medical procedures [22, 23]. While self-supervised learning, in which data points are extracted and used to prepare methodologies has successfully pushed this ground forward into completely unsupervised classification, which would not require labels [24], although completely unsupervised learning is still in its early stages. The employment of these ideas in the field of medicine will lower the costs of design and implementation.

Access to medical data is crucial in this field, and key ethical and legal concerns must be addressed. Do patients have control over their de-identified data? What if data re-identification algorithms become advanced over time? Is it appropriate for the community to make significant volumes of data available to the public? A small number of datasets combining data acquired through commercial solutions have been the primary sources of information for academia and industry up until now. The characteristics of data exchange as well as the availability of resources in different countries will affect deployment options. Federation learning, wherein centralized methods are trained on samples in the dataset that never leave secured enclosures, may be able to provide a workaround in more stringent regimes [25].

Multiple applications, including multimodal learning [26] (figure 10.1), which integrates vision with extra dimensions such as language (figure 10.2), time information, and genetic data have benefited from these advancements. Using these techniques in conjunction with 3D vision [27], it is possible to transform depth cameras [28] into privacy-preserving sensors, which makes deployment in patient situations such as the critical care units [8, 29] much easier. The range of employment opportunities available in video is far broader. Activity recognition [30] and live scene interpretation [31, 32] can help you recognize and respond to noteworthy or unfavorable clinical conditions

10.3 Computer vision in practice

Recent years have seen a rise in the number of verified articles that use machine learning technology to investigate stationary medical imaging images, from hundreds to thousands [33]. Due to the diagnostics task of various specialties and directions giving emphasis to formal disciplined images in computer vision practices, fields such as pathology, radiography and dermatology and ophthalmology are examples which have recently been attractive due to computer vision practice.

10.3.1 Medical imaging

Medical imagery presents a variety of issues for computer vision based on deep learning. For one thing, the photographs might be quite large. Normal CNN image inputs are 200 by 200 pixels, whereas histopathology slides are digitized into gigapixel images with a resolution of 100 000 by 100 000 pixels. In addition, differing composition preparation will result in distinct presentations for the same body part, and different digitization procedures or settings will result in diverse photos of the same slide. When working with radiological modalities such as CT and MRI, which can provide comparably enormous 3D images, conventional CNNs must work with a group of two-dimensional images or change their inner structure in order to deal with 3D. The decision has been made that DL will begin to consider the unique challenges that medical data brings. Using multiple-instance learning (MIL), for example, is a way to understand datasets that contain many images but very few labels (for example, histopathology) [34]. CNNs featuring 3D convolution layers [35] are better at learning from 3D volumes than other CNNs (e.g. for MRI and CT). Working with time-series pictures (e.g. ultrasound) is made possible by spatial-temporal models and image registration [36].

Hundreds of businesses have received the certification of the FDA and CE for medical image processing AI in the United States, and commercial marketplaces are forming as long-term business models are developed [37]. Technological advances such as diabetic retinopathy screening devices, for example, have been well received in healthcare regions such as India and Thailand. The United States' Centers for Medicare and Medicaid Services (CMS) has approved funding for a radiological cardiovascular triage use-case that will shorten the time it takes for patients to receive treatment [38, 39]. This rapid expansion is now having a direct influence on patient outcomes.

CV integration into current physical systems is required in medical modalities with non-standardized data collection. In otolaryngology, for example, CNNs can be utilized with mountable devices coupled to smartphones to assist primary care physicians in managing patients' ears, nose and throat conditions [40–42]. Microscope-integrated artificial intelligence (AI) can help in hematological parameters and serology by identifying common conditions [43] and counting different types of white blood cells, which are repetitive tasks that CNNs can easily enhance. The capabilities of AI in gastroenterology have been astounding [44]. Video-based CNNs can be used for scope guidance, lesion identification and diagnosis in endoscopic procedures [45]. Screening for esophageal cancer [46], identifying gastric cancer, detecting stomach illnesses such as *Helicobacter pylori*, and even locating hookworms are some of the applications. Scientists have gone even further in this area by inventing complete medical AI devices enabling surveillance, including self-development and self-smart bathrooms integrating diagnostics CNNs on cameras [47] and intelligent healthcare devices for surgical planning. CV can help the advancement of healthcare for humankind and methods in addition to only disease analysis, such as implantation assessment of reproductive cloning [48].

Despite the fact that image enhancement in diagnostic imaging is still a relatively new field of study, a considerable body of work [49–51] has been published that covers all imaging modalities with a focus on x-rays, CT and MRI. Models have been established in the investigation of chest x-rays, which is a main clinical focus area. Over 1 million annotated open-source photos have indeed been accumulated, making it the most similar to ImageNet [9] in the medical CV field to date [52–54]. Brain imagery [55] and abdominal imagery [56] are attracting more attention. For the overwhelming majority of instances where data are available, models for sickness classification [57], lesion detection [58] and tissue delineation (e.g. cardiac) [58] have been established. A result of this is that the industry has been able to respond more quickly in moments of emergency, such as when developing and deploying COVID-19 detection models [59]. Imaging interpretation (e.g. transferring noisy visualization methods onto MRI), categorization and advancement, and individual automatic vehicle report generation, and temporal tracking (e.g. image registration to track tumor growth over time) are some of the topics being addressed at the moment. A more in-depth discussion of vision implementations in a number of disciplines will be provided in the next sections of this chapter.

10.3.2 Cardiology

Using cardiovascular imaging in a variety of therapeutic clinical procedures is now becoming increasingly prevalent in the medical field. Among other methods, deep learning has the potential to be used in a number of therapeutic activities such as detection and monitoring. Cardiovascular echocardiography, known colloquially as ultrasonography, is the most widely utilized imaging technique in the area of cardiac therapeutic applications. Echocardiography is a cost-effective, radiation-free technique for DL because of its easy data collection and interpretation. The majority of acute inpatient hospitals, outpatient clinics, and emergency rooms use this treatment [60]. Moreover, digital imaging technologies such as CT and MRI are being used to better comprehend the structure of the heart chambers and to better analyse supply–demand imbalances. Furthermore, the US Food and Drug Administration has authorized a CT segmentation technique for blood vessel visualization [61].

An enormous number of applications are available to choose from. According to view classification [67], DL could be taught on a massive database of electrocardiographic investigations and exceed board-certified echo cardiographers in their respective fields of expertize. Computational DL procedures can be used to diagnose cardiac amyloidosis, pulmonary arterial hypertension and hypertrophic cardiomyopathy among other conditions. The discipline has lately made strides as a result of the development of EchoNet, a supervised neural algorithm that can discern heart architecture, assess functionality and anticipate the overwhelming majority of cases that are difficult to detect using traditional human interpretation methods.

In order to account for data access constraints, information computational techniques, including such moderate GANs that are good at regression tasks, have been designed (e.g. predicting left ventricular hypertrophy). To accommodate for the fact that the majority of medical imaging datasets are privately owned, 10 000 annotated echocardiogram videos were recently made available. In connection with this release, the EchoNet-Dynamic video-based model was also developed. Using results from an independent database and human professionals who can measure left ventricular hypertrophy and diagnose cardiomyopathy, it provides a comprehensive evaluation criterion.

10.3.3 Pathology

Pathologists are crucial in the prevention and treatment of breast cancer. Pathological analysis is mostly subjective in nature because it relies on visual evaluation of clinical specimens under a microscope. Diagnostic and prognostic judgments that are inconsistent can be attributed to variance in the sensory acuity and medical experience [62]. Diagnosis, predictions of the future of outcomes and response to treatment, pathological classification, disease surveillance, and other critical medical tasks can all be made easier using deep learning.

The use of tissue scanners having partial resolution and the ability to record gigapixel whole-slide images (WSIs) has grown increasingly widespread in the last few years. This discovery, combined with advancements in CV, has prompted interest in artificial intelligence-driven electronic histopathology, as well as development and commercialization efforts in the field. In this field researchers have the possibility to (i) enhance the functionality and accuracy of routine activities by overcoming visual processing perception and neurocognitive limitations, (ii) combine pathological changes with radioactive, sequencing and proteomic measuring techniques to continue enhancing diagnosis and therapy, and (iii) build stronger illness and pharmacological biomarkers from morphological characteristics that are invisible to the human eye.

There has been some interest in automating the difficult task of morphological feature localization and quantification, which has been pursued in one area of study. A few examples are the detection and classification of lymphocytes, nucleus, including distant metastases; the localization and segmentation of morphological components including proteins, glands, channels, and tumors; and the identification and classification of morphological elements such as malignant tumors and the localization and subdivision of histopathological primitives such as malignancies. As training data, these techniques frequently involve the manual identification of human tissues by pathologists, which is time-consuming and expensive.

Another field of research provides a direction of diagnoses and diagnostic systems for a variety of tumors utilizing WSIs or tissue microarrays (TMA) for breast, prostate, lung and other malignancies. WSIs and TMAs are being used to diagnose and prognosticate a variety of tumors. Studies have shown that even morphological characteristics obtained using a hematoxylin and eosin (H&E) stain can be utilized to predict nanoscale drug delivery used in the diagnosis of cancer in some cases.

Despite of the fact that histopathology slides are being digitized into large data-rich gigapixel images, comments at the area level are rare and expensive. As a solution to this problem researchers have developed deep learning algorithms associated with different learning approaches that make use of slide-level 'weak' annotation and take advantage of the extensive number of images available to improve performance.

As a result of the large amount of data available in this area, activities such as simulated coloring, wherein the algorithms are educated to predict one type of image from some other (for example, a stained image), have become possible (e.g. a raw microscopy image).

10.3.4 Dermatology

Some of the most important clinical roles for DL in dermatology are making lesion-specific differential diagnoses, identifying concerning lesions among a large number of benign lesions and assisting with the tracking of lesion growth over time [63]. According to a number of studies, CNNs are capable of performing on par with board-certified dermatologists when it comes to discriminating between normal and cancerous skin lesions. These studies have investigated a rising number of dermatologist in a series of tests, with the results consistently demonstrating classification sensitivity and specificity that are on par with or even better than those of physicians. In most cases, these experiments were restricted to binary classification tasks, such as separating benign from malignant cutaneous lesions, or detecting malignant tumors and nevi or carcinomas from seborrheic keratoses, among other things.

It has only recently become possible to use non-visual characteristics (such as patient demographics) as classifier inputs in this area of research, which now includes diagnostic evaluation for thousands of skin related problems, which include non-neoplastic lesions such as rashes and hereditary problems. These initiatives have been prompted by accessible image repositories and artificial intelligence competitions that allow teams to play to achieve specific standards.

With the integration of these algorithms into clinical workflows, they can help with other critical tasks such as the large-scale detection of malignant tumors in patients with multiple lesions, as well as tracking tumor growth and color changes across images in order to acquire dynamic behavior such as economic expansion and color changes. The preliminary research that concurrently trains CNNs to detect and monitor lesions [64] has shown promise, although the field is still largely unexplored.

10.3.5 Ophthalmology

The medical branch of ophthalmology has experienced a sudden popularity in machine learning and data mining, with thousands of studies indicating clinical diagnostic and computational capabilities that are superior to those of human experts. Considering that the equipment used to inspect the eye is portable, it is likely that pop-up clinics and telemedicine will be utilized to spread testing facilities to remote areas, which might achieve a significant clinical improvement. Optical coherence tomography (OCT) and fundus imaging (fundus photography) are two techniques used extensively in the profession to diagnose and manage patients (OCT).

CNNs are capable of making reliable diagnoses of a wide range of disorders. In recent years, diabetic retinopathy, a condition in which blood vessels in diabetic patients' eyes 'leak' and can lead to blindness, has received a lot of attention. After CNNs routinely displayed physician-level evaluations generated from fundus photographs, the FDA recently approved a system in the United States. These tests can also be used to identify or forecast the development of illnesses including diabetic macular edema, age-related neurodegenerative disorders, glaucoma, apparent visual field loss, infantile blindness and other factors that affect the central retina.

There are a variety of non-human interpretable features in the eyes that can be detected by CNNs and are indicative of relevant medical information. Convolutional networks can categories vascular and diabetes risk variables from fundus photos based on age, gender, smoking, hemoglobin A1c, body mass index, and systolic and diastolic blood pressure, to name a few. CNNs can also detect anemia and chronic renal illness in fundus photographs taken by patients. As a result of this discovery, future artificial intelligence investigations that anticipate non-ocular material from eye scanners will have intriguing prospects. This could lead to a shift in hospital treatment, with eye exams being used to monitor for both ophthalmology and non-ocular sickness, something that traditional doctors are currently unable to accomplish due to educational limits.

10.3.6 Video for medical purposes

10.3.6.1 Applications in surgery

Surgery and endoscopy are examples of procedural fields where CV could be quite valuable. Deep learning can be used to improve the performance of surgeons in a variety of clinical settings, including authentic contextual awareness [65], skills assessments and training, to name a few. Early research has mostly focused on video-based robotic and laparoscopic surgery in order to achieve this goal. A number of articles have proposed approaches for distinguishing surgical tools and instruments. The Worldwide Operating Evaluation of Laparoscopy Abilities standards for laparoscopic surgery are used in some research to assess surgeon performance. Some studies, for example, analyse tool motions and other indicators to assess operator achievement using predefined ratings. CV methods were also used in another study to discriminate between different phases of surgery during operations, with the goal of developing situational laptop modeling software to be used in the operating theater CADS (computer aided design system). CV is also beginning to pick up traction in the field of open surgery, where it is frequently employed. The numerous video recording views (e.g. head-mounted, side-view and overhead cameras) and procedures to be recorded provide a difficult problem to resolve. The translation of CV assessment into tools and apps that might assist patients achieve better outcomes is a reasonable next step in the research process for all types of surgical video.

10.3.7 The presence of humans

CV can differentiate between human processes in real-world settings such as hospitals and clinics, which is useful for a range of 'ambient intelligence' applications, such as environmental and intrusion detection. Ambient intelligence is a non-invasive, continuous awareness of behavior in external surroundings that can be used to assist clinicians, nurses and other healthcare practitioners to carry out their responsibilities, including healthcare management, completely automated documentary evidence, and methodology monitoring and enforcement, among others. AI can be used to help with tasks such as patient monitoring, automated record-keeping, as well as security policy compliance monitoring (figure 10.3). Preliminary hospital-based research has proven the use of CV-based situational computation in hospitalized patients in order to monitor for security actions such as infection control activities and client mobilization. As well as being used in the emergency room to document the operations performed while a patient is being revived, CV was created to be used in the operating theater (OR) to distinguish activities and enhance workflow efficiency and productivity. According to the National Institutes of Health, CV is a scalable and comprehensive method for labor and resource monitoring that may be utilized to optimize resource allocation for optimal treatment at the hospital operations level.

Integrating image processing techniques with sensing and video feeds, medical practitioners may expand their capacity to diagnose patients as their workloads increase. This technology can be employed in a variety of clinical and residential settings for a variety of safety applications. Modeling techniques for smooth alright activity recognition have been applied in the development of areas including healthcare management in hospitalized patients, adequate hygiene practices and physical interaction policies and procedures in clinics and hospitals, and outlier action recognition, among others.

Ambient intelligence has the potential to enhance access to healthcare outside hospitals. Through surveillance for safety and anomalies in continuing operations

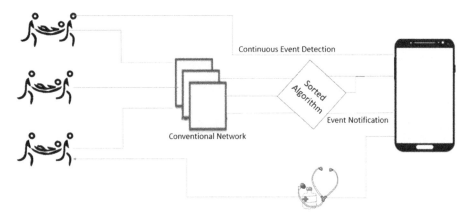

Figure 10.3. Intelligence in the environment. The phone image in this figure has been obtained by the authors from the Pixabay website where it was made available under the Pixabay License. It is included within this article on that basis.

(for instance, detecting falls, which are particularly dangerous for the elderly), supported living and physiological evaluation, it may well be reasonable to allow at-risk elderly people to remain freely at home in some circumstances. A similar level of research has been done on a wide range of routine chores. Strong implication analysis of activities such as resting, moving and sitting can be used to discover therapeutically substantial improvements or irregularities in patients by recognizing and calculating these changes or abnormalities as they occur over time. For the purpose of protecting the confidentiality of their patients, researchers have developed CV algorithms that operate using infrared video data. In supportive housing or rehabilitation, CV may be utilized for a variety of applications, including continual sign language recognition to aid persons with communication issues and monitoring physiotherapy exercises for stroke recovery [66]. Physiological evaluations that are performed at a distance have the possibility of being achieved using CV. Video-based systems, for example, may be used to assess heart and respiration rates in patients. As telemedicine visits become increasingly popular, the use of CV in patient triaging may become more common, in particular during periods of high demand, such as the current COVID-19 pandemic. CVs integrated with ambient intelligence systems have the potential to improve access to high-quality treatment in a variety of ways. On the other side, the advancement of these technologies will raise new ethical and legal concerns.

10.3.8 Implementation in the clinic

Medical artificial intelligence's integration into the clinic has the potential to be extremely beneficial to society while also having the potential to exacerbate long-standing disparities and perpetuate medical errors. If deployed properly and ethically, medical artificial intelligence (AI) has the potential to become a propeller for more equitable treatment; the more it is used, the more data it gathers, and the more precise and ubiquitous it becomes. Understanding the data on which the models are formed, as well as the ecosystem in which they are deployed, is important to their effectiveness. Data evaluation, model limits design, community engagement and trust building are all essential components of utilizing machine learning in healthcare, and we discuss them in detail here.

In large part the quality of the data influences the quality of the models; identifying and correcting for inequalities in the information will lead to more equal healthcare. It may be necessary to run human-in-the-loop programmers or to employ broad-reaching data collecting techniques in order to locate appropriate datasets. Eliminating prejudice in data may be accomplished via the use of a number of different approaches. Individual-level prejudice may be addressed in a variety of ways, including expert discussion and labeling assessment, among others. It is possible to correct for population-level bias by using missing data supplementation and distribution of income changes. International multi-institutional assessment is a rigorous approach for establishing the generalizability of models over a wide range of demographics, medical equipment, resource circumstances and practice patterns, among other things. Additionally, teaching algorithms to perform a wide range of activities rather than simply a single tightly specified goal, such as multi-cancer detection from histopathological images, makes systems more general and robust [67].

Using transparent reporting, one can detect and rectify model faults before they become a problem in the future. Safe-guards must be put in place to defend against the worst-case scenarios, such as being a minority, being dismissed, or being subjected to algorithmic prejudice. When it comes to accomplishing clinical outcomes, the capacity to report and be satisfied with excellent performance metrics on generic datasets is not enough; there must also be an understanding of the specific situations under which the model fails. The use of saliency maps in conjunction with demographic performance analysis allows you to examine what the model looks like and search for potential biases. Using the Fitzpatrick type of skin and other population information, the efficacy of a computational intelligence method of developing a clinical assessment for skin disorders was evaluated. The model was used, for example, to identify physician classifications for which there have been insufficient occurrences and to suggest potential data gathering. Aside from that, they used saliency masks to make sure that they were modeling skin abnormalities instead of skin type.

A well-known challenge is the effectiveness of teaching algorithms on out-of-distribution data samples that are not observed during model training. The creation of 95% confidence intervals to help in the discovery of anomalies, as well as the detection of out-of-distribution events, has made significant strides. Aside from that, methods for assessing the level of uncertainty connected with model findings are being developed. This is, in particular, essential when generating patient-specific predictions that have a detrimental impact on patient safety, which is a common occurrence.

The participation of patients, physicians, computer scientists and other important stakeholders is essential for the success of an implementation. In particular, this has aided in the detection and characterization of structural causes of unconscious discrimination in medical diagnoses, in particular, bias in datasets, as well as the identification of demographics for which models fail. User-centered assessments are an important approach for ensuring that a system's usability and appropriateness in the real world are properly assessed. What is the most effective method of delivering a model's output to doctors in order to assist them make better decisions? When deploying a mobile application in low source of energy situations, such as rural locations with intermittent Internet connections, what is the most effective method to use? Following the implementation of machine learning-powered age-related macular degeneration simulations in Vietnam and Thailand, the researchers discovered that the most effective model was affected by socioeconomic factors. They came to the conclusion that the location where a model is most effective may not be the location where the model was developed. Because of access restrictions in a unique local environment, it is possible that ophthalmology models will be employed in endocrinology care rather than eye centers in the future. Another good way to improve physician confidence in AI discoveries is to install machine learning models side-by-side with existing clinical workflows (e.g. manual grading). As seen in figure 10.3, machine intelligence systems definitely require extensive testing through clinical trials to ensure that they are safe to use and that they function properly. AI and CV can also aid clinical trials through a range of applications, including as medical diagnostics, tumor surveillance and adverse event detection, among others. This offers an environment in which AI can aid in the development of reliable artificial intelligence and machine learning, which is quite exciting.

Here we present an example process that demonstrates the favorable compounding impact of AI-aided workflows, as well as the trust that can be created as a result of using them. Physicians gain instant benefits from artificial intelligence projections, which become more accurate over time as larger datasets are amassed as explained in figure 10.4. The applications of artificial intelligence in healthcare necessitate the confidence of both healthcare staff and patients in the technology. Clinical confidence will be built on the foundation of rigorous clinical trials that assess artificial intelligence technology in real-world healthcare situations. These surroundings include the social reactions of humans, which seem to be difficult to predict and manage, but which must be taken into account by AI systems in order for them to function well. In contrast to retrospective studies, which cannot capture the unpredictability and human aspect that characterize clinical situations, prospective trials that are more representative of clinical reality will move the debate to the provable advantages of new technologies in real-world settings. Prediction analytics will need to be prepared to describe why particular features of just the patient or the environment lead to their projections, which will need the development of AI interpretability capabilities.

Patient trust, like physician trust, must be earned, and this is particularly true when it comes to concerns about privacy. Next-generation regulations, which take into account advancements in privacy-preserving technologies, are a critical area of need in today's environment. When it comes to machine learning, traditional

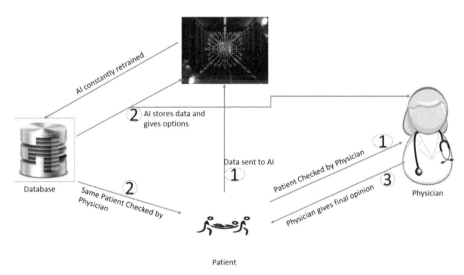

Figure 10.4. Clinical deployment.

identities are not always necessary to obtain effective results, but there are major indicators in data that might be deemed sensitive. The development of privacy-preserving methods, as well as advancements in fields such as federated learning and federated analytics, are required in order to glean insights from these sensitive data types.

Each technological breakthrough provides us with the potential to shape our own destiny. Applied to healthcare delivery, machine intelligence, learning techniques and computer vision provide a significant opportunity for making healthcare services considerably more accessible, egalitarian, accurate and inclusive than they have ever been.

10.4 A case study of vision based machine learning

In this study we will provide a comprehensive introduction and characterization of the deep learning principles and techniques as well as the deep learning architectures that we uncovered while researching medical image analysis studies.

Although there are many intricacies, machine learning algorithms are generally separated into supervised and unsupervised learning algorithms. A dataset $D = x$, $yN n = 1$ of input features x and label pairs y is submitted to a model in supervised learning. It is possible for this y to take on a variety of shapes, depending on the learning aim; for example, in a classification context, it is often represented as a scalar representing a class label, while in a regression setting it may be represented as a vector of continuous variables. A multi-dimensional label image may be utilised to train a segmentation algorithm while learning a segmentation model. Unsupervised training is typically defined as the process of selecting model parameters that largely determine the information using a loss function $L(y, y)$. The output of the model is indicated by y, and it is acquired by inputting a piece of evidence x into the model's function f, which returns the result of the model $(x;)$. Unsupervised learning algorithms are trained to find patterns in unlabeled data, such as latent subspaces, by seeing patterns in previous data. Unsupervised learning techniques such as hierarchical clustering and clustering are examples of classic unsupervised learning algorithms. One example is the reconstruction loss $L(x, x)$, in which the model must learn to rebuild its input from a lower-dimensional or noisy representation, which is commonly used in practice.

10.4.1 Networks of neurons

The vast majority of computational intelligence methods are based on neural network models, which are a type of learning algorithm in their own right. A neural network is composed of neurons or units that have some level of engagement a and parameters w and b, where w denotes weights and b denotes biases, and where W denotes activation a. Following element-wise nonlinearity (also known as a transfer function), the activation is a linear combination of the neuron's input x and the parameters, followed by the following:

$$a = (W^T x + b)\ldots\ldots \tag{10.1}$$

The sigmoid and hyperbolic tangent functions are common transfer functions for conventional neural networks. The most well-known of the classic neural networks, the multi-layered perceptron (MLP), has several layers of these transformations:

$$\begin{aligned}
&(wL(wL_1 \ldots (w_0 x + b_0) + bL_1) + bL) \\
&= (wL(wL_1 \ldots (w_0 x + b_0) + bL_1) + bL) \\
&= (wL(wL_1 \ldots (w_0 x + b_0) + bL_1) + bL) \\
&= (wL(wL_1 \ldots (w_0 x + b_0) + bL_1) \ldots \ldots \ldots \ldots .
\end{aligned}$$

(10.2)

w_n is a matrix with rows wk associated with activation k in the output, n denotes the current layer's number, with L denoting the ultimate layer. 'Hidden' layers are those that exist between the input and the output. A neural network with several hidden layers is referred to as a 'deep' neural network, therefore the name 'deep learning'.

The activations of the network's last layer are frequently mapped to a distribution over classes $P(y|x;)$ using the softmax function [7, 10].

Figure 10.5 shows a schematic illustration of three-layer MLP. The most prevalent method for fitting parameters to a dataset D is maximum likelihood with stochastic gradient descent. Instead of using the entire dataset for each gradient update, stochastic gradient descent uses a small portion of it called a minibatch. In practise, maximizing the maximum likelihood equates to lowering the negative log-likelihood: $\text{argmin}N$, $n = 1$, $\log P(y_n|x_n;)$.

As a result of this, a binary cross-entropy loss is experienced for two-class issues, while a categorical cross-entropy loss is experienced for three-class or higher problems. This technique has the problem of seldom directly optimizing the quantity we are interested in, including the region underneath the receiver operating

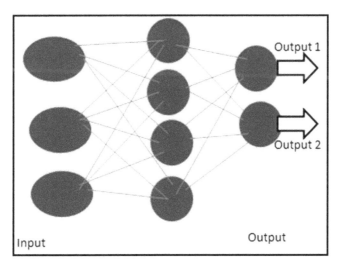

Figure 10.5. Schematic illustration of a three-layer MLP.

characteristic (ROC) curves or popular segmentation assessment metrics such as the Dice coefficient, which are both important.

Deep neural networks (DNNs) were formerly considered to be difficult to properly train because of their complexity. First proposed in 2006 [68], the idea of training DNNs layer-by-layer in an unsupervised manner (pre-training), following by supervised fine-tuning on something like a stacked network, might provide promising results. Stack autoencoders (SAEs) and deep belief networks (DBNs) are two common designs that have been trained in this method. These procedures, however, are quite complicated and necessitate a large amount of engineering to provide excellent results. The most common models are currently trained in a supervised method from beginning to end, considerably simplifying the training procedure. Convolutional neural networks (CNNs) and recurrent neural networks (RNNs) are the most prevalent architectures. Although RNNs are gaining popularity, CNNs are now the most extensively utilized in (medical) image analysis. These techniques will be discussed in detail in the following sections, commencing with one of the most often used and progressing to the least popular, highlighting the distinctions between them as well as any potential obstacles that may arise when they are applied to medical issues.

10.5 Data preparation overview

Before medical photographs can be utilized to create an artificial intelligence system, a number of steps must be accomplished. When using medical data to build a research or commercial artificial intelligence system, it is typically necessary to obtain approval from an ethical committee in the area. Before the research can begin, an institutional review board must assess the risks and benefits to patients. Retrospective studies are usually required since existing data is regularly used. Because the patients would not be subjected to any additional therapies, it is common practise to forgo the requirement for explicit informed consent in this sort of study. In clinical trials it is possible that each main investigator may be asked to provide consent for information about their subjects to be shared with other investigators. For prospective research when study data are gathered prospectively, informed consent must be obtained from the participants before the study can begin. Following ethical clearance, it is necessary to retrieve relevant data, search data, de-identify it appropriately and keep it securely. It is necessary to delete any protected health information (PHI) from of the Digital Imaging and Communications in Medicine (DICOM) infrastructure, including that of the metadata and images themselves [68]. Given that some images contain free-form remarks that have been scanned but cannot be eliminated using automated techniques, a second human evaluation of each photograph is required if the data are to be used for open-source research. The quality and number of images produced vary depending on the job and domain. The data must then be organized in a homogenized and machine-readable way [69]. Linking the pictures to ground-truth data, such as labels, segmentations, or electronic phenotypes, is the final step (e.g. biopsy or

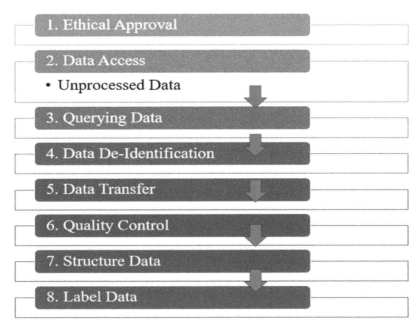

Figure 10.6. Depicts the full process of preparing medical photos for AI development.

laboratory results). Figure 10.6 depicts the entire procedure of preparing medical images for AI development.

10.5.1 Data access and querying

Because artificial intelligence researchers are not always based in hospitals, they do not always have direct access to medical image sequences via a image repository and operational changes in picture archiving and communication system (PACS), which is crucial for building algorithms for the healthcare industry. Patients' information and communications technology, i.e PACS, settings are only available to experts who have been accredited. These professions include physicians, technologists, PACS managers and clinical scientists. The method of producing the data available to artificial intelligence researchers is time-consuming and requires several stages, including de-identification of data before it can be used (described later). In-house or through collaborative research partnerships, clinical engagement with artificial intelligence researchers is the most successful strategy.

In the event that artificial intelligence developers gain access to data, they can employ a variety of ways to study medical images and clinical data. From strings to international classifications of disease codes and current procedural terminology code sets, custom search queries can encompass a wide range of information. Using radiometric information system search engines, including PACS or radiological information system search engines, data from hospital PACS and electronic health records may be used in a systematic review and accessed. Users can gain access to information such as as comments, creators, series and picture numbers as well as distinct target lesion names and linkages, among other things, from several PACS vendors, to mention a few. It is possible for these data to be exported and controlled through other systems, including health records, cancer databases, oncology databases or even other providers' databases, all of which are accessible in some PACS systems [69]. It is reasonable to implement the data searching procedure more efficiently by using different software solutions [70–72].

10.5.2 De-identification

This is required by both the Information Portability and Accountability Act of the US, commonly referred to as the Health Insurance Portability and Accountability Act (HIPAA), as well as the European General Data Protection Regulation (GDPR) that data collected from the patient be appropriately de-identified, regardless of the fact that specific informed consent from patients is not typically required. Among the personal information that should be kept secret are: name, health record number and date of birth, to name a few examples. In DICOM metadata (the header), personally identifiable information is commonly included, and many methods can be used to eliminate this relevant information [73]. In order to build de-identification procedures for a range of applications, the Radiological Association of North America Clinical Research Processors and the Medical Image Archive both use DICOM de-identification profiles [74]. Pictures including protected health information, in addition to DICOM metadata, may be included in the images, as is commonly the case with US exams or radiographs scanned into a healthcare system. To completely eliminate embedded information, more advanced de-identification techniques, such as optical character recognition [75] and human evaluation for handwriting on scanned pictures that is not usually recognized by automated systems, are necessary. Also crucial is not to combine datasets by mistake, since this raises the likelihood of re-identification by cross-linking of data points that are not linked to one another [76]. Finally, medical data may be anonymized through the use of k-anonymity [77], which modifies an original dataset including protected health information in such a way that potential intruders are unable to establish the identity of the patient. If you want to upload radiology data to an open-source research project and want to keep the metadata from DICOM, you can use another format such as the Neuroimaging Informatics Technology Initiative (NIFTI), which only conserves voxel size and patient position, instead of keeping the metadata from DICOM. Because metadata is critical for the development of artificial intelligence algorithms, entirely removing DICOM information from open-source research projects reduces privacy concerns while decreasing the value of the data.

10.5.3 Data retention

A lot of data are transmitted to local data storage (in single-center research) or external data storage (in a multi-center study or commercial AI development) to be processed. Although data are generally saved on a local server, thanks to recent

Cloud-based advancements they are now increasingly being stored in the Cloud as well.

10.5.4 Medical image resembling

Medical image perception tests are more challenging compared to tasks involving nonmedical picture perception. For classification tasks, a large number of convolution neural networks are trained and assessed on two-dimensional images with a quality of less than 300×300 pixels, which is the lowest resolution possible. Medical images, on the other hand, are larger, with a spatial resolution of more than 300×300 pixels, and many brain tumor detection investigations are three-dimensional in presentation rather than two-dimensional.

10.5.5 Choosing an appropriate label and a definition of ground truth

The supervised learning approach is used by the vast majority of contemporary artificial intelligence systems for medical image classification issues. The above indicates that before an artificial intelligence system can be taught and evaluated, it is necessary to establish and relate the ground truth to the image in question. 'Ground truth' is a word that is often used to describe facts that have been discovered via empirical evidence (such as biopsy or laboratory results). Picture labels, which are comments given by medical professionals such as radiologists, are shown on a digital image. If imaging is used as the calibration curve, these comments might be viewed as a technique to ensure accuracy. To learn reliably from ground truth information, supervised techniques sometimes need large dataset quantities. Data complication is a key factor in most corporate business difficulties. To answer the majority of real-world enterprises AI uses cases that generate significant commercial value, at least five or six distinct IT and operational software platforms will be needed. Independent IT source systems were not meant to interoperate in most enterprises, and they generally have widely varying definitions of business entities and ground truth.

10.5.6 The truth or the label's quality

In order to construct advanced healthcare imaging AI models, accurate regression coefficient parameters or picture labels for a wide range of radiological tests are required [78, 79]. There are reported proposals for imaging techniques that aim for organized presentation, which would substantially reduce the amount of time and effort necessary to extract meaningful imaging labels from the image data stream. However, a large percentage of these studies are still entirely made up of textual data, as has been the case today [80].

10.6 The future of computer vision and natural language processing in healthcare

Computer vision and natural language processing in healthcare offer a lot of potential for improving the quality and standard of care all around the world.

Photographs, scans, in-person vision, the patient's answers and medical research are used to make diagnoses. With the help of computer vision and natural language processing, these diagnoses may be performed faster and comprehensively, resulting in rapid and higher-quality healthcare for everyone. Unfortunately, while there have been many advances and technological developments in healthcare, due to the way the business operates the majority of these AI applications in healthcare are unlikely to be widely adopted for another decade. By then, we will be discussing the most recent advances in computer vision and natural language processing in healthcare.

10.7 Research related problems in computer vision

In recent years, there has been an increase in interest in creating machine learning methods for computer vision based applications, particularly in the field of computer vision. This interest stems from both commercial endeavors to create functional products based on computer vision tactics and from a general trend within the computer vision field to include machine learning techniques into their efforts. A contemporary frontier for computer vision research is learning, which has been receiving more attention in recent years.

10.7.1 View of CNN through computer vision

Constitutional networks are large-scale networks that have a high set of variables that are learned from data. Another technique to monitor overall training progress is to draw an error curve and objective function on the training and validation sets against the training process. Unfortunately, this method does not provide information about the CNN layers' real parameters and activation. It is typically helpful to see what CNNs have acquired throughout a training process or or after it has been completed. The following sections present some basic methods for presenting convolution neural networks and their operation.

10.7.2 Visualizations based on gradients

Balduzzi *et al* [81] proposed that viewing gradient distributions could provide valuable insights into deep neural network convergence behavior. According research findings, blindly boosting the complexity of a neural network causes the issue of gradient shattering (i.e. the gradients have a distribution akin to white noise). When batch normalization and skip interconnections were applied in a very deep network, they demonstrated that the gradient distribution approximated brown noise.

Figure 10.7 shows the gradient of the network for inputs $x2[2, 2]$ and its covariance matrix and panel (d) shows a discrete approximation to Brownian motion:

$$B^n(t) = (x + a)^n = \sum_{s=1}^{t} w_s, \quad \text{where } w_s \sim \mathcal{N}\left(0, \frac{1}{N}\right).$$

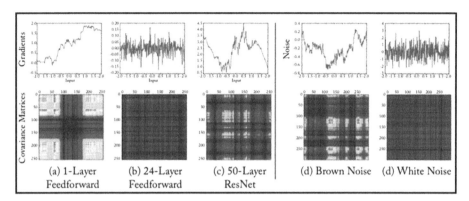

Figure 10.7. The top row shows the gradient distributions for a range of uniformly sampled inputs. The bottom row shows the covariance matrices. The gradients for the case of a 24 layered network resemble white noise, while the gradients of high-performing ResNet resemble brown noise. Note that the ResNet used skip connections and batch normalization which results in better convergence even with much deeper network architectures. Reproduced from [81] with permission of the authors.

The plots are strikingly similar and both clearly exhibit a spatial covariance structure. The resemblance is not coincidental: this section implies Donsker's theorem to show the gradient converges to Brownian motion as $N \to \infty$. Gradients of deep networks resemble white noise. Figure 10.7(b) shows the gradient of a 24-layer fully connected rectifier network. Figure 10.7(e) shows white noise given by samples $wk \leftarrow N(0, 1)$. Again, the plots are strikingly similar. Since the inputs lie on a one-dimensional grid, it makes sense to compute the autocorrelation function (ACF) of the gradient. Figures 10.7(a)–(d) compare this function for feedforward networks of different depths with white and brown noise. The ACF for shallow networks resembles the ACF of brown noise. As the network becomes deeper, the ACF quickly comes to resemble that of white noise. Figure 10.7 explains this phenomenon. We show that correlations between gradients decrease exponentially $\frac{1}{2^1}$ with depth in feedforward rectifier networks.

Shattering is reduced by using skip connections in conjunction with appropriate rescaling. We show that for feedforward typologies, the rate at which correlations between gradients decays is exponential, whereas for ResNets, the rate is sub-linear. Our investigation reveals a surprising and (at least to us) unexpected side effect of batch normalization. Designing non-shattering initialization, such as the LLinit, is an alternative solution to the shattering gradient problem. Future research could look into hybrid architectures that combine the LLinit with skip connections.

References

[1] Esteva A *et al* 2021 Deep learning-enabled medical computer vision *NPJ Digit. Med.* **4** 5
[2] Szeliski R 2010 *Computer Vision: Algorithms and Applications* (Berlin: Springer)
[3] LeCun Y, Bengio Y and Hinton G 2015 Deep learning *Nature* **521** 436–44

[4] Sanders J and Kandrot E 2010 *CUDA by Example: an Introduction to General-Purpose GPU Programming* (Upper Saddle River, NJ: Addison-Wesley) .

[5] Deng J *et al* 2009 ImageNet: a large-scale hierarchical image database *Conf. on Computer Vision and Pattern Recognition* (Piscataway, NJ: IEEE) pp 248–55

[6] Topol E J 2019 High-performance medicine: the convergence of human and artificial intelligence *Nat. Med.* **25** 44–56

[7] Esteva A *et al* 2017 Dermatologist-level classification of skin cancer with deep neural networks *Nature* **542** 115–8

[8] Yeung S *et al* 2019 A computer vision system for deep learning-based detection of patient mobilization activities in the ICU *NPJ Digit. Med.* **2** 11

[9] Russakovsky O *et al* 2015 ImageNet large scale visual recognition challenge *Int. J. Comput. Vis.* **115** 211–52

[10] Krizhevsky A, Sutskever I and Hinton G E 2012 ImageNet classification with deep convolutional neural networks *Advances in Neural Information Processing Systems* ed F Pereira, C J C Burges, L Bottou and K Q Weinberger (Red Hook, NY: Curran) pp 1097–105

[11] Sermanet P *et al* 2013 OverFeat: integrated recognition, localization and detection using convolutional networks arXiv: 1312.6229

[12] Simonyan K and Zisserman A 2014 Very deep convolutional networks for large-scale image recognition arXiv: 1409.1556

[13] Szegedy C *et al* 2015 Going deeper with convolutions *Proc. IEEE Conf. on Computer Vision and Pattern Recognition (CVPR)* pp 1–9

[14] He K, Zhang X, Ren S and Sun J 2016 Deep residual learning for image recognition *Proc. IEEE Conf. on Computer Vision and Pattern Recognition* pp 770–8

[15] Gebru T, Hoffman J and Fei-Fei L 2017 Fine-grained recognition in the wild: a multi-task domain adaptation approach *Int. Conf. on Computer Vision* (Piscataway, NJ: IEEE) pp 1358–67

[16] Gulshan V *et al* 2014 Performance of a deep-learning algorithm vs manual grading for detecting diabetic retinopathy in India *JAMA Ophthalmol.* **137** 987–93

[17] Ronneberger O, Fischer P and Brox T 2015 U-net: convolutional networks for biomedical image segmentation *Int. Conf. on Medical Image Computing and Computer-Assisted Intervention* (Cham: Springer) pp 234–41

[18] Isensee F *et al* 2018 nnU-Net: self-adapting framework for U-Net-based medical image segmentation arXiv: 1809.10486

[19] LeCun Y and Bengio Y 1996 *The Handbook of Brain Theory and Neural Networks* (Cambridge, MA: MIT Press) pp 255–8

[20] Cubuk E D, Zoph B, Mane D, Vasudevan V and Le Q V 2018 AutoAugment: learning augmentation policies from data arXiv: 1805.09501

[21] Goodfellow I *et al* 2014 Generative adversarial nets *Advances in Neural Information Processing Systems* pp 2672–80

[22] Ørting S *et al* 2019 A survey of crowdsourcing in medical image analysis arXiv: 1902.09159

[23] Créquit P, Mansouri G, Benchoufi M, Vivot A and Ravaud P 2018 Mapping of crowdsourcing in health: systematic review *J. Med. Internet Res.* **20** e187

[24] Jing L and Tian Y 2020 Self-supervised visual feature learning with deep neural networks: A survey *IEEE Trans. Pattern Anal. Machine Intell.* **43** 4037–58

[25] McMahan B, Moore E, Ramage D, Hampson S and Arcas B A 2017 Communication-efficient learning of deep networks from decentralized data *Artificial Intelligence and Statistics* (PMLR) pp 1273–82

[26] Karpathy A and Fei-Fei L 2015 Deep visual-semantic alignments for generating image descriptions *Proc. Conf. on Computer Vision and Pattern Recognition* (Piscataway, NJ: IEEE) pp 3128–37

[27] Lv D *et al* 2017 Research on the technology of LIDAR data processing *First Int. Conf. on Electronics Instrumentation Information Systems* (Piscataway, NJ: IEEE) pp 1–5

[28] Lillo I, Niebles J C and Soto A 2017 Sparse composition of body poses and atomic actions for human activity recognition in RGB-D videos *Image Vis. Comput.* **59** 63–75

[29] Haque A *et al* 2017 Towards vision-based smart hospitals: a system for tracking and monitoring hand hygiene compliance *Proc. of the 2nd Machine Learning for Healthcare Conf.* vol 68 (PMLR) pp 75–87

[30] Heilbron F C, Escorcia V, Ghanem B and Niebles J C 2015 ActivityNet: a large-scale video benchmark for human activity understanding *Conf. on Computer Vision and Pattern Recognition* (Piscataway, NJ: IEEE) pp 961–70

[31] Liu Y *et al* 2019 Learning to describe scenes with programs *Int. Conf. on Learning Representation*

[32] Singh A *et al* 2020 Automatic detection of hand hygiene using computer vision technology *J. Am. Med. Inform. Assoc.* **27** 1316–20

[33] Litjens G *et al* 2017 A survey on deep learning in medical image analysis *Med. Image Anal.* **42** 60–88

[34] Maron O and Lozano-Pérez T 1998 A framework for multiple-instance learning *Advances in Neural Information Processing Systems 10* M I Jordan, M J Kearns and S A Solla (Cambridge, MA: MIT Press) pp 570–6

[35] Singh S P *et al* 2020 3D deep learning on medical images: a review *Sensors* **20** 5097

[36] Ouyang D *et al* 2020 Video-based AI for beat-to-beat assessment of cardiac function *Nature* **580** 252–6

[37] Benjamens S, Dhunnoo P and Meskó B 2020 The state of artificial intelligence-based FDA-approved medical devices and algorithms: an online database *NPJ Digit. Med.* **3** 118

[38] Beede E *et al* 2020 A human-centered evaluation of a deep learning system deployed in clinics for the detection of diabetic retinopathy *Proc. 2020 CHI Conf. on Human Factors in Computing Systems* (New York: Association for Computing Machinery) pp 1–12

[39] Viz.ai 2020 Viz.ai granted medicare new technology add-on payment *CISION PR Newswire*

[40] Crowson M G *et al* 2020 A contemporary review of machine learning in otolaryngology-head and neck surgery *Laryngoscope* **130** 45–51

[41] Livingstone D, Talai A S, Chau J and Forkert N D 2019 Building an otoscopic screening prototype tool using deep learning *J. Otolaryngol. Head. Neck Surg.* **48** 66

[42] Chen P-H C *et al* 2019 An augmented reality microscope with real-time artificial intelligence integration for cancer diagnosis *Nat. Med.* **25** 1453–7

[43] Gunčar G *et al* 2018 An application of machine learning to haematological diagnosis *Sci. Rep.* **8** 411

[44] Alam M M and Islam M T 2019 Machine learning approach of automatic identification and counting of blood cells *Health. Technol. Lett.* **6** 103–8

[45] El Hajjar A and Rey J-F 2020 Artificial intelligence in gastrointestinal endoscopy: general overview *Chin. Med. J.* **133** 326–34

[46] Park S-M *et al* 2020 A mountable toilet system for personalized health monitoring via the analysis of excreta *Nat. Biomed. Eng.* **4** 624–35

[47] VerMilyea M *et al* 2020 Development of an artificial intelligence-based assessment model for prediction of embryo viability using static images captured by optical light microscopy during IVF *Hum. Reprod.* **35** 770–84

[48] Choy G *et al* 2018 Current applications and future impact of machine learning in radiology *Radiology* **288** 318–28

[49] Saba L *et al* 2019 The present and future of deep learning in radiology *Eur. J. Radiol.* **114** 14–24

[50] Mazurowski M A, Buda M, Saha A and Bashir M R 2019 Deep learning in radiology: an overview of the concepts and a survey of the state of the art with focus on MRI *J. Magn. Reson. Imaging* **49** 939–54

[51] Johnson A E W *et al* 2019 MIMIC-CXR, a de-identified publicly available database of chest radiographs with free-text reports *Sci. Data* **6** 317

[52] Irvin J *et al* 2019 Chexpert: a large chest radiograph dataset with uncertainty labels and expert comparison *Proc. of the AAAI Conf. on Artificial Intelligence (Honolulu, HI)* vol 33 pp 590–7

[53] Wang X *et al* 2017 Chestx-ray8: hospital-scale chest x-ray database and benchmarks on weakly-supervised classification and localization of common thorax diseases *Proc. IEEE Conf. on Computer Vision and Pattern Recognition (Honolulu, HI)* pp 2097–106

[54] Chilamkurthy S *et al* 2018 Deep learning algorithms for detection of critical findings in head CT scans: a retrospective study *Lancet* **392** 2388–96

[55] Weston A D *et al* 2019 Automated abdominal segmentation of CT scans for body composition analysis using deep learning *Radiology* **290** 669–79

[56] Ding J, Li A, Hu Z and Wang L 2017 *Medical Image Computing and Computer Assisted Intervention—MICCAI* (Berlin: Springer) pp 559–67

[57] Tan L K, Liew Y M, Lim E and McLaughlin R A 2017 Convolutional neural network regression for short-axis left ventricle segmentation in cardiac cine MR sequences *Med. Image Anal.* **39** 78–86

[58] Zhang J *et al* 2020 Viral pneumonia screening on chest x-ray images using confidence-aware anomaly detection arXiv: 2003.12338

[59] Zhang X, Feng C, Wang A, Yang L and Hao Y 2020 CT super-resolution using multiple dense residual block based GAN *Syst. Signal Image Video Technol.* **15** 725–33

[60] Papolos A, Narula J, Bavishi C, Chaudhry F A and Sengupta P P U S 2016 Hospital use of echocardiography: insights from the nationwide inpatient sample *J. Am. Coll. Cardiol.* **67** 502–11

[61] clinicaltrials.gov 2017 HeartFlowNXT—heart flow analysis of coronary blood flow using coronary CT angiography—study results

[62] Perkins C, Balma D and Garcia R 2007 Why current breast pathology practices must be evaluated. A Susan G Komen for the Cure white paper: June 2006 *Breast J.* **13** 443–7

[63] Esteva A and Topol E 2019 Can skin cancer diagnosis be transformed by AI? *Lancet* **394** 1795

[64] Li Y *et al* 2016 Skin cancer detection and tracking using data synthesis and deep learning arXiv: 1612.01074

[65] Maier-Hein L *et al* 2017 Surgical data science for next-generation interventions *Nat. Biomed. Eng.* **1** 691–6

[66] Webster D and Celik O 2014 Systematic review of kinect applications in elderly care and stroke rehabilitation *J. Neuroeng. Rehabil.* **11** 108

[67] Wulczyn E *et al* 2020 Deep learning-based survival prediction for multiple cancer types using histopathology images *PLoS One* **15** e0233678

[68] Hinton G E and Salakhutdinov R R 2006 Reducing the dimensionality of data with neural networks *Science* **313** 504–7

[69] Goyal N *et al* 2017 ENABLE (exportable notation and bookmark list engine): an interface to manage tumor measurement data from PACS to cancer databases *J. Digit. Imag.* **30** 275–86

[70] Nuance 2019 mPower clinical analytics for medical imaging *Nuance*

[71] Stanford Research Informatics Center 2019 STAnford Research Repository (STARR) Tools, https://med.stanford.edu/starr-tools.html

[72] Poglitsch A, Waelkens C, Bauer O H, Cepa J, Feuchtgruber H, Henning T and Van Hoof C *et al* 2010 The Herschel Photodetector Array Camera & Spectrometer (PACS): design and in-flight operation and scientific performance *38th COSPAR Scientific Assembly* **38** 13

[73] Aryanto K Y, Oudkerk M and van Ooijen P M 2015 Free DICOM de-identification tools in clinical research: functioning and safety of patient privacy *Eur. Radiol.* **25** 3685–95

[74] Moore S M *et al* 2015 De-identification of medical images with retention of scientific research value *RadioGraphics* **35** 727–35

[75] Google-Healthcare 2019 De-identifying DICOM data

[76] Price W N 2nd and Cohen I G 2019 Privacy in the age of medical big data *Nat. Med.* **25** 37–43

[77] El Emam K and Dankar F K 2008 Protecting privacy using k-anonymity *J. Am. Med. Inform. Assoc.* **15** 627–37

[78] Brodley C E and Friedl M A 1999 Identifying mislabeled training data *J Artif. Intell. Res* **11** 131–67

[79] Sheng V S, Provost F and Ipeirotis P G 2008 Get another label? Improving data quality and data mining using multiple, noisy labelers *Proc. of the 14th ACM SIGKDD Int. Conf. on Knowledge Discovery and Data Mining (Las Vegas, NV, 24–27 August)* (New York: Association for Computing Machinery) pp 614–22

[80] European Society of Radiology (ESR) 2018 ESR paper on structured reporting in radiology *Insights Imaging* **9** 1–7

[81] Balduzzi D, Frean M, Leary L, Lewis J P, Ma K W D and McWilliams B 2017 The shattered gradients problem: If resnets are the answer, then what is the question? *Int. Conf. on Machine Learning* pp 342–50

Chapter 11

Machine learning in medicine: diagnosis of skin cancer using a support vector machine (SVM) classifier

Siddarth Shah, Dipen Gohil, Rutvik Shah and Manan Shah

Exceptional advancements in computer vision and automated systems in recent years have demonstrated high potential in many fields, one of the most significant fields being medicine, which benefits from the insights that computer vision can extract from imaging. The development of modern computer vision techniques, backed by machine learning (ML) and artificial intelligence (AI), are used for medical applications such as medical imaging. One of the most common and dreadful types of cancers, which is primarily caused due to high sensitivity to ultraviolet (UV) rays from the sun, is skin cancer (scientifically known as malignant melanoma). The diagnosis of skin cancer has now been made easier and more convenient by using the techniques of computer vision and machine learning, as these are more reliable and also reduce human effort and errors. Computer vision, coupled with a supervised machine learning model (such as SVM) based diagnosis systems are now being used in many dermatology clinics which aim to achieve the early diagnosis of skin cancer. The detection of malignant cells can be carried out using different techniques in computer-aided diagnosis (CAD) systems such as pre-processing, extraction of features, classification and segmentation. Various algorithms for the detection and segmentation of skin tumor images based on colors have been developed. Color segmentation techniques have proven successful in identifying areas affected by tumors and the success rate of diagnosis by segmentation reaches as high as 93%.

11.1 Introduction

Skin cancer is described as the abnormal growth of skin cells, and it most often occurs on areas of the skin which have been exposed to the sun for an extended length of time. It is the most prevalent form of human cancer. The three types of skin cancer are squamous cell carcinoma, basal cell carcinoma and malignant melanoma [1].

Skin cancer begins at the outermost layer, which is composed of squamous cells, basal cells and melanocytes, which are the first, second and third or innermost layers, respectively. Non-melanoma cancers include squamous cell and basal cell carcinomas [2], which spread to other tissues of the skin. Melanoma, on the other hand, is the least common but most malignant deadly cancer.

The signs and symptoms of the different types of skin cancers are as follows:

- *Basal cell carcinoma.*

    This type of cancer usually appears in areas exposed to the sun, such as the neck and face. It can appear as a pearly or waxy bump or a smooth flesh-colored scar-like lesion on the skin. This can result in a bleeding or scabbing sore on the infected areas of the skin.

- *Squamous cell carcinoma.*

    These are similar to basal cells, however, skin that has a dark gradient is more prone to develop squamous cell carcinoma in areas that are generally obscured from the sun. It generally manifests as a firm, red-colored lump or as a flat, crusty lesion.

- *Melanoma.* In the case of melanoma, it can appear anyplace on the body. It commonly affects men's faces or trunks, while women's lower legs are infected. It could take the form of a huge brownish area with dark flecks, a mole with varying color and dimensions, a painful abrasion that causes itching and burns, or mucous membrane linings around the mouth, nose, vagina or anus.

For the detection of skin cancer, the biopsy procedure is a recognized diagnostic approach for detecting skin melanoma and 'is a procedure that involves removing a section of tissue or cell samples from a patient's body so that it may be analyzed in a laboratory. It is a cumbersome process' [3]. The biopsy method is complex and time-consuming for both the patient and the medic because testing takes a long time. Biopsies are performed by extracting skin tissues (skin cells), which are then subjected to a range of laboratory tests.

Given the risks associated with biopsies, skin cancer diagnosis using machine learning techniques such as support vector machines (SVMs) is advocated, 'utiliz [ing] digital image processing techniques followed by SVM for the purpose of classifying the images' [4]. According to [5] '[t]his technology has inspired the early identification of skin malignancies and does not entail applying oil on the skin in order to obtain clear, crisp pictures of your moles'. Further, according to [6], '[i]t's a faster and cleaner method this way. Most significantly, because of the greater magnification, skin cancer detection can be performed'. SVM may help to avoid the needless removal of completely innocuous moles and skin lesions. We will discuss the SVM methodology in detail in this chapter.

11.2 Technologies used in skin cancer detection

According to [7], 'computer vision is used to analyze lesions on pictures by providing computers with abilities that are comparable to those of humans'. There are numerous datasets available that can be used for skin imaging, e.g. the International Skin

Imaging Collaboration (ISIC) 2018 dataset of HAM10000 pictures [8]. A convolution neural network (CNN) with multi-categorization may be employed for classifying the 2018 dataset.

A camera lens can obtain a wide-angle photograph of large skin areas of a patient in a primary care environment. All pigmented skin lesions seen in the wide-field picture can be detected, extracted and analyzed by an automated method. This can be done through a pre-trained deep convolutional neural network (DCNN) which 'detects individual pigmented lesions, evaluates their suspiciousness, and tags them (yellow = consider an additional investigation, red = demands further inspection or referral to a dermatologist)' [9]. Extracted characteristics are then utilized to evaluate pigmented lesions and provide the results.

Machine learning is applied for automatic identification of skin lesions, which is done by utilizing approaches for detecting lesions with better accuracy, efficiency and performance criteria. For early identification of skin lesions, the following three techniques of feature extraction can be employed: ABCD rule, GLCM and HOG (Histogram of Oriented Gradients) feature extraction.

An image is made to undergo several processes before segmentation and classification. This is called pre-processing and it is done to increase the quality and precision of skin lesions in order to decrease artifacts, skin color, hair and other factors in the proposed study. A geodesic active contour (GAC) was used to segment the lesion, which was then used for feature extraction. The ABCD scoring technique was used to extract symmetry, border, color and diameter characteristics, while the HOG and GLCM methods were deployed to extract textural data. The collected characteristics were immediately given to classifiers, which use various machine learning techniques such as SVM to identify and differentiate between benign and malignant skin lesions (figure 11.1).

11.3 Support vector machines (SVMs)

SVMs are a robust machine learning approach that is used for efficient and accurate categorization. SVMs are used for an eclectic range of applications, for example, object identification, for recognizing speech, bioinformatics, picture classification and identification, medical diagnosis, and many more. Vladimir Vapnik and colleagues

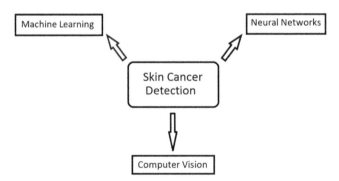

Figure 11.1. Classification of skin cancer detection.

created the SVM at AT&T Bell Laboratories. SVMs, which are based on statistical learning frameworks or the VC (Vapnik–Chervonenkis) theory established by Vapnik and Chervonenkis, are among the most resilient prediction approaches.

The method of supervised learning is divided into two phases: training/learning and classification: 'a differentiating hyperplane is created during the training stage utilizing an input training dataset including data samples' and '[t]he ideal hyperplane that forms the decision boundary is the one that optimally splits the data into two classes (positive and negative samples)' [10].

The sample points that lie on or near the boundaries are called support vectors (SVs). The SVs are illustrated in figure 11.2. These SVs are then employed for the classification step to predict the right class for the test data input.

Support vector machines have the following advantages:
- They work well in three-dimensional areas.
- SVs can be used if the number of parameters exceeds the amount of class samples.
- It uses a subset of training points (called SVs) in the output function, which saves memory.
- It is versatile as 'different kernel functions can be used for the decision function. Common kernels are provided, however custom kernels can be specified' [11].

The drawbacks of support vector machines include:
- They '[p]revent over-fitting when picking kernel functions if the number of attributes is considerably more than the number of samples' [12].

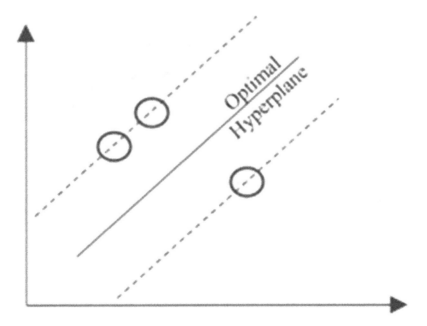

Figure 11.2. The SVM separating hyperplane.

- Considering the SVM, the regularization term is critical and as such cannot be ignored.
- SVMs cannot directly deliver probability evaluations. These need to be calculated by means of an expensive five-fold cross-validation.

11.4 The SVM in skin cancer detection

11.4.1 Image acquisition

This section discusses how to use publicly available skin cancer image databases (figure 11.3).

According to [13], '[s]kin cancer researchers mostly employ two distinct types of pictures—images gathered through dermoscopy or digital images available on the Internet. Dermoscopic pictures are taken at a pathological center by specialist dedicated equipment. These are zoomed in on a specific area of interest'. Digital pictures, on the other hand, are captured using any image capturing device with minimal attention on the region of interest. Dermoscopy pictures are better for diagnosis, but they require the expertise of a dermatologist to diagnose skin cancer. Digital image-based skin cancer diagnostic technology is in high demand.

11.4.1.1 Pre-processing
Image pre-processing comprises two steps:
   A. *Image filtering.*
        Skin pictures feature a variety of undesirable figures or defects, for example, hair, air bubbles and noise. As a result, each and every picture in the collection must be de-noised. This is accomplished through the employment of a variety of methods. The median filter is a method utilized by the majority of researchers to remove hair and de-noise skin pictures.

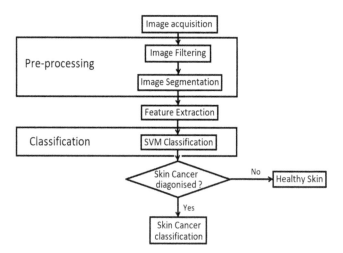

Figure 11.3. SVM classification flowchart.

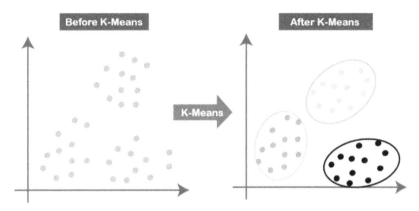

Figure 11.4. *k*-means clustering.

Sharpening filters and dull razor software are also used by some throughout the skin picture pre-processing stage.

The filter which is most prominently used in digital image processing (DIP) is the median filter, because it may preserve the edge while decreasing noise in certain situations: 'The median filter works by going over the picture window by window and replacing individual entry with the median of the surrounding entries. The median filter is a non-linear levelling method that efficiently eradicates noise while maintaining the edge' [14]. The fact that the border of skin cancer cells has a nodular shape is one of the most essential characteristics of skin cancer. The border structure is utilized to obtain an accurate diagnosis. As a result, the median filter is critical for pre-processing of skin images since it preserves the border structure. This effectively preserves the spatial resolution of a picture [13].

B. *Image segmentation*. Image segmentation can be defined as the process of separating an image into numerous pieces in order to classify an item and screen out irrelevant data. Pre-processing of the picture of skin is performed initially, after which it is necessary to segment the picture and remove the regions other than region of interest to skin cancer detection technologies. The classification algorithm's quality can be improved if skin image segmentation is done properly and rapidly. Various segmentation methods employed by various researchers are described below.

11.4.1.2 k-*means clustering*

According to [15], '*k*-means is a clustering, unsupervised pre-processing step that is implemented to classify data into diverse alike groups'. It is a widely used picture segmentation approach in machine learning. In image processing, *k*-means has been used to take out the region of interest from the background of the picture. *k* determines the number of groups into which we wish to split the image in the *k*-means approach. This *k* value must be defined. The *k*-means method is divided into two steps: (i) estimating the average of each grouping, after the distance of each point from each group or cluster is calculated by subtracting the point's length from the matching cluster's mean, and (ii) each point is given to the cluster to which it is the most closely related.

These two phases are repeated in k-means until the summation of squares of each point within each group reaches a user-defined minimal threshold error. To cluster randomly, the beginning points must be defined. Throughout iteration the k-means algorithm tries to minimalize the total across all groups as well as the sum of the square of errors inside each group, as well as changing the center of a group dynamically throughout the run time. At the segmentation step, when the k-means segmentation method is applied to a grayscale picture, it divides it into two distinct sets. One group is designated as zero, while the other is classified as one. The two clusters combine to form a matrix called a mask, which contains the black and white versions of the original picture [16]. The white picture labeled one indicates skin lesion, whereas the black image labeled zero represents normal skin. After this, multiplication of the mask matrix is done pixel by pixel using a greyscale/color picture, yielding just the skin lesion portion [13].

11.4.1.3 Region of interest (ROI) clustering

ROI clustering is a sophisticated thresholding segmentation algorithm that computes intensity values from grayscale pictures. It can distinguish between dark and bright substances in a given picture. Normal skin is permanently lighter in color compared to skin lesions. As a result, the distribution of normal skin is likewise greater [13]. There is a strong sign of a dramatic reduction in pixel intensity distribution. This inferior distribution can be utilized as the histogram's threshold and '[i]f the pixel value is more than the threshold, it is considered a lesion, and if the pixel value is less than the threshold, it is considered normal skin' [17].

11.4.2 Feature extraction

Extracting features is the next part of the recognition and classification procedure. The segmented picture separates the features, and feature extraction is performed on images using techniques such as the gray-level co-occurrence matrix (GLCM) and ABCD rule techniques.

ABCD rule. In computerized skin cancer analysis, the qualities known as ABCD are used to extract features. As described in [18], '[t]he ABCD rule-based recognition extracts the cutaneous lesion using the ABCD rule that has four characteristics: A—asymmetry, B—border, C—color, and D—diameter'. These are as follows:

Asymmetry: Melanoma lesions have an asymmetric appearance. Because of this, the asymmetry index is used to determine the entity's level of symmetry. This is accomplished by dividing the picture into parallel or upright halves.

Border: 'The border of melanoma is uneven, ragged, and indistinct' [18]. The compactness index is used to determine the extent of the border irregularity.

Color: Melanoma is not always the same color as a normal mole. The color consistency is determined by the normalized Euclidean distance between each pixel.

Diameter: In the case of a melanoma lesion, it is larger than 6 mm in diameter. The diameter in the picture is determined and equated to a measurement of 6 mm.

Gray-level co-occurrence matrix features. The GLCM investigates the dimensional connection of pixels using an arithmetic technique. The gray-level spatial dependency matrix is another name for the gray-level co-occurrence matrix. The GLCM calculates the combination of pixels in a picture that has definite principles and appears in a specific dimensional association [19]. These statistics provide information about an image's surface.

11.4.3 SVM classification

Classification techniques group the image and distinguish it from other skin disorders. For simplicity of usage, the SVM classification technique is employed to reorganize the images into hazardous and harmless groups. The support vector machine is utilized because of its excellent accuracy for multi-class characterization, ease of analytical application and direct geometric transformation [20]. The SVM can be defined as a supervised and non-linear classifier that generates an optimum n-dimensional hyperplane to categorize each input point. By maximizing the separation hyperplane between them it assigns a class to each piece of data in the dataset. The maximum margin classifier is another name for the SVM. During model training, the SVM attempts to maximize the distance between the hyperplane and the separating hyperplane [21]. As a result, the input sample data in SVM classification is seen as an n-dimensional vector, and our goal is to create a hyperplane with $n - 1$ dimensions. This approach uses the hyperplane to maximize the distance, on all sides, between it and the nearest data point. In figure 11.5 the exact architecture of the SVM is shown in a linear way, with the three hyperplanes represented by H, H_1 and H_2, which correctly distinguishes the two classes. Because H has the greatest deviation from the support vectors, it is picked as the best classification hyperplane.

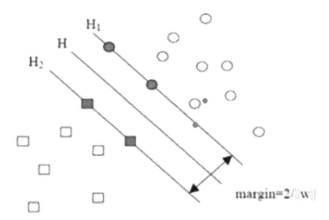

Figure 11.5. Schematic of linear SVMs.

An SVM is capable of learning both linear and non-linear classifiers. SVM classifiers are trained via a Lagrangian dual. SVMs can perform linear classification as well accomplishing non-linear classification effectively by adopting a technique known as the kernel technique, in which the inputs are implicitly translated onto high-dimensional feature spaces [22]. When the data in the original feature space are not linearly separable, an SVM employs a kernel to convert the feature space to a higher dimension.

11.5 Brief description of skin cancer detection

The different forms of skin cancer reported in this study include basal cell and squamous cell carcinoma, malignant melanoma and actinic keratosis (solar keratosis). A new DE-ANN-based feature extraction and classification technique with high accuracy is described. The recommended technique begins with some pre-processing to smoothen, improve and remove noise from a given image. In this case the segmentation method is employed to reduce noise. It enhances the look of facial features while also eliminating wrinkles and oiliness from the image of the face. Image classification is the next stage, which splits a picture into distinct sections based on criteria such as intensity, color and surface characteristics. Here, the fuzzy C-means clustering technique is used to segment or build homogeneous clusters. The local binary pattern (LBP), RGB color scheme and GLCM algorithms are then used to extract picture characteristics from a segmented image. RGB is used to estimate color characteristics such as contrast, association, monotony, mean and kurtosis, whereas GLCM is used to estimate texture features such as contrast, correlation, homogeneity, mean and skewness. The suggested technique employs 500 pictures, both malignant and non-cancerous, from the HAM dataset. The DE-ANN classified around 325 pictures as carcinogenic and about 175 as benign. With 97% accuracy, the suggested approach retrieves the skin lesion portions of the image and the assessed characteristics, which are subsequently utilized for training the DE-ANN classifier [19].

For real-time applications, SVM classifiers integrated into hardware can enhance computation speed while reducing the energy consumption in real-time applications. The goal of this research is to create a real-time embedded classifier capable of detecting melanoma early on, utilizing a low-cost portable device. SVM is an abbreviation for support vector machine, and it is used for precise and effective classification in a variety of applications such as object recognition, clinical diagnosis and others. The two primary phases of the SVM method are training/learning and classification. The embedded system design was also reduced using the HLS (high level synthesis) approach, resulting in less accuracy. When related to other published variants in the literature, the system utilised in this study is considered a low-power system. As a consequence, the suggested technique might be utilised to create a real-time embedded system that delivers accurate cancer classification while using the least amount of money, space and power. The suggested integrated SVM classifier might be utilised for a variety of virtual real identification applications in the future. Furthermore, other designers may find the

the Zynq design and HLS approach beneficial for creating new embedded systems. In the future, further analysis and implementation approaches, such as the multiplier-less methodology and the DPR (dynamic partial reconfiguration) methodology, will be utilised [10].

Early detection is critical for a better chance of survival. Because melanoma is mostly seen on the outside of the body, a skin doctor can employ computer-assisted diagnostics with digital image processing to help detect it. The authors used the ABCD rule to identify melanoma. Traditional image processing is used in their method (image enhancement, mean shift segmentation and feature extraction). The retrieved features are then utilised to train and predict whether a picture is positive or negative using an SVM classification model, and experiments demonstrate that high accuracy may be achieved with a small number of usable features. They employed the GrabCut method to segment an input image into melanoma-like lesions of interest, and then used image processing techniques to extract specific properties such as shape, color and geometry. Using a support vector machine with a Gaussian radial basis kernel, these obtained features are classified as cancerous (malignant) or benign (benign) moles. Out of the 200 photos examined, only six features were found to be adequate for diagnosing the majority of malignant cases and providing reliable information for skin cancer diagnosis [22].

The authors of [23] proposed an algorithm for early detection of skin lesions that uses feature extraction based on the ABCD rule, GLCM and HOG feature extraction. In the study proposed by Vidya *et al*, pre-processing is utilised to improve the quality and clarity of skin lesions in order to reduce artefacts, skin color and hair, among other things. To detect the skin lesion automatically, methods for lesion identification that meet accuracy, efficiency and performance requirements can be applied. The procedure includes data collection, pre-processing, segmentation, feature extraction and classification. As experiment data, the scientists used skin lesion photographs obtained from ISIC. There were 328 benign photographs and 672 melanoma photographs in the databases. The geodesic active contour (GAC) is used in segmentation to locate lesion regions. After that, properties such as symmetry, border, color and diameter were extracted using the ABCD scoring system. HOG and GLCM are used to extract textural information. To handle classification, several machine learning algorithms were added, including SVM, k-nearest neighbors (k-NN) and naive Bayes. Using SVM classifiers, the classification results in an output with 97.8% accuracy (AC) and 0.94 area under the curve (AUC). With an AC of 97.8% and an AUC of 0.94, the SVM beats all the other classification algorithms. k-NN has a sensitivity of 86.2% and a specificity of 85% [23].

Jayade and colleagues [24] offer a method for extracting features from skin photos and classifying them with a support vector-based classifier. Skin cancer is identified using an SVM-based classification technique. The gray-level co-occurrence matrix approach is used to extract features. This technique is used to extract features from photographs, which are then used to categorize the images.

The input image is first pre-processed with techniques such as grayscale conversion, then a median filter is used to minimize noise and finally the error-free image is utilised to extract features by implementing the GLCM extraction approach. The collected attributes are then sent into the SVM classifier, which uses them to differentiate between cancerous and non-cancerous pictures. The experiment was carried out on 100 different photographs, and the correctness of the results was determined. This technique outperforms previous systems, with empirical studies indicating that the suggested system has an accuracy of 94.05%.

The skin cancer detection technology pipeline is described in detail in the Jana *et al* [13] paper, which begins with the collection of worrisome skin images. They achieved this goal by using a small set of publicly available skin imaging data. There may be a lot of flaws and artefacts in the obtained skin images. As a result, air bubbles, hairs and noise are removed, and the image is de-noised before further processing. The de-noised image is then segmented to retrieve the region of interest. Before any classification method is applied, a feature set is determined that might be drawn out from the segmented image. Then, to identify cancer, a machine learning or deep learning classification system is applied. The authors undertook a comprehensive study and comparison of current skin cancer screening methods. As a result, of all the algorithms examined for skin cancer diagnosis, SVM produces the best results. In addition, a review as well as an analysis of the various types of ANN architecture, as well as the application of SVM for skin cancer picture sorting, are presented, along with accuracy and performance results.

In [6] the authors looked at textural information to see if it could be used to diagnose skin cancer. Their ultimate goal was to improve the DSS's overall decision-making capabilities and to use texture information to distinguish between benign and malignant skin lesions. The authors exploited a three-layered mechanism innate in the SVM approach to improve the generalization error rate and processing productivity. They presented an SVM-based texture classification approach for early melanoma diagnosis. All of the tests were carried out using AR features, which are a basic texture feature. Following that, the approach was tested on a binary texture classification benchmark problem, and the best window size 17×17 and fourth-degree polynomial kernel for SVM were chosen based on performance analysis. The best window size was 35×35, and the fourth-degree polynomial kernel was the best degree, according to the same performance study procedure. Experiments were carried out on 22 sets of skin lesion pictures with non-disputable class labels using this set of parameters. The average accuracy for binary classification is determined to be around 70% when 200 feature vectors are picked from each image [6].

In [25] the authors proposed employing the power of texture feature extraction to acquire the characteristics of lesions. They also used a multi-class SVM (MSVM), which is an amalgamation of binary SVMs, for training and categorizing the different versions of skin cancer previously identified. The author gives a brief description of the global color histogram (GCH) and color coherence vector (CCV), both of which are implemented in the proposed framework. For 75 training photographs, the proposed method has an accuracy of 81.43%, which is higher than the CCV and GCH approaches. Using a MSVM in conjunction with numerous binary support vector machines, a strategy for detecting different malignancies is proposed [25].

The watershed segmentation technique is used to segment the data in [18]. A photograph is pre-processed using the median filtering approach when it is first uploaded to the system. Feature extraction is applied to the extracted segments. The ABCD rule and the GLCM are used to extract attributes. Skin lesions can be segmented more precisely using watershed approaches. The lowest region is reached by following the raindrop transit and executing the fundamental watershed rainfall characteristics. The data are then classified using the attributes collected. Three different types of classifiers are used in this classification. The k-NN, random forest and SVM algorithms are included. The proposed method compares the SVM, random forest and k-NN classifiers and finds that the SVM outperforms the others in terms of skin lesion categorization. Even when the training data contained significant bias, the SVM proved to be dependable and durable [18] (table 11.1).

Table 11.1. A comparison of various skin cancer detection approaches.

Author's name	Methodology	Detection accuracy
Ansari *et al* [32]	Uses thresholding and segmentation by an SVM classifier.	95%
Bakheet *et al* [33]	SVM framework for skin cancer detection using HOG features.	97.32
Kumar *et al* [34]	Carcinoma detection using an SVM by flattening the image into an array.	90%
Salem *et al* [35]	Extraction of features from symmetry, border irregularity, color fluctuation and dimension, as well as a genetic algorithm-based approach.	76.17%
Lingaraj *et al* [36]	Uses a modified version of SVMs, known as veritable SVMs (VSVMs) evaluated on HIS2828 and ISIC2017.	The results of the experiments show that the VSVM achieved accuracies of 82.11% and 88.10%, respectively, on the HIS2828 and ISIC2017 medical image datasets.
Tang *et al* [37]	Particle swarm optimization and probability distributions are used in this technique.	95.23%
Csabai *et al* [38]	The ultrasound picture is used as a complement to the dermoscopic image. AdaBoost and an SVM are used for classification.	Both classifiers achieved specificity of at least 19% at 100% sensitivity and an AUC of 84%.

11.6 Challenges faced by SVMs

The volume of data in various classes is uneven in some classification tasks. As a result, several researchers have recommended that alternative penalty parameters be used in SVM formulations, which complicates the proper methods [33], table 11.1. Also, when a large number of samples or high-dimensional space kernels are provided, the quadratic is not always a straightforward task.

The selection of kernel functions is interesting from both a theoretical and a practical standpoint. The objective function of a quadratic program defines both the functional form of the approximation and the type of regularization that is employed to restrict the estimate [34]. Despite the fact that different kernels create different types of learning machines, it appears that the kernel choice is less crucial than it looks at first glance.

Regardless of the fact that the usage of SV techniques in applications is still in its early stages, 340 application developers have already claimed cutting-edge performance in a variety of applications, such as pattern recognition, regression estimation and time series prediction [35, 36]. Nevertheless, an application in which SV techniques surpass any other existing algorithm or tackle a traditionally difficult-to-address problem is likely to be absent. In the latter instance, SV techniques for tackling inverse problems are an excellent choice.

The implementation of kernels in other algorithms seems to be a potential route for evolving innovative learning techniques. The kernel methodology to predicting dot products in feature spaces could be used to generate non-linear extensions to every algorithm that can be represented using dot products. To begin, we will perform principal component analysis (PCA), which is the most often used data analysis approach. As a consequence, a kernel approach is developed that uses linear PCA to perform non-linear PCA in feature space. Resolving a linear eigenvalue issue for a matrix whose elements are calculated using the kernel function is part of the technique. The architectures of the feature extractors that emerge are identical to those of the SVMs. A lot of scholars have begun to 'kernel' various linear techniques.

Although only a few collections of popular functions are widely recognized, the VC dimension is sought in nature since it is the foundation of the SVM. Furthermore, SVM research is even more recent than theoretical research, and all possible approaches to dealing with these issues are promising.

11.7 Future aspects in skin cancer detection

The majority of skin cancer detection research focuses on determining if a particular lesion picture is malignant. When a patient inquires about a specific skin cancer symptom appearing on any area of their body, however, existing research is unable to offer a response [37]. The study has so far been limited to the subject of signal picture categorization. To find an answer to the issue that frequently occurs, future studies might involve full-body photography. The picture acquisition process will be automated and sped up with autonomous full-body photography.

Auto-organization is a relatively new idea in the domain of deep learning. Auto-organization is an unsupervised learning approach that attempts to discover features and reveal relationships or patterns in image samples from a collection. Convolutional neural networks, which use auto-organization procedures, increase the amount of feature representation that expert systems recover. It is currently a paradigm that is constantly being investigated and expanded. Its discoveries, on the other hand, may help to enhance the precision of image processing technologies in the future, in particular in the field of diagnostic imaging, where minute details of characteristics are crucial for effective disease detection.

The model in the context of the SVM classifier may be utilised in a variety of on-going online classification techniques. Furthermore, the suggested hardware design, which was created on the Zynq platform using the HLS technique, might be useful to other hardware developers when developing intelligent systems. In the future, further structural optimization approaches, such as the multiplier-less approach and the DPR methodology, will be used [38]. The model might be linked to a variety of existing clinical decision support systems and/or healthcare networks.

11.8 Conclusion

Squamous cell carcinoma, melanoma and basal cell carcinoma are three kinds of skin malignancies. Melanoma is the deadliest cancer, with an extremely low survival rate. Melanoma may be detected early, which may increase the chances of survival. Various methods can be used to detect skin cancer. In this chapter an analysis of vision-based skin cancer detection methods using machine learning approaches is provided.

All the methods start with pre-processing of the image and thereafter it is segmented to obtain the region of interest. Subsequently, an SVM is used to classify features of the image and determine whether skin cancer is present or not. The categorization of the obtained picture into different areas is referred to as segmentation. The expanded stage assessed using the new classifier approach is seen in the SVM simulation for the ABCD rule. The SVM has several advantages, including being accurate and resilient even when the training example is biased.

References

[1] Gloster H M and Neal K 2006 Skin cancer in skin of color *J. Am. Acad. Dermatol.* **55** 741–60

[2] Lu K, Bhat M, Peters S, Mitra R, Oberyszyn T and Basu S 2021 Suppression of beta 2 adrenergic receptor actions prevent UVB mediated cutaneous squamous cell tumorigenesis through inhibition of VEGF-A induced angiogenesis *Mol. Carcinog.* **60** 172–8

[3] Nault A, Zhang C, Kim K, Saha S, Bennett D D and Xu Y G 2015 Biopsy use in skin cancer diagnosis: comparing dermatology physicians and advanced practice professionals *JAMA Dermatol.* **151** 899–902

[4] Masood A and Al-Jumaily A 2015 Differential evolution based advised SVM for histo-pathological image analysis for skin cancer detection *Proc. Annu. Int. Conf. IEEE Eng. Med. Biol. Soc. (November)* (Piscataway, NJ: IEEE) pp 781–4

[5] Jana E, Subban R and Saraswathi S 2018 Research on skin cancer cell detection using image processing *IEEE Int. Conf. Comput. Intell. Comput. Res. (ICCIC)* (Piscataway, NJ: IEEE)

[6] Yuan X, Yang Z, Zouridakis G and Mullani N 2006 SVM-based texture classification and application to early melanoma detection *Annu. Int. Conf. IEEE Eng. Med. Biol.* (Piscataway, NJ: IEEE) pp 4775–8

[7] Jain S, Jagtap V and Pise N 2015 Efficient Gabor filter using Vedic mathematic for high speed convolution in skin cancer detection *Proc. 1st Int. Conf. Comput. Commun. Control Autom. (ICCUBEA)* pp 800–4

[8] Codella N C F *et al* 2019 Skin lesion analysis toward melanoma detection 2018: a challenge *2017 Int. Symp. on Biomedical Imaging (ISBI), hosted by the international skin imaging collaboration (ISIC) 2018 IEEE 15th Int. Symp. on Biomedical Imaging (ISBI 2018)* pp 168–72 https://doi.org/10.1109/ISBI.2018.8363547

[9] Bruner A and Schaffer S D 2012 Diagnosing skin lesions: clinical considerations for primary care practitioners *J. Nurse Pract.* **8** 600–4

[10] Afifi S, Gholam Hosseini H and Sinha R 2016 A low-cost FPGA-based SVM classifier for melanoma detection *IECBES 2016—IEEE-EMBS Conf. Biomed. Eng. Sci.* pp 631–6

[11] Amarappa S and Sathyanarayana S V 2014 Data classification using support vector machine (SVM), a simplified approach *Int. J. Electron. Comput. Sci. Eng.* **3** 435–45

[12] Zhang M, Zhang J, Su J and Zhou G 2006 A composite kernel to extract relations between entities with both flat and structured features *21st Int. Conf. on Computational Linguistics and 44th Annual Meeting of the Association for Computational Linguistics* vol 1 pp 825–32

[13] Jana E, Subban R and Saraswathi S 2017 Research on skin cancer cell detection using image processing *Int. Conf. on Computational Intelligence and Computing Research* (Piscataway, NJ: IEEE) pp 1–8

[14] Sharma S and Selva Kumar J 2015 Image denoising using median filter having SDC comparator *Int. J. Sci. Technol. Eng.* **1** 18–23

[15] Feng Z M and Su Y D 2013 Application of using simulated annealing to combine clustering with collaborative filtering for item recommendation *Appl. Mech. Mater.* **347–50** 2747–51

[16] Rashad M W and Takruri M 2017 Automatic non-invasive recognition of melanoma using support vector machines *Int. Conf. on Bio-Engineering for Smart Technologies* (Piscataway, NJ: IEEE)

[17] Agarwal A, Issac A, Dutta M K, Riha K and Uher V 2017 Automated skin lesion segmentation using k-means clustering from digital dermoscopic images *40th Int. Conf. Telecommun. Signal Process. (January)* pp 743–8

[18] Murugan A, Nair S A H and Kumar K P S 2019 Detection of skin cancer using SVM, random forest and kNN classifiers *J. Med. Syst.* **43** 269

[19] Kumar M, Alshehri M, AlGhamdi R, Sharma P and Deep V 2020 A DE-ANN inspired skin cancer detection approach using fuzzy C-means clustering *Mob. Networks Appl.* **25** 1319–29

[20] Jayade S, Ingole D T and Ingole M D 2020 Skin cancer detection using gray level co-occurrence matrix feature processing *5th Int. Conf. Devices, Circuits Syst.* pp 49–53

[21] Melgani F and Bruzzone L 2004 Classification of hyperspectral remote sensing images with support vector machines *IEEE Trans. Geosci. Remote Sens.* **42** 1778–90

[22] Mustafa S and Kimura A 2018 A SVM-based diagnosis of melanoma using only useful image features *Int. Work. Adv. Image Technol.* pp 1–4

[23] Vidya M and Karki M V 2020 Skin cancer detection using machine learning techniques *Int. Conf. on Electronics, Computing and Communication Technologies* (Piscataway, NJ: IEEE) pp 1–5

[24] Jayade S, Ingole D T and Ingole M D 2020 Skin cancer detection using gray level co-occurrence matrix feature processing *5th Int. Conf. on Devices, Circuits and Systems* (Piscataway, NJ: IEEE) pp 49–53

[25] Maurya R, Singh S K, Maurya A K and Kumar A 2014 GLCM and multi class support vector machine based automated skin cancer classification *Int. Conf. on Computing for Sustainable Global Development* (Piscataway, NJ: IEEE) pp 444–7

[26] Farooq M A, Azhar M A M and Raza R H 2016 Automatic lesion detection system (ALDS) for skin cancer classification using SVM and neural classifiers *Proc. 16th Int. Conf. Bioinforma. Bioeng.* pp 301–8

[27] Ercal F, Chawla A, Stoecker W V, Lee H C and Moss R H 1994 Neural network diagnosis of malignant melanoma from color images *IEEE Trans. Biomed. Eng.* **41** 837–45

[28] Hameed N, Shabut A M and Hossain M A 2019 Multi-class skin diseases classification using deep convolutional neural network and support vector machine *Int. Conf. Software, Knowl. Information, Ind. Manag. Appl. Ski. (December 2018)*

[29] Salem C, Azar D and Tokajian S 2018 An image processing and genetic algorithm-based approach for the detection of melanoma in patients *Methods Inf. Med.* **57** 74–80

[30] Jaleel J A, Salim S and Aswin R B 2013 Computer aided detection of skin cancer *Proc. IEEE Int. Conf. Circuit, Power Comput. Technol.* pp 1137–42

[31] Tan T Y, Zhang L, Neoh S C and Lim C P 2018 Intelligent skin cancer detection using enhanced particle swarm optimization *Knowl. Based Syst.* **158** 118–35

[32] Csabai D, Szalai K and Gyöngy M 2016 Automated classification of common skin lesions using bioinspired features *IEEE Int. Ultrason. Symp. IUS (November)*

[33] Yue S, Li P and Hao P 2003 SVM classification: its contents and challenges *Appl. Math.* **18** 332–42

[34] Weston J, Gammerman A and Stitson M 1997 Density estimation using support vector machines *Technical report* Royal Holloway College, Report number CSD-TR-97-23

[35] Smola A J, Schölkopf B and Müller K R 1998 The connection between regularization operators and support vector kernels *Neural Netw.* **11** 637–49

[36] Chang C C, Hsu C W and Lin C J 2000 The analysis of decomposition methods for support vector machines *IEEE Trans. Neural Networks* **11** 1003–8

[37] Dildar M, Akram S, Irfan M, Khan H U, Ramzan M, Mahmood A R, Alsaiari S A, Saeed A H M, Alraddadi M O and Mahnashi M H 2021 Skin cancer detection: a review using deep learning techniques *Int. J. Environ. Res. Public Heal.* **18** 5479

[38] Kaur K, Boddu L B and Science C 2018 Computer vision for skin cancer detection TechRxiv. Preprint. https://doi.org/10.36227/techrxiv.12089514.v1

CPSIA information can be obtained
at www.ICGtesting.com
Printed in the USA
BVHW010838010722
640031BV00012B/75